AF264375

Systematic Theology Study Guide and Workbook for Beginners

How to Easily Understand the Bible and Christian Doctrine Through a Clear Study with Practical Lessons and Exercises

TABLE OF CONTENTS

PART 1: SYSTEMATIC THEOLOGY FOR BEGINNERS 5-IN-1

OVERALL INTRODUCTION 3

BOOK ONE - KNOW THE LIVING GOD 9

Chapter 1 - Begin with God's Self - Revelation: Learn How God Makes Himself Known 11

Chapter 2 - Confess One God in Three Persons: Grasp the Trinity without Confusion 17

Chapter 3 - Trust God's Character: Study His Holiness, Love, Justice, and Mercy 23

Chapter 4 - Receive God's Word: Understand Inspiration, Authority, and Clarity of Scripture 28

Chapter 5 - Rely on God's Providence: See His Rule over Nature, Nations, and Daily Life 34

Chapter 6 - Worship God as Creator: Connect Creation, Order, and Human Purpose 40

BOOK TWO - UNDERSTAND HUMANITY UNDER GOD 47

Chapter 1 - Accept Human Worth: Learn What "Image of God" Means for Daily Life 49

Chapter 2 - Face the Fall Honestly: Trace How Sin Entered and Spread 55

Chapter 3 - Recognize Sin's Patterns: Name Pride, Idolatry, and Self-Rule 61

Chapter 4 - Measure the Heart by God's Law: Use the Commandments as a Mirror 68

Chapter 5 - Understand Guilt and Shame: Tell the Difference and Seek True Cleansing 74

Chapter 6 - Explain Human Relationships: Study Marriage, Family, and Neighbor - Love..80

Chapter 7 - Admit Human Limits: Accept Why You Cannot Save Yourself 86

BOOK THREE - SALVATION: RECEIVE GOD'S RESCUE IN CHRIST 93

Chapter 1 - Trace God's Rescue Plan: Follow the Covenants from Promise to Fulfillment..95

Chapter 2 - Know the Promised Savior: Confess Jesus Christ as God and Man.. 101

Chapter 3 - Trust the Cross and Resurrection: Receive Atonement, Victory, and Peace with God.. 107

Chapter 4 - Receive Grace through Faith: Stop Earning and Start Trusting Christ 112

Chapter 5 - Be Born Again: Repent, Believe, and Walk in New Life.. 117

Chapter 6 - Grow in Grace Daily: Follow How God Applies Salvation and Changes You 122

BOOK FOUR - THE SPIRIT: LIVE BY GOD'S PRESENCE AND POWER 127

Chapter 1 - Meet the Holy Spirit as God: Trust His Presence and Follow His Leading.. 129

Chapter 2 - Trace the Spirit's Work in the Old Testament: See God's Presence Before Pentecost.. 135

Chapter 3 - Follow the Spirit in Jesus' Life: See the Messiah Anointed for His Mission 141

Chapter 4 - Receive the Spirit's Promise: Understand Pentecost and the Church's New Covenant Strength.. 146

Chapter 5 - Live Filled with the Spirit: Practice Daily Dependence, Holiness, and Wisdom.. 150

Chapter 6 - Endure with the Spirit's Comfort: Face Suffering, Stand Firm, and Keep Hope.. 154

Chapter 7 - Guard Unity by the Spirit: Build Peace, Practice Truth, and Keep the Church Strong.................................... 159

BOOK FIVE - THE FUTURE: LIVE READY FOR CHRIST'S RETURN 165

Chapter 1 - Fix Your Hope on Christ's Return: Live Watchful, Faithful, and Unafraid 167

Chapter 2 - Trace the Spirit's Work in the Old Testament: See God's Presence Before Pentecost.. 172

Chapter 3 - Follow the Spirit in Jesus' Life: See the Messiah Anointed for His Mission 178

Chapter 4 - Study Views with Charity: Compare Major End - Times Frameworks Fairly 183

Chapter 5 - Long for the New Creation: See Heaven and Earth Made New 187

Chapter 6 - Live Ready Now: Practice Faithfulness, Watchfulness, and Joy 190

OVERALL CONCLUSION: HOLD TO CHRIST, LIVE WITH CLARITY, AND FINISH WELL 193

PART 2: SYSTEMATIC THEOLOGY WORKBOOK 5-IN-1

INTRODUCTION.. 197

BOOK ONE - KNOW GOD AS HE HAS REVEALED HIMSELF.......... 203

Chapter 1 - Start with God's Self-Disclosure................................ 205

Chapter 2 - See God as Trinity: One in Three............................... 209

Chapter 3 - Recognize God's Sovereignty in All Things 213

Chapter 4 - Trust God's Moral Goodness.................................... 218

Chapter 5 - Understand God's Relationship with Time.................... 223

Chapter 6 - Worship God in Truth 229

BOOK TWO - UNDERSTAND WHAT IT MEANS TO BE HUMAN .. 237

Chapter 1 - Created in God's Image.. 239

Chapter 2 - Human Purpose and God's Design.............................. 247

Chapter 3 - The Fall: What Broke in Us 253

Chapter 4 - How Sin Affects Our Thinking and Desires 260

Chapter 5 - Human Worth and Dignity After the Fall...... 268

Chapter 6 - Living as God's Image Bearers Today............ 276

BOOK THREE - GRASP HOW SALVATION REALLY WORKS.......... 283

Chapter 1 - Salvation Begins with God's Initiative............ 285

Chapter 2 - Christ's Work Secures Our Salvation 293

Chapter 3 - Faith and Repentance Are Both Required.......... 300

Chapter 4 - Justified by Faith Alone 307

Chapter 5 - Sanctified for a New Way of Life 314

Chapter 6 - Assurance and Endurance in Salvation 322

BOOK FOUR - LIVE BY THE SPIRIT GOD HAS GIVEN.......... 331

Chapter 1 - The Spirit Is God - Not an Influence 333

Chapter 2 - The Spirit Brings Life 340

Chapter 3 - The Spirit Unites Believers to Christ 347

Chapter 4 - The Spirit Produces Fruit, Not Just Gifts.......... 355

Chapter 5 - The Spirit Builds and Guides the Church 363

Chapter 6 - Walking by the Spirit Daily 371

BOOK FIVE - HOLD FAST TO THE FUTURE GOD HAS
PROMISED 379

Chapter 1 - Jesus Will Return in Power...................... 381

Chapter 2 - The Dead Will Be Raised 388

Chapter 3 - Heaven and Hell Are Real and Final 395

Chapter 4 - God Will Make All Things New.................. 402

Chapter 5 - Live Today in Light of the End 409

Chapter 6 - Hope That Never Fades........................ 417

Conclusion - Hold the Whole Counsel of God Close.......... 424

APPENDIX - BIBLE STUDY PLANS AND MEMORY WORK.......... 432

HERE'S ANOTHER BOOK BY JAMES NORTHWELL THAT YOU
MIGHT LIKE 472

PART 1: SYSTEMATIC THEOLOGY FOR BEGINNERS 5-IN-1

A Simple Guide to God, Humanity, Salvation, the Spirit, and the Future

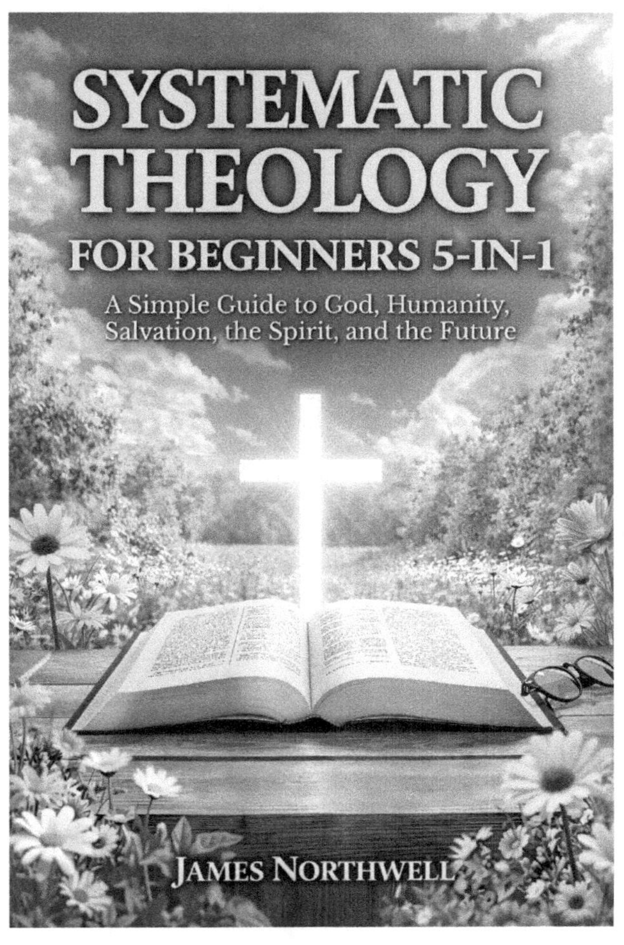

OVERALL INTRODUCTION

Start Systematic Theology with Confidence: What It Is, Why It Matters, and How to Use This 5-in-1 Guide

Systematic theology sounds like a classroom word. Many believers hear it and picture thick books, long footnotes, and debates they did not ask for. Yet the basic idea is simple. Systematic theology is the careful practice of gathering what the whole Bible teaches about a topic, then stating it clearly and faithfully. It helps you connect Scripture's many parts into one coherent confession.

Every Christian already does some form of theology. When you say "God is good," you are making a theological claim. When you say "Jesus saves," you are making another. The question is not whether you will form beliefs. The question is whether your beliefs will be shaped by Scripture or by habit, emotion, culture, or personal preference. Scripture calls believers to grow in knowledge that leads to love and steady obedience (Colossians 1:9–10). That growth does not happen by accident.

This book exists for readers who want clarity without pretension. You may be new to the Bible. You may have been in church for years but still feel unsure when hard questions come. You may love God deeply and still struggle to explain what you believe. This guide aims to help you speak with conviction and humility, because your foundation is the Word of God.

What Systematic Theology Is (and What It Is Not)

Systematic theology is not a replacement for reading the Bible. It is not a shortcut around prayer, worship, and discipleship. It is a tool that supports them. It gathers the Bible's teaching the way a good map gathers roads. The roads are still real places. The map simply helps you see how they connect.

Systematic theology is also not an excuse to win arguments. The goal is not to sound clever. The goal is to know God, love Him, and live faithfully. Scripture warns against knowledge that inflates pride (1 Corinthians 8:1). At the same time, Scripture commands believers to handle the Word with care and to guard the truth once delivered to the saints (2 Timothy 2:15; Jude 1:3). A healthy theology produces steadiness, worship, repentance, and courage.

A simple way to define systematic theology is this: it is Bible truth organized for faithful living. It takes doctrine out of the clouds and puts it into daily decisions.

Why This Matters for Real Life

Bad theology does not stay on a page. It shows up in the way we pray, the way we raise children, the way we treat money, and the way we face suffering. If we view God as distant, our prayers shrink. If we view people as accidents, human dignity weakens. If we treat salvation as self-improvement, guilt never lifts. If we treat the Holy Spirit as a vague force, we become confused about guidance and holiness. If we treat the future as unclear or irrelevant, hope fades and fear rises.

Good theology also does not stay on a page. It shapes the heart. It strengthens faith under pressure. It steadies believers who feel tossed around by social media claims, sensational teachers, and shifting moral norms. Scripture itself ties doctrine to stability: believers should no longer be like children, carried by every wind of teaching (Ephesians 4:14). That is not a call to suspicion. It is a call to maturity.

Here is the promise of this book: if you learn to think biblically about God, humanity, salvation, the Spirit, and the future, you will gain a stronger grip on reality. You will also gain a gentler posture toward others, because you will know the difference between essential truths and secondary debates.

One Question You Might Be Asking

Do I need theology if I just want to love Jesus? Yes, because the Jesus you love must be the Jesus Scripture reveals. Love is not sustained by sentiment alone. Love grows when truth becomes clear, and when trust becomes deeper. The Bible does not separate love from knowledge. It joins them.

How This 5-in-1 Guide Is Built

This volume is arranged as five "Books" inside one collection. Each chapter is written for beginners, but it does not treat you like a child. The chapters aim for plain speech, clear structure, and direct application.

Scripture First, Then Clear Reasoning

This book is Biblically centered by design. We treat Scripture as the final authority for doctrine. That does not mean we ignore church history. It means we place church history in its proper role. Christians have wrestled with doctrine for two thousand years. Councils, creeds, and confessions often clarify what Scripture teaches, especially when false views arise. For example, the early church fought for clear language about the Trinity and the full deity and humanity of Christ. Those were not academic games. They were matters of worship and salvation.

So, throughout this book, you will see careful use of church history. You will see how faithful believers argued, where they agreed, and why certain conclusions became standard. You will also see where Christians differ today on secondary matters. In those places, you will be given the strongest biblical arguments on each side, with a steady emphasis on charity and truth.

We will also define key terms in plain language. Systematic theology uses words like "attribute," "incarnation," "atonement," "justification," and "sanctification." These words can feel heavy at first. But they exist because they serve clarity. When you learn them, you can speak precisely, and you can avoid confusion that harms faith.

The Method You Will Learn (So You Can Keep Growing)

You will repeatedly practice a simple method:

1. **Gather the relevant Scriptures.**

    We look at passages that directly teach the topic.

2. **Read each passage in context.**

    One verse should not be forced to say what it does not say.

3. **Summarize the Bible's teaching in one clear statement.**

    We aim for faithful sentences, not slogans.

4. **Test that statement against the whole Bible.**

    Scripture does not contradict itself.

5. **Apply the doctrine to worship, obedience, and endurance.**

    Truth is meant to shape life.

If you learn this method, you will not depend on a single teacher. You will become a steady reader of Scripture who can evaluate claims with care.

A Word About Disagreements

Some doctrines are non-negotiable in historic Christianity. The Trinity is essential. The true humanity and true deity of Christ are essential. Salvation by grace, through faith, because of Christ's work, is essential. The bodily resurrection of Jesus is essential. God's final judgment and the promised renewal of creation are essential.

Other doctrines have faithful Christian disagreement. Timing details about end-times events often fall here. Some questions about spiritual gifts, church governance, and baptism practices also vary across traditions. This book will treat essential truths with firmness. It will treat secondary matters with honesty and respect. You do not need to fear those differences. You need to learn how to sort them.

What is the point of learning both agreement and disagreement? It helps you avoid two common errors. The first error is to treat every issue as equally important, which leads to constant conflict. The second error is to treat no issue as important, which leads to drifting and confusion. Scripture calls for both conviction and love.

How to Use This Book Well

If you read alone, take one chapter at a time. Do not rush. After each chapter, answer the discussion questions in writing. If possible, speak your answers out loud. Doctrine settles into the mind when we put words to it.

If you read with a group or family, set a weekly rhythm. Read a chapter during the week. Then meet for 45–60 minutes. Start with prayer. End with one specific action step. For example, after a chapter on God's holiness, you might choose a focused confession of sin and a plan to reconcile a strained relationship. After a chapter on providence, you might choose to pray through a current worry in a more structured way.

If you are a teacher or ministry leader, use the chapters as a framework. Each chapter is structured to support teaching. You can expand the Scripture reading, add historical quotes, and bring in examples from pastoral life.

What You Can Expect as You Read

You should expect your mind to sharpen. You should also expect your heart to be confronted. Biblical truth does both. Scripture often comforts, but it also corrects. It warns, it invites, and it calls for change. If you encounter a doctrine that challenges your assumptions, do not panic. Slow down. Return to Scripture. Pray for humility and clarity. God honors honest seeking.

You should also expect to gain confidence without arrogance. Confidence comes from knowing that your beliefs are rooted in God's Word, not in personal mood. Arrogance comes from forgetting that everything we know is received. The posture of a student never ends. Even the most mature believer remains a learner.

This book uses the **NSV** for Scripture references unless otherwise noted. When we cite a passage, the goal is not to sprinkle verses on top of our ideas. The goal is to let Scripture lead. Theology is faithful only when it echoes God's voice.

One more question: what if you feel unqualified to study theology? You are qualified if you belong to Christ and you are willing to learn. Scripture was given to the church, not only to scholars. The Spirit teaches believers through the Word, within the life of the church (John 16:13; Acts 2:42). Begin with humility, consistency, and a desire to obey.

Now we start where Scripture starts: with God. The most practical thing you can do for your life is to know Him as He truly is.

BOOK ONE
KNOW THE LIVING GOD
A Simple Guide to God's Being, Words, Works, and Ways

CHAPTER 1

BEGIN WITH GOD'S SELF - REVELATION: LEARN HOW GOD MAKES HIMSELF KNOWN

If you want to know God, you must start with a simple fact: God is not silent. We do not climb our way up to Him by intelligence, effort, or emotion. God makes Himself known because He chooses to do so. The Bible does not present faith as guessing. It presents faith as hearing God's voice and responding.

Hebrews 1:1-2 (NSV) sets the tone. God spoke in many ways in earlier times, and He has spoken with final clarity in His Son. That means Christianity stands or falls on revelation. If God does not reveal Himself, then theology becomes speculation. If God does reveal Himself, then theology becomes obedience: we learn, we worship, and we live in line with what He has shown.

1) Define Revelation the Way Scripture Does

Revelation means "making known what would otherwise remain hidden." The key idea is not that humans discover God. The key idea is that God discloses Himself. He shows His character, His will, and His saving plan.

Deuteronomy 29:29 (NSV) makes a crucial distinction. Some things belong to God alone, but what He has revealed belongs to His people so they can obey. This verse protects you from two opposite mistakes. One mistake is to demand answers God has not given. The other mistake is to neglect what God has clearly said.

So revelation is both a gift and a boundary. It is a gift because God gives real knowledge of Himself. It is a boundary because God sets the limits of what we can know.

Do you need to know everything about God to know Him truly? No, because God gives true knowledge without giving exhaustive knowledge. A child can know a parent truly without knowing every detail of the parent's life.

That is how Scripture trains our minds. God is infinite. We are creatures. We can know Him truly because He speaks truly. We cannot know Him fully because we are not God.

2) Learn the Two Main Categories: General and Special Revelation

Christians often use two terms that help organize the Bible's teaching: **general revelation** and **special revelation**.

General Revelation: God Makes His Existence and Power Plain

General revelation refers to what God shows through creation and providence. Psalm 19:1–4 (NSV) teaches that the created order communicates God's glory. Romans 1:19–20 (NSV) teaches that God's invisible attributes are seen through what He has made, so people are accountable.

General revelation is real, constant, and universal. Everyone lives in God's world. Everyone receives breath, food, seasons, and the order of nature. God's power and wisdom shine through what He made.

But general revelation has limits. It can tell you that God exists, that He is powerful, that He rules, and that you are responsible to Him. It cannot tell you the gospel. It does not tell you the name of the Savior, the meaning of the cross, or the promise of forgiveness. It can expose guilt, but it cannot cleanse guilt.

That is why Scripture never treats nature as a substitute for God's Word. Creation points. Scripture explains.

Special Revelation: God Speaks for Salvation and Covenant Life

Special revelation refers to God's direct self-disclosure through His spoken and written Word, fulfilled in Jesus Christ. Hebrews 1:1–2 (NSV) highlights both the diversity of God's past communication and the finality of His revelation in the Son.

Special revelation includes God's words through prophets and apostles. It includes God's mighty acts interpreted by God's own speech. It includes Scripture as the written, enduring form of that revelation.

And it reaches its center in the person and work of Jesus.

John 1:18 (NSV) teaches that the Son makes the Father known. This is decisive. God does not merely send information. He sends His Son. Christianity is not first a set of ideas. It is God giving Himself to us through Christ, then giving words that explain that gift.

3) See Why Sin Makes Revelation Necessary and Grace Makes It Possible

If humans were morally neutral, they might respond to God's world with clear-eyed gratitude. But Scripture teaches that sin twists perception. Romans 1 does not describe people as lacking evidence. It describes people as suppressing the truth. Sin does not merely break rules. Sin bends the heart away from God.

That means revelation is not only about information. It is about rescue. God does not speak because He is lonely. He speaks because He is gracious and because we need truth to live.

You also need to understand another point: even special revelation does not produce faith automatically. People can hear God's words and still resist. That is why Scripture also speaks about the Spirit's work of illumination. 1 Corinthians 2:10–12 (NSV) teaches that God's Spirit helps believers grasp what God has given.

4) Learn the Main Ways God Reveals Himself in Scripture

God reveals Himself through several channels across redemptive history. The Bible does not flatten them into one method. It shows God speaking and acting in complementary ways.

God Reveals Himself Through His Names

Names in Scripture often carry meaning. In Exodus 3:14 (NSV), God identifies Himself in a way that emphasizes His self-existence and faithfulness. He is not defined by the world. He is not dependent on anything outside Himself. He simply is.

This matters for beginners because it clears away common errors. God is not a larger version of you. God is not a force inside nature. God is personal, living, and free. He stands over creation as Creator, and He draws near by covenant grace.

God Reveals Himself Through His Acts

God's works interpret God's character. Creation displays His wisdom and generosity. The exodus displays His power to save and His commitment to His promises. Judgment displays His justice. Provision displays His care.

But here is the key: Scripture does not leave God's acts open to personal interpretation. God often explains His acts with His words. He tells Israel what the exodus means. He tells the church what the cross means. He tells believers what the resurrection means.

If you separate acts from words, you will misread the acts. If you receive acts through God's words, you will learn to worship rather than speculate.

God Reveals Himself Through His Spoken Word

Throughout the Bible, God speaks. He speaks commands, promises, warnings, and comfort. He speaks in covenant language: "I will be your God, and you will be my people." His speech is not casual. His speech creates obligations and hope.

God's spoken Word also exposes the heart. When God speaks, you learn what you love, what you fear, and what you excuse. That is why Scripture often feels personal. It is personal, because God addresses persons.

God Reveals Himself Through Scripture as Written Word

God's revelation did not end as scattered memories. God gave Scripture as an enduring witness. 2 Peter 1:20–21 (NSV) teaches that prophecy did not arise from human initiative, but from God's Spirit moving human authors.

This is where systematic theology begins to feel practical. If Scripture is God's written Word, then you have a stable source of truth. You do not need to chase rumors, impulses, or trending voices. You can open your Bible and read what God has spoken.

5) Hold to Four Commitments That Keep You Steady

If you want to grow without drifting, commit to four simple principles. These principles show up across historic Christian teaching because they reflect how Scripture functions.

Commitment 1: Treat Scripture as Your Highest Authority

Many voices compete for authority: personal experience, family tradition, cultural pressure, and even fear. Scripture must govern them all. This does not mean you despise learning. It means you test every claim by God's Word.

When a belief conflicts with Scripture, Scripture wins. When a practice contradicts Scripture, Scripture corrects it.

Commitment 2: Read Passages in Context

A single verse can be misunderstood when you detach it from its chapter, its book, and the full storyline of Scripture. Context protects you from forcing Scripture to support ideas it does not teach.

This also guards you from shallow reading. God's Word is coherent. Themes repeat. Promises develop. Fulfillment arrives in Christ. You will understand more when you read whole sections, not only isolated lines.

Commitment 3: Let Clear Passages Interpret Less Clear Passages

Scripture contains poetry, visions, and difficult statements. Do not build a major doctrine on an unclear verse. Use the plain teaching of Scripture to guide your reading of the harder parts.

This principle reduces confusion and conflict. It also increases confidence, because the Bible speaks plainly about the truths that matter most.

Commitment 4: Connect Revelation to Worship and Obedience

The goal is not to store facts. The goal is to know God and honor Him. True knowledge produces reverence. It also produces repentance, gratitude, patience, and courage.

If your study makes you harsh, you are studying wrongly. If your study makes you prayerless, you are studying wrongly. Scripture aims for faith working through love.

6) Avoid Common Traps That Disfigure Theology

Beginners often face predictable dangers. Naming them helps you resist them.

Trap 1: Treat Feelings as Revelation

Feelings matter, but they do not define truth. A strong impression may be wisdom, fear, habit, or temptation. God may comfort you through Scripture, but that comfort comes through His Word, not apart from it.

So measure impressions by Scripture. If the impression contradicts Scripture, reject it. If it aligns with Scripture, hold it with humility, and seek wise counsel.

Trap 2: Treat Theology as a Private Project

God reveals Himself to form a people. Scripture assumes community: worship, teaching, correction, and shared life. If you try to build doctrine alone, you will likely build blind spots into your beliefs.

Read Scripture personally, yes. But also learn within the church. Listen to faithful teachers. Study the great creeds and confessions as summaries, not as replacements. Let the body of Christ sharpen you.

Trap 3: Demand Certainty Where Scripture Allows Humble Patience

Some questions have firm answers. Others require careful thought and charity. Wisdom knows the difference.

When Scripture is clear, speak clearly. When Scripture is less specific, speak carefully. Do not turn opinions into tests of fellowship. At the same time, do not use "mystery" as an excuse for laziness.

CHAPTER 2

CONFESS ONE GOD IN THREE PERSONS: GRASP THE TRINITY WITHOUT CONFUSION

Christians are often told the Trinity is "too advanced" for ordinary believers. Scripture disagrees. The Bible does not hide God's identity behind a locked door. It calls God's people to worship Him as He truly is. If you want to pray with confidence, read the Bible with clarity, and guard the gospel from distortion, you must understand the Trinity.

The Trinity does not mean "three gods." It does not mean "one person wearing three masks." It means the one true God eternally exists as three distinct persons: Father, Son, and Holy Spirit. God is one in being, and three in person. That is the Christian confession.

This chapter will help you say that confession with understanding. We will build from Scripture first. Then we will use careful language shaped by the church's early teaching. We will also name common errors and show why they fail.

1) Start Where the Bible Starts: God Is One

The Bible is clear that there is only one God. Deuteronomy 6:4 (NSV) states it plainly: the Lord is one. This is not a minor theme. It is the foundation of biblical faith. Israel was called to worship the one Creator, not the many gods of the nations. The church inherits that same confession.

So any explanation of the Trinity must protect monotheism. The Trinity does not add gods. It clarifies the identity of the one God who saves.

A helpful way to state this first truth is simple: **Christianity is strict monotheism.** There is one God, not three.

While Scripture insists God is one, it also speaks of the Father, Son, and Spirit in ways that cannot be reduced to mere titles or roles.

One of the clearest places is the command of Jesus in Matthew 28:19 (NSV). He tells His disciples to baptize in the name of the Father, and of the Son, and of the Holy Spirit. Notice "name" is singular. Yet three are named. Jesus does not treat Father, Son, and Spirit as three separate deities. He places them together under the one divine name.

Another key text is 2 Corinthians 13:14 (NSV). Paul blesses the church with grace from the Lord Jesus Christ, love from God, and fellowship of the Holy Spirit. This is not casual language. The church's life is described as coming from the Father, through the Son, in the Spirit.

This pattern appears across the New Testament. Christians did not invent it later. They recognized what Scripture already gave them.

3) Affirm What Scripture Affirms About the Son

The Trinity becomes clearer when you see what Scripture teaches about Jesus. The Son is not a created helper. The Son is not a lesser deity. The Son is fully God, and truly distinct from the Father.

John 1:1–3 (NSV) teaches that the Word was with God and was God, and that all things were made through Him. This guards two truths at once. First, the Son is truly God. Second, the Son is personally distinct, because He is "with" God.

Jesus also receives honors that belong to God alone. In John 20:28 (NSV), Thomas addresses Jesus as "my Lord and my God." Jesus does not correct him. He receives that confession.

Hebrews speaks of the Son as the exact imprint of God's nature and the one who upholds all things (Hebrews 1:3, NSV). That is divine work. Creatures do not uphold the universe.

So Scripture forces a decision. If you take the Bible seriously, you cannot treat Jesus as merely a moral teacher or a high angel. He is the eternal Son.

Many believers understand the Father and the Son but remain unsure about the Spirit. Scripture will not allow the Spirit to be treated as an "it" or as a mere force.

In Acts 5:3–4 (NSV), Peter confronts Ananias. He says Ananias has lied to the Holy Spirit, and then he says Ananias has lied to God. The Spirit can be lied to because He is personal. The Spirit is identified with God because He is divine.

The Spirit also acts with divine authority. He speaks, directs, appoints, and searches the depths of God (see Acts 13:2; 1 Corinthians 2:10–11, NSV). These are not descriptions of impersonal energy. They are descriptions of a divine person.

5) Use Careful Words: One Being, Three Persons

Once you see Scripture's teaching, the next step is to speak about it accurately. The church did not create the Trinity out of thin air. It created language to protect what Scripture teaches and to reject false summaries.

Here is the classic wording that helps most beginners:

- **There is one God in being (or essence).**
- **There are three persons: Father, Son, and Holy Spirit.**
- **The persons are distinct, not identical.**
- **The persons are not three gods, because the being is one.**

"Being" answers the question, "What is God?" The answer: God is one.

"Person" answers the question, "Who is God?" The answer: Father, Son, and Spirit.

This is careful, but it is not complicated once you practice it. It is also necessary. If you blur "being" and "person," you will fall into error quickly.

6) Learn from History: Why the Creeds Matter

In the early centuries, the church faced teachers who claimed to honor Scripture while denying its meaning. Two major errors forced the church to speak with precision.

Arianism taught that the Son was the first and greatest created being. This view sounded respectful, but it destroyed salvation. A created savior cannot bring you to God. Only God can save. The church answered with the Council of Nicaea (AD 325), confessing that the Son is of the same essence as the Father.

Later, the church clarified the Spirit's full divinity more explicitly at Constantinople (AD 381). The result is what many call the Nicene Creed, a summary meant to guard biblical teaching in worship and instruction.

Why does this matter for you today? Because the same old errors return with new packaging. Creeds help you recognize them quickly. They also show you that the Trinity is not a modern theory. It is the church's settled reading of Scripture.

7) Reject Three Common Errors

If you can name the common mistakes, you can avoid them.

Error 1: Modalism (One Person, Three Masks)

Modalism says God is one person who appears sometimes as Father, sometimes as Son, sometimes as Spirit. This fails because Scripture shows the persons relating to one another at the same time. At Jesus' baptism, the Son is baptized, the Spirit descends, and the Father speaks from heaven (Matthew 3:16–17, NSV). That is not one person acting three parts in sequence. It is three persons acting together.

Error 2: Tritheism (Three Separate Gods)

Tritheism treats Father, Son, and Spirit as three independent divine beings. This fails because Scripture insists God is one. The Father, Son, and Spirit share one divine life, one will, and one glory. Christianity is not a committee of deities. It is the worship of the one true God.

Error 3: Subordinationism (Son and Spirit as Lesser Deities)

Some say the Son and Spirit are divine, but not fully divine. Scripture does not speak that way. The Son creates and rules all things. The Spirit is identified with God and acts with God's authority. To reduce their divinity is to rewrite the Bible.

8) Handle Illustrations with Caution

Many people try to explain the Trinity with simple pictures. Most of them mislead.

Water as ice, liquid, and steam suggests one substance shifting forms. That leans toward modalism. The three-leaf clover suggests three parts that make a whole. That leans toward tritheism or partialism, as if each person is one-third of God.

Is there any illustration that works perfectly? No, because God is not like anything in creation. Creation can hint. It cannot match.

So use illustrations only as temporary supports, and always return to Scripture's words. The Trinity is not a puzzle to solve. It is a truth to confess.

9) Understand the Trinity in Salvation

The Trinity is not an abstract doctrine. It is the shape of the gospel.

- The **Father** plans salvation and sends the Son (John 3:16, NSV).
- The **Son** accomplishes salvation through His life, death, and resurrection (Romans 5:8–10, NSV).
- The **Spirit** applies salvation by giving new birth and uniting us to Christ (Titus 3:5–6, NSV).

This means your salvation is not a vague kindness from an unknown deity. It is the coordinated work of the triune God. The Father's love is not separate from the Son's grace. The Spirit's work is not detached from the Father's purpose. One God saves, in a triune manner.

Here is a practical result: when you struggle with assurance, the Trinity steadies you. The Father chose to save. The Son finished the saving work. The Spirit brings that finished work home to your heart. Your hope rests on God's action, not your mood.

10) Pray and Worship as a Trinitarian Christian

Many believers say they believe in the Trinity, but they do not practice trinitarian worship. Scripture teaches you to pray to the Father, through the Son, by the Spirit. This is not a rule meant to limit your words. It is a pattern meant to deepen your reverence and confidence.

When you pray to the Father, you approach the source of every good gift. When you pray through the Son, you rely on the one mediator who brings you near. When you pray by the Spirit, you depend on the one who helps you in weakness and shapes your desires toward holiness (Romans 8:26–27, NSV).

This also shapes church worship. Christian worship is directed to the Father, centered on the Son, and empowered by the Spirit. If you remove any person, you damage the whole.

11) Speak with Humility and Confidence

The Trinity is a mystery in one sense: you could never invent it. It is also clear in another sense: Scripture teaches it, and the church confesses it. Mystery does not mean confusion. It means God is greater than our categories.

So be humble. Do not pretend to explain God fully. But also be confident. God has revealed enough for worship, faith, and obedience.

A good summary you can remember is this:

The Father is God. The Son is God. The Spirit is God.

The Father is not the Son. The Son is not the Spirit. The Spirit is not the Father.

There is one God.

CHAPTER 3

TRUST GOD'S CHARACTER: STUDY HIS HOLINESS, LOVE, JUSTICE, AND MERCY

Many people believe in "a god" who feels like them, changes like them, and excuses what they excuse. Scripture will not let us settle for that. The living God reveals His character so we can trust Him, fear Him, and draw near to Him with clean hands and steady hope.

This chapter focuses on four core traits that Scripture highlights again and again: **holiness, love, justice, and mercy**. These traits do not compete. They belong together. If you pull them apart, you will misread God and misunderstand the gospel.

1) Begin with Holiness: God Is Set Apart and Morally Pure

Holiness means God is set apart from all creation and morally perfect in all He is and does. Holiness is not one attribute among many. Scripture often presents it as the "atmosphere" of God's presence.

Isaiah 6:1–3 (NSV) gives a famous scene. Isaiah sees the Lord high and exalted. Seraphim call out, "Holy, holy, holy." They repeat the word three times, not because they lack vocabulary, but because holiness stands at the center of God's revealed majesty. The vision does more than inform Isaiah. It crushes his pride and exposes his sin. He responds with confession because holiness reveals reality.

God's holiness means He never bends toward evil. He never adjusts His standards to fit our excuses. He never grows numb to sin. Scripture says, "Be holy, for I am holy" (1 Peter 1:15–16, NSV). That command does not imply we can become divine. It means God's moral purity sets the standard for His people.

Holiness also guards you from sentimental theology. Some people speak as if love means God ignores evil. Scripture rejects that. Holiness means God's love never becomes moral indifference.

2) Understand Love Correctly: God Gives Himself for Our Good

Scripture teaches that God is love (1 John 4:8, NSV). That statement is often quoted, and often misused. Many people define love as approval. Scripture defines love as holy self-giving that seeks the true good of the beloved.

In 1 John 4:9–10 (NSV), love appears in action. God shows love by sending His Son. The text ties love to atonement, not to vague kindness. God's love does not float above sin. It deals with sin through sacrifice.

This protects you from another error: treating love as God's only defining trait. God is love, but God is not only love in the way modern culture uses the word. Biblical love works with holiness and justice. It does not erase them.

Church history helps here. Pastors and theologians often said God's love is not random affection. It is covenant faithfulness. God commits Himself to His people and keeps His promise even at great cost. That is why Scripture links love to God's steadfast love and faithfulness, not merely to His emotions.

3) Hold to Justice: God Always Does What Is Right

God's justice means He always acts in perfect righteousness. He judges without corruption. He shows no partiality. He never makes mistakes. He never "grades on a curve." He does what is right because He is right.

Psalm 89:14 (NSV) says righteousness and justice are the foundation of God's throne. That means God's rule rests on moral perfection, not raw power. God does not rule like a tyrant. He rules like a righteous King.

God's justice also explains why Scripture takes sin seriously. If God shrugged at evil, He would not be good. If He ignored oppression, He would not be righteous. If He excused lies, violence, and abuse without judgment, He would become the opposite of the God the Bible reveals.

This matters in daily life. When you see injustice in your home, workplace, or nation, you may feel rage, despair, or cynicism. God's justice gives you another option: you can grieve honestly and still refuse despair. God sees. God knows. God will judge.

Romans 2:6–8 (NSV) teaches that God repays each person according to deeds. Scripture never uses this truth to produce smugness. It uses it to call for repentance and to assure the oppressed that evil will not have the last word.

4) Receive Mercy: God Shows Compassion to the Guilty and Weak

Mercy means God's compassion toward those who deserve judgment and cannot rescue themselves. Mercy does not deny guilt. Mercy addresses guilt with grace.

Exodus 34:6–7 (NSV) stands among the clearest places where God describes Himself. God declares that He is compassionate and gracious, slow to anger, and abounding in steadfast love. In the same breath, He also says He will not clear the guilty. That combination is not a contradiction. It is the tension Scripture forces us to hold until we see its fullest resolution in the saving work God provides.

Mercy also appears in daily faithfulness. Lamentations 3:22–23 (NSV) says God's steadfast love does not cease, and His mercies are new each morning. That statement comes from the middle of suffering and ruin. The writer does not deny pain. He affirms mercy within pain.

Many believers think mercy is only for the moment of conversion. Scripture treats mercy as God's ongoing posture toward His people. Mercy sustains the weak, restores the repentant, and invites the sinner to return.

5) Refuse to Separate What God Joins

Here is where many Christians get stuck. Some emphasize holiness and justice but forget love and mercy. Their theology becomes cold, suspicious, and harsh. Others emphasize love and mercy but downplay holiness and justice. Their theology becomes sentimental and permissive.

Scripture joins the traits. God's holiness does not cancel His love. God's love does not cancel His justice. God's justice does not cancel His mercy. God's mercy does not cancel His holiness.

Micah 6:8 (NSV) gives a simple pattern for God-centered living: do justice, love mercy, and walk humbly with your God. Notice the balance. Justice and mercy belong together. Humility keeps you from using either one as a weapon.

James 2:13 (NSV) adds another helpful note: mercy triumphs over judgment. The context does not erase judgment. It condemns favoritism and calls God's people to reflect God's heart. Mercy "triumphs" because God does not leave repentant sinners under condemnation. He provides a way to forgive and restore without abandoning righteousness.

6) See How the Cross Holds These Truths Together

The clearest display of God's character appears where many people least expect it: in the suffering and death of Jesus Christ. At the cross, God does not choose between justice and mercy. He reveals both.

Romans 3:25–26 (NSV) explains that God presented Christ as a sacrifice of atonement. The purpose is moral clarity. God shows His righteousness, and He justifies the one who has faith. This matters because forgiveness is not God pretending sin did not happen. Forgiveness is God dealing with sin in a way that satisfies righteousness and grants mercy.

This is why the gospel is not moral advice. It is divine action. God remains just, and God shows mercy. God keeps His holiness intact, and God extends love to sinners.

When you understand this, you gain a strong answer to two common fears:

- The fear that God is too holy to receive you.
- The fear that God is too kind to correct you.

The cross answers both. God receives repentant sinners because He provides cleansing. God corrects His people because He loves them enough to make them holy.

7) Learn to Trust God's Character in Real Situations

Doctrine becomes valuable when it steadies you under pressure.

When you feel condemned: remember God's mercy and love. Confess sin with honesty. Do not hide. God calls you into light so He can restore you.

When you feel casual about sin: remember God's holiness and justice. Do not treat grace as permission. Grace trains you to obey.

When you suffer unfair treatment: remember God's justice. You can pursue help, seek protection, and speak truth without sinking into bitterness. God's throne rests on righteousness.

When you doubt God's goodness: remember that Scripture defines goodness by God's character, not by your comfort. God's love remains steady even when circumstances feel confusing. Mercy does not mean an easy path. Mercy means God does not abandon His people.

A mature Christian learns to say, with calm confidence, that God is good even when life hurts. That confidence does not come from denial. It comes from knowing God's character.

8) Practice a Simple "Four-Part" Worship Pattern

If you want these truths to shape your life, apply them in worship. Use a four-part pattern in prayer:

1. **Praise God for His holiness** (reverence).
2. **Thank God for His love** (gratitude).
3. **Submit to God's justice** (humility and integrity).
4. **Ask God for mercy** (confession and help).

CHAPTER 4

RECEIVE GOD'S WORD: UNDERSTAND INSPIRATION, AUTHORITY, AND CLARITY OF SCRIPTURE

If you want to know God rightly, you must know how He speaks. Christians do not treat the Bible as a helpful religious guide among many. We treat it as God's written Word. That single conviction shapes everything else: how we worship, how we make choices, how we correct sin, and how we endure suffering.

Many people today respect the Bible in theory but ignore it in practice. Others read it but do not trust it. Some treat it like a book of inspiring thoughts. Some treat it like a codebook for winning arguments. Scripture calls us to a better posture: hear God's voice, submit to it, and live by it.

This chapter will explain three closely linked truths: **inspiration** (where Scripture comes from), **authority** (what Scripture requires), and **clarity** (how Scripture speaks). We will also look at how the church has defended these truths across history, and how you can read the Bible with confidence and care.

1) Start with Inspiration: Scripture Is God-Breathed

The central text for inspiration is 2 Timothy 3:16–17 (NSV). It teaches that all Scripture is God-breathed and useful for teaching, correction, and training in righteousness, so God's people are equipped for good works.

"God-breathed" means Scripture originates from God. It does not mean the human authors became robots. It means God spoke through human writers in such a way that what they wrote is truly God's Word.

2 Peter 1:20–21 (NSV) adds important detail. Prophecy did not come by human will. Men spoke from God as they were moved by the Holy Spirit. The Spirit's work did not erase personality, style, or historical context. It ensured the final message was God's intended Word.

This protects you from two mistakes:

- **Mistake one:** treating the Bible as a merely human book that can be dismissed when it conflicts with preference.
- **Mistake two:** treating the Bible as if God dropped it from heaven without human language, history, or genre.

Inspiration means God used real people, in real times, using real words, to communicate a message that is fully trustworthy.

2) Understand What Inspiration Does and Does Not Mean

Inspiration does not mean every biblical writer knew every implication of what they wrote. It also does not mean every verse is equally easy to interpret. The Bible contains poetry, narrative, prophecy, proverbs, letters, and visions. Each genre communicates in its own way.

Inspiration does mean that Scripture is reliable in what it teaches. Jesus treats Scripture this way. He quotes it as decisive. He appeals to it as the final court. He teaches that Scripture cannot be broken (John 10:35, NSV).

The apostles do the same. They reason from Scripture, correct error by Scripture, and call the church to submit to Scripture. The pattern is consistent: God speaks, and God's people listen.

3) Move to Authority: Scripture Carries God's Right to Command

Authority means Scripture is not merely informative. It is binding. When Scripture speaks, God speaks. That is why Scripture carries the right to correct you even when you disagree.

A key passage is 1 Thessalonians 2:13 (NSV). Paul thanks God that the believers received the apostolic message not as the word of men, but as what it truly is: the word of God, which works in those who believe. The church is not free to treat Scripture as optional. Scripture addresses the church with God's authority.

Authority also means you cannot place your conscience above the Word. Your conscience matters, but it is not infallible. It can be misinformed or hardened. Scripture is the standard that informs the conscience. When conscience and Scripture conflict, Scripture corrects conscience.

This is one reason Christians have historically emphasized preaching. Preaching is not entertainment. It is the public reading and explanation of God's Word so God's people can obey.

4) Receive Scripture as Sufficient for Faith and Life

Another key principle is sufficiency. Sufficiency means Scripture contains everything necessary for salvation and godly living. It does not contain every fact about science, medicine, or engineering. It does contain everything you need to know God, trust Christ, repent of sin, and walk in obedience.

2 Timothy 3:16–17 (NSV) points in this direction. Scripture equips believers for every good work. That does not mean it answers every curiosity. It means it provides what is necessary to live faithfully.

Across church history, this principle has guarded the church from two dangers:

- **Adding to Scripture** as if God's Word is incomplete.
- **Replacing Scripture** with personal experiences or traditions as final authority.

Tradition can be helpful. Church history can clarify. Teachers can guide. But none of these can take the place of Scripture's final authority.

5) Grasp Clarity: Scripture Is Understandable in Its Main Message

Some people avoid the Bible because they assume it is too hard. Others avoid it because they want to keep control. The doctrine of clarity confronts both.

Clarity does not mean every passage is equally plain. It means the Bible's main message is clear enough for ordinary believers, using normal means, to understand what God requires for salvation and faithful living.

Psalm 119:105 (NSV) describes God's word as a lamp to the feet and a light to the path. A lamp does not show you everything at once. It shows you enough to take the next faithful step. That is the Bible's practical clarity.

The New Testament assumes believers can read and understand Scripture. Paul's letters were read to whole churches, including people with different levels of education. He expects them to learn, apply, and grow.

Clarity also means Scripture interprets Scripture. When you are confused by one passage, you look for other passages that speak more directly. Over time, the Bible becomes its own teacher.

6) Use Sound Reading Habits: Context, Genre, and Repetition

Clarity becomes real in your life when you adopt good habits.

Read in context.

Ask: Who is speaking? To whom? What problem is being addressed? What comes before and after?

Recognize genre.

Poetry uses imagery. Proverbs give general patterns, not guaranteed outcomes in every case. Narratives describe events, but not every event is a command. Letters contain direct instruction for church life.

Notice repetition.

Scripture repeats key truths. God's holiness is repeated. Human sin is repeated. God's promise to save is repeated. Christ's resurrection is repeated. Repetition signals emphasis.

Summarize in your own words.

After reading a section, state the main point in one sentence. This simple practice exposes misunderstandings early.

7) Learn How the Church Has Protected Scripture's Authority

Throughout history, the church has faced pressure to lower Scripture's status. Sometimes the pressure comes from government power. Sometimes from intellectual fashion. Sometimes from church leaders who want to control people.

During the Protestant Reformation, one major emphasis was that Scripture is the final standard for doctrine and practice. The church did not reject all tradition. It rejected tradition as the highest authority. That debate still matters because many believers today feel pulled between Scripture and strong voices—online teachers, political movements, or popular therapy language.

The church's enduring need is the same: receive God's Word as God's Word.

8) Face Common Challenges without Fear

You will meet common objections. Many are sincere questions. Some are excuses. Either way, you should learn to respond calmly.

"There are many interpretations, so we cannot know what Scripture means."

There are many interpretations because humans disagree, not because Scripture is meaningless. On central matters—God's nature, sin, Christ, salvation, holiness—Scripture is clear. Disagreements often arise from ignoring context or forcing the text to serve an agenda.

"The Bible was written long ago, so it cannot address modern life."

Scripture addresses the heart, and the heart has not changed. Technologies change, but pride, fear, lust, greed, bitterness, and unbelief remain. Scripture speaks to the roots. Wise application brings it into present situations.

"My experience feels more real than what I read."

Experiences are powerful, but they are not final. Scripture corrects experiences and interprets them. If you let experience overrule Scripture, you will drift into confusion.

9) Put Scripture's Authority into Practice

Here is where this chapter becomes personal. Many people claim the Bible is authoritative. Few let it correct them.

Scripture's authority shows up in three measurable ways:

1. **Your willingness to obey when it is costly.**
2. **Your willingness to change your mind when Scripture corrects you.**

3. **Your willingness to submit desires to God rather than bending God to desires.**

Jesus compares obedience to building on rock (Matthew 7:24–27, NSV). The storm reveals the foundation. It is easy to claim authority during calm days. It is harder when obedience brings tension, loss, or ridicule.

A steady Christian learns to obey Scripture before the storm arrives.

10) Read the Bible as a Means of Grace

The Bible is not only a source of doctrine. It is a means God uses to strengthen faith. When you read Scripture, you are not merely gathering data. You are meeting God through His Word.

That does not mean every reading session feels warm. Some sessions feel dry. Some confront sin. Some expose confusion. Keep going. Over time, Scripture shapes instincts. It reforms priorities. It rebuilds hope.

To keep it simple, use this weekly pattern:

- **Daily:** read one chapter and write a one-sentence summary.
- **Weekly:** choose one key passage to memorize.
- **Ongoing:** bring your questions to a local church, not only to the internet.

Scripture was not given to isolate you. It was given to form you within God's people.

CHAPTER 5

RELY ON GOD'S PROVIDENCE: SEE HIS RULE OVER NATURE, NATIONS, AND DAILY LIFE

Most believers say, "God is in control," until life stops feeling controlled. A diagnosis arrives. A job ends. A child wanders. A conflict hardens. In those moments, the doctrine of providence moves from a word you recognize to a truth you must lean on.

This chapter will help you rely on providence with clarity. We will define it, show it in Scripture, address common misunderstandings, and apply it to fear, suffering, planning, and prayer.

1) Define Providence in Plain Words

Providence includes three inseparable truths:

1. **God preserves**: He sustains the world and every creature moment by moment.
2. **God governs**: He rules events, choices, and outcomes without losing control.
3. **God provides**: He cares for His people with wise fatherly care.

A key text is Psalm 103:19 (NSV): the Lord has established His throne in the heavens, and His kingdom rules over all. That is comprehensive. Nothing sits outside His royal authority.

Another key text is Ephesians 1:11 (NSV): God works all things according to the counsel of His will. Scripture does not say God reacts to history. It says God works within history to accomplish His purpose.

Providence is not fate. Fate is impersonal. Providence is personal rule by the living God. Providence also is not a vague optimism. It is the conviction that God is present and active in every season.

A common worry appears quickly. If God rules all things, do human choices matter? Yes, because Scripture affirms both God's sovereignty and real human responsibility.

Proverbs 16:9 (NSV) says the heart of a man plans his way, but the Lord establishes his steps. That verse does not cancel planning. It places planning under God's rule. Humans make meaningful choices. God governs outcomes.

Here is the point you must keep: God's providence does not turn people into puppets. Scripture treats human decisions as morally significant and accountable. At the same time, Scripture refuses to place God at the mercy of human will.

This balance protects you from two opposite errors:

- **Passive fatalism**: "Nothing I do matters, so I will do nothing."
- **Anxious control**: "Everything depends on me, so I must manage everything."

Providence produces a third posture: **responsible action with settled trust**.

3) See Providence in Creation and Daily Provision

Jesus points to small details to teach big trust. In Matthew 10:29–31 (NSV), He speaks about sparrows that do not fall apart from the Father's care, then He says you are worth more than many sparrows. The argument is simple: if God attends to small creatures, He does not ignore His children.

That passage does not promise comfort at every moment. It promises attention. God's care is not distant. It is direct.

Acts 17:26–28 (NSV) adds another layer. Paul tells the Athenians that God determined times and boundaries for nations, and that in Him we live and move and have our being. Providence covers biology, geography, history, and breath. God is not locked inside religious spaces. He rules the ordinary world.

This means your daily life is not spiritually empty. Meals, work, schedules, setbacks, and relationships all sit under God's rule. The

Christian does not divide life into "God's territory" and "real life." All of life is lived before God.

4) Learn How Providence Works in Suffering

Providence becomes hardest when you face pain. You may be tempted to choose between two bad options: either God is good but weak, or God is strong but harsh. Scripture rejects that false choice. God is both sovereign and good.

Romans 8:28 (NSV) is one of the clearest statements: God works all things for good for those who love Him and are called according to His purpose. The verse does not say all things are good. It says God works in all things for good. That difference matters.

What does "good" mean in that verse? The context points to being conformed to the image of Christ (Romans 8:29, NSV). God's goal is not short-term comfort. God's goal is Christlike maturity, steadfast faith, and final glory.

Does this make suffering easy to bear? No, but it prevents despair. It anchors suffering in a purposeful story rather than chaos.

Church history reflects this same conviction. Augustine wrote often about God's rule even in a broken world, insisting that evil is never equal to God. Centuries later, many Reformers emphasized providence not to produce cold theory, but to provide comfort in unstable times. The point was pastoral: believers can rest because the Father reigns.

Many confessions echo that pastoral aim. They speak of providence as God's fatherly hand that governs all things for the good of His people. That language has helped generations stand firm in persecution, illness, poverty, and uncertainty.

5) Use Joseph's Story as a Case Study

Genesis 50:20 (NSV) gives one of the clearest windows into providence in human history. Joseph speaks to the brothers who betrayed him. He says they meant evil against him, but God meant it for good, to preserve many lives.

Notice what the verse does and does not do.

- It **does** call their action evil. Providence does not rename sin as virtue.

- It **does** say God had a good purpose that overruled their evil intent.
- It **does not** say God excused their guilt.
- It **does not** remove Joseph's pain or deny his years of hardship.

This is providence with moral clarity. Humans can intend evil. God can intend good through the same event without being the author of sin. Scripture is comfortable saying both.

If you want a mature view of providence, return to Joseph often. It teaches patience. It teaches forgiveness without pretending. It teaches that God can bring life out of what looked like ruin.

6) Avoid Common Distortions of Providence

Distortion 1: "Everything That Happens Must Be Good"

This sounds pious, but it is careless. Scripture calls many things evil: oppression, deceit, violence, abuse. To call evil "good" is to mis-speak. It can also harm the wounded.

A better statement is this: **God is good, and God can work good through evil without approving evil.**

Distortion 2: "Providence Means I Do Not Need Wisdom"

Some believers stop planning and stop seeking counsel. Scripture never teaches that. Proverbs is filled with calls to wisdom, diligence, and restraint. Providence does not cancel means. God often provides through ordinary means: work, medicine, wise counsel, and faithful planning.

Distortion 3: "Providence Means God Does Not Care About My Tears"

Providence can be misused as a cold answer: "God is sovereign, so stop crying." That is not biblical. Scripture includes lament and grief. Jesus Himself wept. God's rule does not erase sorrow. It gives sorrow a place to go.

Here is the question many people fear to ask: *If God rules, why pray?* Because God ordains both the ends and the means, and prayer is one of His appointed means. Scripture presents prayer as real participation in God's work. You do not pray to inform God. You pray to honor God, ask for help, and align your will with His.

Providence gives you a stable approach to choices.

1. **Use wisdom**: gather facts, seek counsel, and consider consequences.
2. **Obey Scripture**: never choose what God forbids, even if it seems efficient.
3. **Act with humility**: make plans, then hold them loosely.
4. **Trust God with outcomes**: do your duty, and leave the result to God.

This does not remove tension. It removes panic. It also guards you from interpreting every closed door as punishment or every open door as approval. Doors open for many reasons. You need Scripture, wisdom, and prayer to interpret them.

A steady life does not require perfect foresight. It requires faithful steps under God's care.

8) Let Providence Produce Four Practical Fruits

Fruit 1: Courage

If God reigns, you can obey even when obedience costs you. Fear loses some of its power when you remember God's throne is not threatened.

Fruit 2: Patience

Providence teaches timing. God often works slowly. He forms character over years, not days. You may not see what He is doing right now, but His work continues.

Fruit 3: Gratitude

Every ordinary good becomes a gift. Food, sleep, friendship, and work are no longer "normal." They are provision from the Father's hand.

Fruit 4: Repentance and Humility

Providence confronts pride. You are not the center. You are not in charge. This is not crushing; it is freeing. You are a creature loved by the Creator.

Use a short pattern that joins trust and action:

1. **Name what you control** (choices, obedience, attitude).
2. **Name what you do not control** (timing, outcomes, other people).
3. **Ask for wisdom and courage** for what you must do.
4. **Entrust outcomes to God** and choose one next faithful step.

This is not a formula. It is a way to pray like a Christian who believes God reigns and listens.

Providence is not meant to satisfy curiosity. It is meant to steady the soul. The Lord's throne stands. His care reaches into your day. So you can plan, obey, repent, work, and rest without living as if the world depends on you.

CHAPTER 6

WORSHIP GOD AS CREATOR: CONNECT CREATION, ORDER, AND HUMAN PURPOSE

Many people treat creation as background scenery. Scripture treats it as testimony. The Bible begins with God creating, not because God needed a world, but because God chose to make one. Creation reveals God's power, wisdom, generosity, and authority. It also tells you something about yourself: you are not self-made, and you are not accidental. You were made by God and for God.

This chapter will help you worship God as Creator in a way that shapes daily life. We will look at what Scripture teaches about creation, why order matters, what it means to be made in God's image, and how creation connects to work, rest, and responsibility. We will also address common confusions that weaken faith.

1) Begin with the Bible's Opening Claim: God Created All Things

Genesis 1:1 (NSV) is direct: "In the beginning God created the heavens and the earth." The verse is not an argument. It is a declaration. Scripture does not introduce God as a discovery. It introduces God as the Creator who already exists.

This single statement sets a clear boundary against two errors:

- The world is not divine. God is not part of the world. God made the world.

- The world is not ultimate. The created order has purpose because it came from a purposeful Maker.

When Christians confess God as Creator, we confess His rightful ownership. Creation belongs to God. Life belongs to God. You belong to God.

2) Learn What Creation Shows About God

Scripture repeatedly links creation to God's glory and power.

Psalm 33:6–9 (NSV) emphasizes God's effective speech: He spoke, and it came to be. This is not a poetic exaggeration. It is the Bible's way of saying God creates with authority. He does not struggle. He does not compete with another power. He commands, and reality responds.

Jeremiah 10:12 (NSV) highlights God's wisdom: He made the earth by His power and established the world by His wisdom. Creation is not random assembly. It reflects design, order, and purposeful arrangement.

These texts do not answer every modern question about processes and timelines. Their primary aim is theological: the world is God's work, so the world is meaningful.

Practical result: worship begins with recognition. You are living in God's world, not your own. That changes the way you treat people, time, money, and the earth itself.

3) Understand Order: God Made a World You Can Live In

Creation is not chaos. God forms and fills. He separates light from darkness, land from seas, and then places living creatures in their proper domains. The repeated pattern in Genesis 1 is "and it was so." God's word brings stability.

Order is not a cage. Order is a gift. It makes life possible. It supports learning, work, community, and stewardship. When Scripture speaks about God's providence and wisdom, it often assumes this ordered creation.

This also connects to moral order. Many people today want the benefits of an ordered world but reject a moral order that comes from God. Scripture ties them together. If God is Creator, then God defines the good. The created world is not a blank canvas for self-definition. It is a world with a Maker, and a Maker's purposes.

Practical result: you can submit to God's design with trust rather than suspicion. God's commands are not random restrictions. They flow from His wisdom as Creator.

4) Receive the Gift of Being Human: Made in God's Image

Genesis 1:26–27 (NSV) teaches that God made humanity in His image. This does not mean humans are divine. It means humans reflect God in a creaturely way. We can know, love, rule responsibly, communicate, create, and live in moral relationship.

The image of God is foundational for human dignity. It applies to every human being, not only the strong, the young, the healthy, or the useful. The unborn, the elderly, the disabled, the poor, and the outsider all bear God's image. That is why Scripture condemns violence and contempt. Human life is sacred because it is God-given.

This truth also corrects pride. Being in God's image does not mean you are the center. It means you are accountable to the One you reflect. Image implies representation. You are meant to live in a way that points beyond yourself.

Practical result: treat people as image-bearers. Speak with care. Refuse cruelty. Practice honesty. Protect the vulnerable. These are not optional ethics. They are consequences of creation.

5) Connect Creation to Calling: Work and Stewardship

Work is not a punishment. Work appears before the fall. Genesis 2:15 (NSV) says God placed the man in the garden to work it and keep it. That means work is part of God's good design. Work is one way humans reflect God's wise rule.

This changes how you view ordinary labor. Work is not only about income. Work is a calling to serve others and honor God. Some work is public; some is hidden. Both matter. A parent caring for children, a mechanic repairing engines, a nurse tending wounds, and a teacher shaping minds are all serving within God's created order.

Stewardship follows naturally. To "keep" the garden implies responsibility. The earth is not a god to worship. It is not a toy to abuse. It is God's possession entrusted to human care.

Church history often emphasized this connection. Many Christian teachers spoke about vocation as service. The value of work was tied to God's creation design, not only to personal ambition.

Practical result: ask a simple question about your labor: "Who does this serve?" When your work serves people and honors God's commands, it becomes an act of worship.

6) Receive Rest as a Created Good: The Pattern of Sabbath

Genesis 2:2–3 (NSV) teaches that God rested on the seventh day and blessed it. God did not rest because He was tired. God rested to set a pattern. Rest declares that the world does not depend on your constant activity.

Rest is both spiritual and practical. It trains you to trust God's providence. It also protects you from burnout and from the pride that assumes your work holds the world together.

The Bible's later teaching about Sabbath is rich and sometimes debated across traditions. Christians differ on how Sabbath observance applies under the new covenant. Yet the core principle remains: God builds rest into faithful living. Jesus also calls the weary to come to Him for rest (Matthew 11:28–29, NSV). That rest is not only a schedule. It is a relationship with the Lord who carries burdens.

Practical result: plan rest. Treat it as obedience, not laziness. Make space for worship, family, and renewal. Your limits are not failures. They are part of creaturehood.

7) Face the Fall without Losing the Goodness of Creation

Genesis teaches creation is good, and it also teaches creation is now broken by sin. The fall affects human hearts, relationships, work, and the wider world. Yet Scripture never treats creation as worthless. It treats creation as damaged and groaning, awaiting renewal.

Romans 8:19–22 (NSV) speaks of creation's longing for liberation from corruption. That passage is not merely poetic. It frames history. God will not discard His world. He will redeem it. That connects creation to the future hope we will study later.

This guards you from two errors:

- **Despising the material world** as if spirituality means escape from creation.
- **Worshiping the material world** as if creation is the highest good.

Christian faith refuses both. The Creator is to be worshiped. Creation is to be stewarded and enjoyed with gratitude.

Practical result: enjoy created goods without making them ultimate. Food, art, music, nature, and friendship are gifts. Receive them with thanks. Do not treat them as saviors.

8) Answer Common Confusions with Calm Clarity

Confusion 1: "Science and Scripture must be enemies."

Scripture and honest observation of the world need not be enemies because God is the author of both creation and revelation. Many historical Christians worked in science precisely because they believed the world is ordered and intelligible.

Still, Scripture's purpose is not to be a modern textbook. Its purpose is to reveal God and His saving plan. So you should not force Scripture into questions it was not written to answer. At the same time, you should not let modern theories erase what Scripture clearly teaches: God is Creator, and humans are His creatures.

Confusion 2: "If God made the world, then the world is perfect as it is."

No. Scripture teaches the fall. The world contains beauty and disorder, pleasure and pain. Creation points to God's goodness, but it also shows the need for redemption.

Confusion 3: "Purpose is self-chosen."

Scripture teaches purpose is received from God. That does not erase creativity or personal calling. It anchors them. You are free to choose many paths, but you are not free to redefine the good apart from the Creator.

9) Let Creation Theology Shape Everyday Ethics

If God is Creator, then certain ethical conclusions follow.

- **Human life has dignity** because God gives it and images Himself in it.
- **Sex and marriage have meaning** because God designs bodies and covenant life.

- **Truth matters** because God is truthful and made humans to communicate.
- **Justice matters** because God rules the world in righteousness.

This does not make Christian ethics simplistic. It makes them grounded. You do not build morality on shifting trends. You build it on creation order and God's revealed will.

10) Practice One Week of "Creator-Focused" Living

Try a simple practice for seven days.

1. Each morning, read one Psalm that praises God as Creator.
2. Each day, thank God for three created gifts (food, air, sunlight, friendship, skill).
3. Choose one act of stewardship: care for a person, care for a space, or care for a task you usually neglect.
4. End each day with one sentence: "I am a creature, and God is faithful."

This is not sentimental. It is honest. It places you back in reality.

God is Creator. You are His creature. That is not a limitation. It is a gift. It means you can worship, work, rest, and hope with purpose.

BOOK TWO

UNDERSTAND HUMANITY UNDER GOD

A Simple Guide to the Image of God, Sin, Conscience, and Community

CHAPTER 1

ACCEPT HUMAN WORTH: LEARN WHAT "IMAGE OF GOD" MEANS FOR DAILY LIFE

People swing between two bad stories about humanity. One story says humans are basically good, so we only need encouragement. The other story says humans are basically worthless, so we should expect little more than selfishness. Scripture refuses both. The Bible teaches real dignity and real ruin at the same time. If you miss either side, you will harm people and confuse the gospel.

This chapter focuses on human worth. That may sound obvious, but it is not. Many Christians carry quiet contempt for themselves, while others carry loud contempt for their neighbors. Both errors grow in the same soil: forgetting what God says about human life. When you accept human worth as Scripture defines it, you gain a steadier view of yourself and others. You also gain a clearer reason to love, protect, and speak truth.

1) Begin with the Source of Human Worth

Human worth does not start with talent, health, strength, age, or productivity. It starts with God's act of creation and God's claim over His creatures. Scripture grounds dignity in God's design, not in social approval.

Psalm 8:4–6 (NSV) captures the wonder well. The writer looks at the vast heavens and asks why God is mindful of man. Then he states the answer: God crowned humanity with glory and honor and appointed humans to a responsible role in His world. The point is not that humans are great by nature. The point is that God gives a gifted status and a calling.

This means your worth is not fragile. It does not rise and fall with mood, income, or appearance. It rests on God's decision to create and honor human life.

2) Learn What the "Image of God" Includes

The Bible teaches that humans are made in God's image. Even when you do not quote the first chapter of Genesis, Scripture keeps returning to that truth in other places and builds ethical conclusions from it.

Genesis 9:6 (NSV) treats human life as uniquely protected because humans bear God's image. That passage appears after the flood, in a fallen world. It shows that the image is still a moral reality after sin entered the human story. Human dignity is not erased by human failure.

So what does "image of God" mean in daily terms?

It means humans are personal.

We are not only biological organisms. We think, choose, communicate, and form moral relationships.

It means humans are moral.

We are accountable. We can do right and wrong. We can repent. We can grow in wisdom.

It means humans are relational.

We are built for family, community, and covenant. Isolation damages us.

It means humans are responsible.

We can steward, build, organize, and serve. We are meant to cultivate and protect.

It means humans can reflect God.

We do not share God's essence, but we can display His character in a creaturely way: truthfulness, justice, mercy, creativity, and love.

Does this mean every person reflects God equally well at all times? No, because sin distorts the image's expression. Yet the image remains the basis for dignity and the reason Scripture condemns contempt.

3) Treat Speech as a Test of Your View of Human Worth

Scripture ties the image of God directly to how you talk about people.

James 3:9–10 (NSV) warns that with the tongue we bless the Lord, and with the same tongue we curse people who are made in God's likeness. James treats this as a moral contradiction. He does not excuse it as a personality trait. He names it as spiritual disorder.

This matters because speech is where contempt often hides. People may never throw a punch, yet they strike with words. They mock weakness. They reduce people to labels. They spread rumors. They talk about others as if they are objects.

If you accept the image of God, your speech must change. You can still confront sin. You can still tell hard truths. But you cannot treat image-bearers as disposable.

A simple practice helps: before you speak about someone, ask what your words are trying to accomplish. Are you aiming to build, correct, protect, or heal? Or are you trying to dominate, shame, and win?

4) Hold Dignity and Difference Together

Scripture teaches equal worth, and it also teaches real difference. God made humans male and female. God gives different gifts. God assigns different roles in families and communities. Yet those differences never cancel dignity.

In Galatians 3:28 (NSV), Paul insists that in Christ there is no hierarchy of worth based on ethnicity, social status, or sex. The verse does not erase all distinctions in life. It does erase any claim that some people are closer to God by nature and others are second-class.

This truth matters for churches and families. It calls leaders to lead with honor. It calls parents to treat children as persons, not projects. It calls husbands and wives to serve one another with respect. It calls believers to welcome the poor, the outsider, and the wounded, not as charity cases, but as neighbors.

5) Connect Human Worth to the Second Adam

The image of God becomes clearer when you see Jesus. Scripture calls Christ the visible image of the invisible God (Colossians 1:15, NSV). Jesus shows what true humanity looks like under God: obedient, truthful, compassionate, strong, and clean.

This protects you from another common error. Many people measure human worth by performance. Scripture measures human worth by creation and then shows restored humanity in Christ. Jesus is not only the Savior from sin. He is also the model of faithful human life.

When you look at Christ, you see dignity without pride and humility without self-hatred. You see authority used for service. You see strength paired with gentleness. That is what God aims to form in His people.

6) Apply Human Worth to the Hard Places

The doctrine of the image of God is not only for debates. It is for the hardest places in life: conflict, weakness, aging, and suffering.

When you face weakness in yourself:

You do not need to despise yourself to grow. You can repent without self-hatred. You can seek help without shame. Worth and weakness can exist in the same person, because worth rests on God's gift, not your power.

When you face weakness in others:

You do not treat people as burdens. You treat them as neighbors. This includes those who cannot "pay you back." It includes the sick, the elderly, and the disabled. The image of God calls for patient honor.

When you face conflict:

You can confront wrong without dehumanizing the person who did it. That does not mean you ignore harm. It means you pursue justice without contempt.

When you face cultural pressure to reduce people to categories:

You resist. Scripture gives you a better lens. You see persons, not stereotypes. You see souls, not talking points.

Is it naïve to treat everyone as an image-bearer in a harsh world? No, because Scripture does not deny evil. It commands love in the presence of evil. It also gives tools for protection, boundaries, and accountability.

7) Watch for Two Dangers: Pride and Despair

The image of God guards you from despair, but it can be twisted into pride.

Pride says: "I am made in God's image, so I answer to no one."

Scripture rejects that. The image includes accountability. You are a representative under the King, not a rival to the King.

Despair says: "I am too broken to matter."

Scripture rejects that too. Even in a fallen world, the image remains the basis for dignity and the reason God calls for mercy and justice.

A balanced view says: "I matter because God made me. I must repent because I have sinned. I have hope because God restores."

8) Practice Honor as a Daily Discipline

Honor is not flattery. Honor means you treat people as weighty because God made them. It changes habits.

- You listen without interrupting.
- You tell the truth without cruelty.
- You keep promises because your word affects image-bearers.
- You refuse gossip because it tears down.
- You protect the vulnerable because God does.

Honor also shapes how you view your own body and life. Your body is not an accident. Your life is not your own possession. This will matter later when we discuss sin, conscience, and the moral life. For now, receive a basic truth: being human is a gift before it is a problem.

9) Bring It into the Church: A Community of Honor

The church should be the safest place to be treated as a person. That does not mean the church is perfect. It means the church should aim for a culture shaped by the image of God.

This includes practical commitments:

- Take repentance seriously, because sin harms people.
- Take forgiveness seriously, because grace restores people.
- Take discipline seriously, because love protects people.

- Take service seriously, because Christ dignifies people.

When a church forgets human worth, it becomes harsh or shallow. When a church remembers human worth, it becomes a place where truth and mercy can meet.

10) Summarize the Point You Must Keep

Human worth is not earned. It is received from God. The image of God explains why human life is sacred, why speech matters, why justice matters, and why love is commanded. It also prepares you for the next chapters, because the same Bible that gives dignity also explains what went wrong in the human heart.

You can accept human worth without denying human sin. In fact, you must hold both, or you will either excuse evil or crush the wounded. Scripture calls you to a stronger path: honor people as God's creatures, and call people back to God's ways.

CHAPTER 2

FACE THE FALL HONESTLY:
TRACE HOW SIN ENTERED AND SPREAD

If you only believe in human worth, you will not understand the world you live in. You will be confused by betrayal, addiction, violence, and hypocrisy—especially in yourself. Scripture honors human dignity, but it also tells the truth about human ruin. The Bible calls that ruin "sin," and it traces sin to a decisive turning point: the fall.

The fall is not a minor detail. It explains why people who know better still do wrong. It explains why good gifts become idols. It explains why shame and blame are so common. It also explains why salvation must be rescue, not self-improvement.

This chapter will trace how sin entered and spread, using Scripture's storyline and the church's careful reflection across history. We will look at the first transgression, the nature of temptation, the results of sin, and the way sin multiplies in families and nations. We will also address common modern misunderstandings that soften sin into mere weakness.

1) Start with God's Good World and a Clear Command

Genesis begins with a good creation. God speaks, orders, blesses, and calls His work good. Humanity is placed in a garden not as prisoners, but as stewards. In that setting, God gives a command.

Genesis 2:16–17 (NSV) records it: God permits wide freedom—every tree except one. The boundary is clear, reasonable, and relational. The command also includes a warning: disobedience leads to death.

This matters because the fall did not come from scarcity. It came from abundance. Sin entered not because God withheld good, but because humans distrusted God's goodness and wanted autonomy.

Modern people often assume rules are signs of oppression. Scripture presents God's command as wise love. The boundary was meant to protect life and preserve trust.

2) Watch How Temptation Works: The Lie Attacks God's Character

Genesis 3 shows the strategy of temptation with frightening clarity. The serpent does not begin by denying God's existence. He begins by questioning God's word.

In Genesis 3:1 (NSV), the serpent twists God's command: "Did God really say...?" The goal is to plant suspicion. Then the serpent escalates: he denies the consequence and promises a different outcome.

The lie attacks three areas:

1. **God's word**: "Did God really say?"
2. **God's justice**: "You will not surely die."
3. **God's goodness**: "God knows ... you will be like God."

Temptation often follows this pattern today. It does not always present itself as rebellion. It presents itself as freedom. It suggests God is holding you back. It suggests obedience is naïve. It suggests you deserve more control.

Notice also how the lie makes sin look small and God's warning look exaggerated. That is a common move. Sin often enters the heart when you minimize consequences and maximize your own right to choose.

3) Identify the Heart of Sin: Self-Rule

At its core, sin is not only breaking a rule. It is turning from God to self-rule. It is choosing independence over trust.

Genesis 3:6 (NSV) describes the act: the woman sees, desires, takes, and eats; then she gives to her husband, and he eats. The language is simple, and that is part of its power. The moment is not described with drama. It is described like ordinary choice. Sin often begins as an ordinary choice that says, "My desire outranks God's word."

Church history has often described this as pride and disordered love. Augustine argued that sin is love turned inward, where the self becomes the center. That is not academic language. It is practical. When the self becomes the center, everything else becomes a tool: people, work, sex, money, even religion.

This also explains why sin spreads. Self-centeredness does not remain private. It shapes relationships.

4) Trace the Immediate Results: Shame, Blame, and Separation

As soon as Adam and Eve sin, the story shifts.

Genesis 3:7–10 (NSV) shows shame. They realize they are naked and hide. Shame is not only embarrassment. It is the sense of exposure and vulnerability before God and others. They cover themselves, and they avoid God's presence.

Then comes blame. Genesis 3:12–13 (NSV) shows each person shifting responsibility. Adam blames the woman and, indirectly, God: "the woman You gave me." The woman blames the serpent. Sin quickly turns people into self-defenders.

Then comes separation. The relationship with God becomes strained. The relationship between man and woman becomes strained. Harmony breaks. The fall fractures communion.

These results matter because they still describe life today. People hide. People cover. People blame. People avoid responsibility. People avoid God.

If you want to understand your own habits, ask where you hide, where you blame, and where you refuse honesty.

5) Understand God's Judgment and God's Mercy in the Same Scene

Genesis 3 includes judgment, and it also includes mercy.

God's judgment is real. The serpent is cursed. The woman's pain and conflict are increased. The man's work becomes hard and resisting. Death enters the human story. God's warning was not empty.

Yet God's mercy appears in several ways.

First, God seeks them. He asks, "Where are you?" (Genesis 3:9, NSV). That is not a request for information. It is a summons to confession.

Second, God provides clothing. Genesis 3:21 (NSV) says God made garments for them and clothed them. Their fig leaves were inadequate. God covers their shame more effectively than they can cover themselves.

Third, God gives a promise. Genesis 3:15 (NSV) speaks of the offspring who will crush the serpent's head. This is the first hint of redemption. The promise is not full detail, but it is a direction: God will act to defeat evil and restore what sin ruined.

This is important for the whole Bible. From the start, God's response to sin includes both judgment and a saving promise. The story does not end in the garden. It moves toward the cross.

6) Follow the Spread of Sin: From One Act to a Flood

Sin does not remain contained. Genesis quickly shows sin multiplying.

Genesis 4 records the first murder. Cain kills Abel. Then Cain denies responsibility: "Am I my brother's keeper?" (Genesis 4:9, NSV). That question captures the fall's logic. Self-rule refuses responsibility for others.

Soon, violence becomes normal. By Genesis 6:5 (NSV), Scripture says the intent of human hearts was continually evil. That statement is sweeping. It describes a moral collapse, not merely isolated mistakes.

The flood narrative is one of Scripture's clearest witnesses that sin is not a small flaw. It corrupts human society. It spreads across generations. It turns culture into a machine for producing harm.

At the same time, Genesis also shows God preserving a line of promise. God keeps His saving purpose moving forward.

7) Learn the Doctrines of "Original Sin" and "Sin's Spread" with Care

The church has used the term "original sin" to describe two related truths:

1. The first sin was the origin point of human rebellion.
2. Human beings now inherit a sinful condition that inclines them toward sin.

You do not need to use the term "original sin" to believe the biblical teaching. But it is useful language because it summarizes what Scripture shows.

Romans 5:12 (NSV) teaches that sin came into the world through one man, and death through sin, and so death spread to all because all sinned. This passage is important because it links Adam's sin to the universal reality of death and sin.

The point is not that humans are forced to sin against their will. The point is that human nature after the fall is bent. We sin because we are sinners, and we are sinners because the human race is now fallen.

Church history debated details of how Adam's sin relates to all humanity, but the central agreement has been strong: sin is universal, deep, and inherited in the sense that all humans are born into a corrupted condition.

This explains why sin appears early in life without needing to be taught. Children do not need lessons in selfishness. They need training in patience and truth. The bent is already present.

8) Face Total Corruption without Despair

Christians have sometimes used the phrase "total depravity." Many misunderstand it. It does not mean every person is as evil as possible. It means sin affects every part of the person: mind, will, desires, and actions.

Ephesians 2:1–3 (NSV) describes people apart from Christ as dead in trespasses, following sinful desires, and by nature children of wrath. That is strong language. It tells you sin is not merely an external habit. It is a spiritual condition.

Yet Scripture also teaches that humans still bear God's image. That means fallen humans can still do acts of kindness, create beauty, and build societies. The problem is that sin distorts motives and aims. Even good deeds can be done for pride, control, or fear. Without God, even "good" can become a path away from God.

Facing this truth should not produce despair. It should produce humility and hope. Humility, because you cannot fix yourself. Hope, because God's salvation is a real rescue.

9) Reject Modern Softening of Sin

Modern culture often avoids moral language. It prefers categories like "mistakes," "brokenness," or "struggle." Those words can describe real pain, but they can also hide guilt.

Scripture speaks more directly. Sin is lawlessness, rebellion, and unbelief. It is refusing God's rightful rule.

Why does this matter? Because you cannot repent of what you will not name. If sin is merely weakness, then you only need support. If sin is guilt before God, then you need forgiveness and change.

The gospel offers both comfort and correction. But it begins with truth.

10) Put the Fall into Your Own Story

The fall is not only a past event. It describes what happens in every human heart when temptation arrives.

The pattern still holds:

- Question God's word.
- Doubt God's goodness.
- Desire control.
- Take what is forbidden.
- Hide, blame, and harden.

If you can see that pattern in your own life, you can interrupt it earlier. You can respond to temptation with confession, Scripture, and prayer before sin grows.

And here is the hope: the story does not end with Adam. Scripture presents Christ as the one who obeys where Adam failed. Later we will study salvation in depth. For now, the truth is simple: the fall explains what is wrong, and God's promise points to what He will do to make things right.

CHAPTER 3

RECOGNIZE SIN'S PATTERNS: NAME PRIDE, IDOLATRY, AND SELF-RULE

Sin rarely announces itself with a warning label. It usually arrives as a pattern, a habit, a reflex. It feels normal because it has been practiced. That is one reason Scripture speaks so often about watchfulness. If you can learn to recognize sin's patterns, you can repent earlier, seek help sooner, and avoid damage that spreads into your relationships.

This chapter will name three core patterns Scripture exposes again and again: **pride**, **idolatry**, and **self-rule**. These patterns overlap. They often appear together. When you learn to spot them, you gain a clearer view of your own heart, and you gain a steadier way to counsel and care for others.

1) Start with the Heart: Sin Grows from the Inside Out

Many people treat sin as a behavior problem. Scripture goes deeper. The Bible treats sin as a heart problem that produces behaviors.

Jeremiah 17:9 (NSV) gives a sober assessment: the heart is deceitful above all things and desperately sick; who can understand it? The verse does not mean you cannot know anything about yourself. It means your inner life can mislead you. You can excuse what is harmful. You can call darkness "light" when you want control.

This is why biblical repentance starts with honesty before God. You do not merely stop a habit. You expose the desires and beliefs that feed it. Then you bring those desires under God's authority.

If that sounds discouraging, remember the purpose of the diagnosis. God exposes the heart so He can heal the heart. Scripture does not reveal sin to shame you into paralysis. It reveals sin so you can be freed from its grip.

Pride is not limited to arrogance and loud self-praise. Pride is any posture that places the self above God and above others. Pride wants to be central. Pride wants to be uncorrectable. Pride wants the final word.

Proverbs 16:18 (NSV) warns that pride goes before destruction, and a haughty spirit before a fall. This is not superstition. It is moral cause and effect. Pride makes you careless. It makes you overconfident. It makes you slow to listen. Then it sets you up for collapse.

Pride also hides under respectable forms:

- **Spiritual pride**: "God is fortunate to have me."

- **Intellectual pride**: "If I understand it, it must be true."

- **Moral pride**: "My sins are smaller than theirs."

- **Victim pride**: "Because I suffered, I can do as I please."

- **Quiet pride**: "I will never ask for help; I will prove myself."

In church history, Augustine wrote at length about pride as a root sin. He described it as the soul turned in on itself. That phrase matters because pride is not only self-love. Pride is self as the reference point for everything. God becomes a tool. People become props. Even good deeds become trophies.

How do you identify pride in daily life? Look for defensiveness when corrected. Look for joy when others fail. Look for resentment when someone else receives honor. Pride reveals itself by how it reacts, not only by what it says.

Idolatry sounds like a problem from the ancient world: statues, temples, and rituals. Scripture teaches a wider meaning. An idol is anything you trust, fear, or love more than God.

Ezekiel 14:3 (NSV) describes "idols in the heart." That phrase is crucial. Idolatry can exist without a statue. It can live in motives, longings, and private loyalties.

Idols often begin as good gifts:

- Work becomes identity.

- Family becomes ultimate.

- Romance becomes salvation.

- Money becomes security.
- Comfort becomes the highest goal.
- Reputation becomes a god you must feed.

Paul makes this concrete when he speaks of greed as idolatry (Colossians 3:5, NSV). Greed is not only wanting more. It is trusting more. It is treating possessions as protection and meaning.

Idolatry also explains why sin can feel necessary. If your idol is approval, then lying feels necessary. If your idol is control, then anger feels justified. If your idol is comfort, then compromise feels reasonable.

Martin Luther often said the human heart functions like an idol factory. His point was practical: if you tear one idol down, you will likely try to build another. That is why repentance is not a one-time event. It is a pattern of turning from false gods to the true God.

4) Name Self-Rule: The Refusal to Be Ruled by God

Self-rule is the engine behind pride and idolatry. It is the quiet decision: "I will decide what is right for me." Scripture treats that decision as rebellion because it rejects God's rightful authority.

Judges 21:25 (NSV) describes a society collapsing into chaos: everyone did what was right in his own eyes. The verse does not celebrate freedom. It warns about moral disorder. When people become their own law, the strong dominate the weak, and truth becomes flexible.

Self-rule appears in small daily forms:

- You obey when it matches your preference, and resist when it costs you.
- You treat Scripture as advice, not command.
- You keep "private sins" because you believe God should not touch that corner.
- You set your own standards and then call them "authentic."

Self-rule also appears in religion. Some people use religious activity to keep control. They serve, give, and volunteer, but they refuse surrender. They want a life that looks faithful without a heart that is submitted.

The early church fathers warned about this. They spoke of sin as disordered desire. When desire rules, God's commands feel like threats. When God rules, desire finds its proper place.

5) Track the Pattern: Desire, Justification, Action, and Covering

Sin often moves through a repeatable sequence. Naming the sequence helps you interrupt it.

1. **Desire awakens**: "I want this."
2. **Justification forms**: "I deserve this," or "This is different," or "No one will know."
3. **Action follows**: words spoken, money spent, boundaries crossed.
4. **Covering begins**: hiding, blaming, minimizing, comparing, or doubling down.

James describes this movement in a clear way: desire conceives, then gives birth to sin, and sin grows into death (James 1:14–15, NSV). James is not describing a rare event. He is describing common spiritual mechanics.

Once you see this, you can respond earlier. You can address desire and justification before action becomes a mess that harms others.

6) Recognize "Respectable" Sin Patterns

Some sins shock us. Others hide behind respectability. Scripture warns about both.

People-Pleasing

People-pleasing can look kind, but it often functions as idolatry. You crave approval, so you avoid truth. You fear conflict, so you stay silent when you should speak. Over time, your integrity weakens.

Galatians 1:10 (NSV) draws a line: if I were still trying to please man, I would not be a servant of Christ. Paul is not promoting rudeness. He is exposing divided loyalty. You cannot serve Christ while treating human approval as the final judge.

Bitterness

Bitterness often starts with real hurt. Then it becomes a settled posture. Hebrews 12:15 (NSV) warns that a root of bitterness can spring up and cause trouble, and many become defiled. Bitterness spreads. It changes how you interpret everything. It also invites revenge fantasies and cold speech.

Self-Pity

Self-pity can feel humble, but it can be pride turned inward. It says, "My pain gives me rights others do not have." Scripture calls you to bring pain to God and seek help, not to build a throne out of suffering.

These patterns matter because they often pass as "personality." Scripture calls them what they are: spiritual issues that require repentance and renewed trust.

7) Connect Sin Patterns to Relationships and Community

Sin is never only private. It affects speech, trust, and community health.

Pride damages relationships because it refuses to listen.

Idolatry damages relationships because it uses people.

Self-rule damages relationships because it rejects accountability.

That is why Scripture places so much emphasis on confession, forgiveness, and reconciliation. James 5:16 (NSV) calls believers to confess sins to one another and pray for one another. This does not mean public exposure of every struggle. It means sin thrives in secrecy, and healing often requires honest community.

Church history supports this. Many early Christian communities practiced regular confession and mutual correction, not to create shame, but to cultivate humility and protection. The point was simple: if sin hides, it grows. If sin is brought into light with repentance, it loses power.

8) Use Practical Tests to Identify Idols and Pride

You can learn a lot about your heart by asking diagnostic questions. You do not ask them to accuse yourself. You ask them to tell the truth.

- What do I fear losing most?
- What do I daydream about when I have time alone?
- What makes me angry fast?
- What do I defend without reflection?
- What do I hide?
- What do I trust when I feel unsafe?

Your answers often point to idols. They also show where pride demands control.

One question people often ask is: "How can I tell the difference between enjoying a gift and turning it into an idol?" The answer is straightforward: you can thank God for a gift and hold it loosely, but an idol demands your loyalty and punishes you with anxiety when it is threatened.

9) Replace Sin's Patterns with New Patterns

Scripture never calls you to stop sin without giving you a better path. Repentance has two sides: turning from sin and turning to God.

Here are three replacement patterns:

Replace Pride with Humility and Teachability

1 Peter 5:5–6 (NSV) calls believers to clothe themselves with humility and to humble themselves under God's mighty hand. Humility is not self-hatred. It is truthful self-placement under God.

Practice: invite correction from a mature believer. Then listen without interrupting. Write down what you heard. Pray over it. Act on one point.

Replace Idolatry with Worship and Gratitude

1 Thessalonians 1:9 (NSV) describes conversion as turning from idols to serve the living and true God. That is the core. Idols lose power when God becomes your primary love.

Practice: list three gifts you tend to treat as ultimate. Thank God for them. Then ask God to help you obey Him even if those gifts change.

Replace Self-Rule with Submission to Scripture

Psalm 119:11 (NSV) says, "I have stored up Your word in my heart, that I might not sin against You." Scripture becomes an inner guide. It confronts excuses early.

Practice: memorize a short passage that targets your common temptation, and speak it when the justification phase begins.

Naming sin patterns can feel heavy. Do not miss the purpose. God reveals sin so you will run to His mercy. You do not overcome pride by trying harder to be humble. You overcome pride by seeing the greatness of God and the grace of Christ. You do not escape idolatry by emptying your life of all desires. You escape idolatry by receiving a better treasure. You do not defeat self-rule by building stricter rules. You defeat self-rule by surrendering to a wiser King.

As you move through Book 2, you will see sin's effects in conscience, relationships, and culture. But you will also see why salvation must be God's work from start to finish. For now, take a clear first step: recognize the patterns. Bring them into the light. Ask God for clean repentance and steady obedience.

CHAPTER 4

MEASURE THE HEART BY GOD'S LAW:
USE THE COMMANDMENTS AS A MIRROR

Many people treat "God's law" like a relic. They picture stone tablets and ancient rules for another time. Scripture treats God's law as a gift that reveals truth, restrains harm, and guides love. The law does not save you, but it does expose what you need saving from. It also trains you to live as God's people.

In the last chapter, we named pride, idolatry, and self-rule as repeating sin patterns. Now we need a reliable measuring line. Feelings cannot measure the heart. Comparisons cannot measure the heart. God's law can. It gives clear categories for truth, worship, speech, sexuality, money, time, and relationships.

This chapter will help you use God's law the way Scripture uses it: as a mirror that shows what is in you, so you can repent with honesty and walk in obedience with clarity.

1) Understand Why God Gives Law at All

God gives law because God is King and Father. Kings set standards for life in their kingdom. Fathers instruct children for their good. God's commands are not random. They flow from His character and His design for human life.

Deuteronomy 10:12–13 (NSV) ties the purpose together: fear the Lord, walk in His ways, love Him, serve Him, and keep His commandments for your good. God's law aims at faithful living, not spiritual confusion.

So the law is not first a ladder to climb. It is light that shows the path. It is also a mirror that shows what is wrong in the heart.

2) Meet the Ten Commandments as a Summary of God's Moral Will

The Ten Commandments in Exodus 20:1–17 (NSV) give a clear summary of God's moral will. They are not the only commands in Scripture, but they function like a backbone. They teach you what love for God and neighbor looks like in concrete terms.

The commandments have a structure:

- The first commands focus on worship and loyalty to God.
- The later commands focus on life with other people.

This matches what Jesus later teaches about the greatest commandments: love God fully and love your neighbor as yourself (Matthew 22:37–40, NSV). Jesus does not replace God's moral will. He summarizes it and presses it deeper into the heart.

Are the commandments only about outward actions? No, because Scripture repeatedly shows that God aims at motives as well as behaviors.

3) Use the Law as a Mirror, Not a Mask

A mirror shows your true condition. A mask hides it. Many people use religion as a mask. They point to visible obedience while ignoring hidden sin.

Romans 3:19–20 (NSV) explains a core use of the law: the law speaks so every mouth may be stopped and the whole world held accountable to God; through the law comes knowledge of sin. That is blunt. The law removes excuses. It ends the habit of self-justification.

This is why moral people sometimes resist God's law. The law does not flatter. It names sin with precision. It exposes pride that hides behind respectability.

If you use the law as a mask, you will become defensive and harsh. If you use the law as a mirror, you will become honest and humble.

4) Learn Three Biblical Uses of God's Law

Across church history, teachers often explained the law's purpose in three broad uses. This is not a clever system. It is a practical summary of how Scripture speaks.

Use 1: The Law Reveals Sin and Drives You to Mercy

Romans 7:7 (NSV) captures it: Paul says he would not have known sin except through the law. The law exposes what hides in you. It identifies coveting, not only theft. It identifies inner desire, not only outward acts.

This use protects the gospel. If you do not see sin clearly, you will not value grace. You will think salvation is improvement, not rescue.

Use 2: The Law Restrains Evil in Society

Even unbelievers benefit from moral clarity. Laws against murder, theft, and perjury restrain harm. Social customs shaped by Scripture can reduce violence and protect families. This restraint does not change the heart. It limits damage.

The Bible assumes this function when it calls rulers to punish wrongdoing and reward good (Romans 13:3–4, NSV). The point is not that governments create righteousness. The point is that God uses order to restrain chaos.

Use 3: The Law Guides Believers in Grateful Obedience

Once you belong to God, you do not obey to earn acceptance. You obey because you are accepted in Christ, and you want to please your Father. Scripture treats obedience as the path of wisdom.

Jesus says plainly, "If you love Me, you will keep My commandments" (John 14:15, NSV). Love does not float above obedience. Love expresses itself through obedience.

This third use keeps believers from drifting into moral fog. Grace does not erase God's moral will. Grace trains you to delight in it.

5) Let the Commandments Expose Pride, Idolatry, and Self-Rule

The Ten Commandments cut through the three patterns we named earlier.

- Pride resists submission. The first command demands loyalty to God alone.
- Idolatry seeks replacements. The commandments forbid worshiping God on your own terms.
- Self-rule rejects boundaries. The commandments define right and wrong outside your feelings.

Here is a simple way to read the commandments as heart-tests:

1. **No other gods**: What do I treat as ultimate?
2. **No carved images**: Do I remake God into a version I prefer?
3. **Honor God's name**: Do I use God to decorate my plans?
4. **Remember the Sabbath**: Do I trust God enough to rest?
5. **Honor parents**: Do I honor rightful authority and responsibility?
6. **Do not murder**: Do I nurture anger and contempt?
7. **Do not commit adultery**: Do I treat people as objects?
8. **Do not steal**: Do I take what is not mine, in money or time?
9. **Do not bear false witness**: Do I shape truth to protect myself?
10. **Do not covet**: Do I resent what God has given others?

Notice how many aim at the inner life. God's law does not stop at public reputation. It reaches the heart.

6) Understand How Jesus Deepens the Law without Changing It

Some people read the Old Testament law and think Jesus lowered the standard. Jesus did the opposite. He exposed the law's true depth.

In Matthew 5:21–22 (NSV), Jesus connects murder to anger. In Matthew 5:27–28 (NSV), He connects adultery to lust. His point is not that external obedience is meaningless. His point is that external obedience can hide a corrupt heart.

This helps you see why you need more than rules. You need a changed heart. The law tells you what love requires. It cannot create love in you. Only God's grace can do that.

So the law and the gospel are not enemies. The law diagnoses. The gospel heals and renews. Then renewed people learn to obey from the heart.

7) Avoid Two Errors: Legalism and Lawlessness

When Christians talk about God's law, two errors show up quickly.

Error 1: Legalism

Legalism uses law to earn God's acceptance. It treats obedience as a payment plan. It often produces pride, fear, and hypocrisy.

Paul rejects this with force. Galatians 2:16 (NSV) teaches that a person is not justified by works of the law but through faith in Jesus Christ. Justification is God's verdict of "righteous" on the basis of Christ, not your performance.

Legalism also harms relationships. It makes you a judge who scans others for failure, while hiding your own. It turns church into a courtroom.

Error 2: Lawlessness

Lawlessness uses grace as an excuse to ignore obedience. It says, "God forgives, so it does not matter how I live." Scripture rejects that too.

James 2:8 (NSV) calls the love command the "royal law." It is royal because it belongs to the King and governs His people. Love is not lawless. Love has shape.

Both errors twist the Bible. Legalism forgets grace. Lawlessness forgets holiness. The gospel preserves both: free forgiveness and real transformation.

8) Practice Using the Law for Self-Examination without Self-Destruction

Some believers fear self-examination because it can spiral into shame. Others avoid it because it threatens comfort. Scripture calls for a healthier path: honest confession under mercy.

Psalm 139:23–24 (NSV) models this: the psalmist asks God to search him, know his heart, and lead him in the everlasting way. This is not self-hatred. It is openness to God's correction with confidence in God's care.

Use this simple process:

1. **Read one commandment slowly.**
2. **Ask what it requires and what it forbids.**
3. **Name one outward way you obey and one inward way you resist.**
4. **Confess specific sin without excuses.**
5. **Ask God for strength to change one concrete behavior this week.**

This process works because it keeps confession specific and action-oriented. It also keeps you anchored in grace. You are not confessing to earn love. You are confessing because you are loved.

The commandments are not private spirituality. They protect real people.

- "Do not bear false witness" protects reputations and justice.

- "Do not steal" protects families and livelihoods.

- "Do not commit adultery" protects marriages and children.

- "Honor your father and mother" protects generational stability.

- "Do not covet" protects the heart from resentment that poisons community.

When a church treats these commands lightly, trust collapses. When believers take them seriously, community grows safer and stronger.

This is why many churches across history taught the Ten Commandments using catechisms and sermons. They wanted believers to understand sin, practice repentance, and learn the shape of love. The goal was not control. The goal was formation.

10) Keep the Main Point Clear:
The Mirror Leads to the Savior and the Path

God's law is a mirror that tells the truth. It shows you God's holy standard. It shows you your real condition. It also shows you the shape of love.

But the mirror cannot wash you. It can only show the dirt. When the mirror exposes sin, you must go to the cleansing God provides. Later books will focus on salvation in depth. For now, keep one truth fixed: the law makes the need clear so grace becomes precious.

So use the commandments the right way:

- Let them humble you, not harden you.

- Let them convict you, not crush you.

- Let them guide you, not inflate you.

When you measure your heart by God's law, you stop bargaining with sin. You also begin to see obedience as the practical path of love.

CHAPTER 5

UNDERSTAND GUILT AND SHAME: TELL THE DIFFERENCE AND SEEK TRUE CLEANSING

Guilt and shame often travel together, but they are not the same. If you confuse them, you will apply the wrong remedy. You may try to silence guilt with excuses. Or you may try to heal shame with achievements. Neither works for long.

Scripture speaks to both with clear realism and real hope. It tells you what guilt is, what shame is, how they damage the heart, and how God provides cleansing that reaches deeper than appearances. This matters for discipleship, counseling, parenting, and daily growth. Many people live for years under a heavy weight because they never learned to name the problem correctly.

In this chapter, you will learn to distinguish guilt from shame, identify how each one operates, and pursue the kind of cleansing God gives through confession, forgiveness, and restored fellowship.

1) Define Guilt: A Legal and Moral Reality Before God

Guilt is objective. It describes real moral liability. When you break God's law, you stand guilty before Him, whether you feel it or not. Feelings may intensify guilt, but feelings do not create guilt.

Scripture presents guilt in courtroom terms. God is Judge. His law is good. Sin violates His law. That makes guilt more than a psychological experience. It is a moral condition.

Psalm 51:4 (NSV) captures David's clarity after grievous sin. He says he has sinned against God and done what is evil in God's sight. David does not begin by explaining himself. He begins by admitting guilt.

This is one reason the Bible treats confession as essential. Confession agrees with God about what happened. It stops bargaining. It stops pretending.

2) Define Shame: A Relational Wound and a Sense of Exposure

Shame is often relational. It says, "I am unacceptable," or "I am stained," or "If they really knew me, I would be rejected." Guilt says, "I did wrong." Shame says, "I am wrong."

Shame can follow real sin. Shame can also follow suffering that was not your fault. People who were abused often carry shame even though they did not cause the harm. Scripture's categories help you respond wisely in both cases.

The Bible shows shame as exposure and hiding. After Adam and Eve sinned, they hid. We studied that earlier. That same impulse still shapes human life. Shame pulls you into concealment. It trains you to manage impressions instead of living in truth.

A key danger appears here: shame often grows stronger in secrecy. The longer you hide, the more shame claims authority over your identity.

3) Learn How Guilt and Shame Can Work Together

Guilt and shame can overlap, but they respond to different kinds of truth.

- Guilt needs pardon and reconciliation with God.
- Shame needs covering, welcome, and restored belonging.

If you try to treat guilt like shame, you may focus on self-esteem while ignoring repentance. If you try to treat shame like guilt, you may keep apologizing without receiving comfort and restoration.

Scripture addresses both. It speaks of forgiveness, and it also speaks of cleansing and clothing. God does not merely cancel a debt. He restores a person.

4) Use Psalm 32 as a Map: Hidden Sin Makes Life Smaller

Psalm 32:3–5 (NSV) offers one of the clearest descriptions of what hidden guilt does to a person. David describes physical and emotional strain while he kept silent, then relief when he confessed.

The pattern is worth noticing:

1. Silence and concealment.
2. Inner pressure and weakness.
3. Confession without excuse.
4. Forgiveness and renewed stability.

This passage shows that guilt does not stay "spiritual." It spills into the body and into daily life. It drains energy. It tightens relationships. It produces irritability, numbness, or constant self-defense.

Confession is not a magic trick. It is the moment you step into light. It is also the moment you stop trying to be your own savior.

5) Learn God's Promise for Guilt: Confession Leads to Forgiveness

A central promise for guilt appears in 1 John 1:9 (NSV). God is faithful and just to forgive sins and cleanse from unrighteousness when we confess. Notice two words: faithful and just. Forgiveness is not God ignoring evil. Forgiveness is God acting in line with His covenant faithfulness and righteous provision.

This is where Christian theology becomes sharply different from self-help. Self-help often says, "Forgive yourself." Scripture says, "Come to God, confess honestly, and receive His forgiveness."

The difference matters. Self-forgiveness can become self-deception. God's forgiveness is grounded in God's verdict and God's mercy.

Church history has emphasized this point in pastoral care. Many historic liturgies include confession and assurance for a reason. They train believers to stop hiding and to rely on God's promise. Public worship reinforces what private conscience forgets.

6) Learn God's Remedy for Shame: Cleansing, Covering, and Welcome

God's answer to shame is not performance. It is cleansing and restored fellowship.

Hebrews 9:14 (NSV) speaks about the blood of Christ cleansing the conscience from dead works to serve the living God. This reaches into the inner life. It addresses the "stained" feeling that shame often produces.

Scripture also speaks of believers being clothed in righteousness. Isaiah 61:10 (NSV) rejoices in being clothed with garments of salvation. Clothing language matters because shame often feels like exposure. God answers with covering that is real, not pretend.

Then Scripture adds welcome. Romans 15:7 (NSV) calls believers to welcome one another as Christ welcomed them. When Christ welcomes sinners, He does not approve sin. He brings sinners into grace, truth, and a new identity.

So shame does not get healed by trying to look acceptable. Shame gets healed as God makes you clean and restores you to belonging.

7) Distinguish True Shame from False Shame

This distinction will protect your conscience.

True shame

True shame can be an appropriate response to real sin. It can push you toward repentance. It can humble you. Yet it should not settle into identity. In Christ, your identity does not remain "unclean." God cleanses.

2 Corinthians 7:10 (NSV) helps here. It describes godly sorrow producing repentance that leads to salvation, without regret. This sorrow is not self-hatred. It is grief over sin that turns into change.

False shame

False shame attaches to things God does not condemn. It may come from abuse, manipulation, unrealistic expectations, or constant criticism. It may come from family patterns that equate worth with performance.

False shame says, "You are dirty because you exist." Scripture never speaks that way. Scripture says you bear God's image. It also says Christ restores sinners and comforts the afflicted.

If you carry shame for harm done to you, you need truth and care. You may need a pastor, a trusted counselor, and a safe community. Bringing pain into light is often necessary for healing.

8) Understand the Conscience:
Why You Can Feel Guilty When You Are Not

The conscience is a gift, but it is not perfect. It can be under-trained or mis-trained. It can accuse wrongly. It can also go quiet when it should warn.

Romans 14:22–23 (NSV) shows a conscience can be tender, even about disputable matters. That tenderness can be good, but it can also become fear-driven if you treat conscience as the highest authority.

So you must train conscience by Scripture. A trained conscience does two things well:

- It convicts you when God's Word convicts you.
- It comforts you when God's Word comforts you.

This is also why some believers struggle with recurring guilt after repentance. They confessed. God forgave. Yet the conscience keeps accusing. In such cases, you must answer the conscience with truth. Romans 8:1 (NSV) states there is no condemnation for those in Christ Jesus. That does not deny discipline or consequences. It does deny condemnation as your standing before God.

9) Practice Cleansing in Real Life: Four Steps That Match Scripture

Here is a steady, action-oriented path for dealing with guilt and shame.

Step 1: Tell the truth without editing

Name the sin or the wound plainly. Avoid vague words that protect pride. Use clear language. God already knows. Honesty is for your healing.

Step 2: Confess to God and receive His verdict

Confess with specificity. Ask forgiveness. Then receive God's promise. Use 1 John 1:9 (NSV) as your anchor, not your emotions.

Step 3: Make amends where possible

If your sin harmed someone, pursue reconciliation when it is safe and wise. Zacchaeus models this impulse by making restitution after repentance (Luke 19:8, NSV). Restitution does not earn forgiveness. It expresses it.

Step 4: Bring shame into safe light

Share with a mature believer, pastor, or counselor when shame traps you in secrecy. James teaches confession and prayer in community for healing (James 5:16, NSV). Choose someone wise, not someone who collects stories.

This is not a quick fix. It is a faithful path. Over time, truth and grace loosen shame's grip.

10) Learn to Speak to Others: A Pastoral Approach

If you want to help others, you must speak differently to guilt than to shame.

- To guilt, you speak repentance and pardon.
- To shame, you speak cleansing and welcome.
- To both, you speak the cross and resurrection.

When someone confesses sin, do not minimize it. Do not intensify it either. Agree with God's Word. Then point them to God's forgiveness in Christ.

When someone carries shame from being sinned against, do not treat them as guilty. Do not demand quick trust. Offer safety, patience, and practical help. Remind them God sees, God judges, and God heals. Then help them take wise next steps.

Many historic pastors emphasized this kind of care. They warned against two failures: harshness that crushes the weak, and softness that refuses to confront sin. Scripture calls for truth and gentleness at the same time.

11) Keep the Center: Jesus Gives a Clean Conscience and a New Identity

The Bible does not leave you in analysis. It brings you to Christ.

Guilt finds its answer in pardon. Shame finds its answer in cleansing and adoption. Scripture speaks of believers being made God's children (John 1:12, NSV). Children may be corrected, but they are not rejected. That relational security changes everything.

When shame says, "You are unworthy," you answer, "Christ cleanses."

When guilt says, "You are condemned," you answer, "Christ has borne my judgment."

When memory says, "This will define you," you answer, "God defines me in Christ."

You will still face consequences at times. You will still need growth. Yet you do not live under the old verdict. You live under God's grace.

CHAPTER 6

EXPLAIN HUMAN RELATIONSHIPS: STUDY MARRIAGE, FAMILY, AND NEIGHBOR - LOVE

Human relationships can be a source of great comfort and deep pain. Scripture does not treat relationships as optional. God made people to live in covenant, community, and responsibility. That is why sin shows up so quickly in the home, in friendships, and in public life. Relationships reveal what is in us.

This chapter builds a clear framework for three major arenas: **marriage**, **family**, and **neighbor-love**. You will see God's design, sin's common distortions, and practical ways to live faithfully. You will also see why the gospel matters here. Doctrine becomes visible in relationships faster than anywhere else.

1) Start with God's Design: Covenant, Not Convenience

The Bible treats relationships as covenantal, not casual. A covenant is a binding commitment that creates obligations and protection. God relates to His people by covenant, and He calls His people to live with covenant faithfulness.

Marriage is the clearest example. Genesis 2:24 (NSV) describes a man and a woman leaving and cleaving, becoming one flesh. This is not presented as a social experiment. It is a created pattern. It includes loyalty ("hold fast"), unity ("one flesh"), and a public re-ordering of priorities ("leave").

This does not mean every person must marry to be whole. Scripture honors singleness and marriage as gifts with different callings. Yet it does mean marriage, when entered, is not a temporary arrangement for personal fulfillment. It is a covenant that requires faithfulness.

Many conflicts in marriage come from a shared mistake: both spouses try to use power rather than give service. Scripture calls for a different posture.

Ephesians 5:25 (NSV) commands husbands to love their wives as Christ loved the church and gave Himself for her. That is sacrificial leadership. It rejects harshness and selfishness. It also gives a clear model: Christ's authority expresses itself through self-giving care.

Ephesians 5 also calls wives to respect and support their husbands in a way that reflects the church's response to Christ. In faithful Christian teaching across the centuries, wise leaders have stressed that this never excuses intimidation, coercion, or harm. Scripture never gives permission for abuse. It calls for holiness, protection, and accountability.

If you want one practical summary: **husbands lead by serving; wives support by honoring; both submit to Christ and to one another's good.** When either spouse treats the other as a tool, covenant life breaks down.

3) Protect Marriage with Clear Boundaries

Marriage does not survive on romance alone. It survives on trust built through repeated faithfulness.

Malachi 2:14–16 (NSV) presents marriage as a covenant and warns against treachery. The passage treats unfaithfulness as serious because it tears apart what God intends to be a safe bond. Scripture is direct about sexual sin, but covenant betrayal can also happen through persistent deceit, financial secrecy, emotional abandonment, and cruel speech.

Here are three boundaries that protect marriage in practical ways:

- **Truthful speech:** no secret lives, no double stories, no hidden accounts.
- **Loyal priorities:** spouse and children are not competing with every other demand.
- **Shared repentance:** when sin appears, confession happens quickly, not months later.

Church history supports this emphasis. Early Christian communities taught marital faithfulness as a public witness in pagan cultures that often treated sex and divorce casually. Later pastors continued the same message, because the same temptations remain.

4) Receive Singleness as a Calling with Real Value

Some people treat singleness as a "waiting room." Scripture does not. Paul teaches that singleness can allow focused devotion to the Lord's work and undivided service (1 Corinthians 7:32–35, NSV). This does not make singleness easy. It does make singleness meaningful.

The church must treat single believers as full members, not as unfinished adults. Single believers also must resist two common traps:

- **Isolation:** withdrawing into private life instead of building strong Christian friendships.
- **Self-protection:** refusing covenant commitments in church and community because they feel risky.

A healthy church treats marriage and singleness as different paths of faithfulness, not different levels of spiritual success.

5) Build a Family Culture with Discipline and Warmth

Family is a training ground for love and responsibility. It is also a place where sin can become normal if no one confronts it.

Ephesians 6:1–4 (NSV) gives direction to children and parents. Children are called to honor and obey. Parents are warned not to provoke children to anger, but to raise them in the instruction and discipline of the Lord.

Notice the balance. Scripture does not support harsh parenting that rules by fear. It also does not support passive parenting that refuses correction. Faithful parenting joins warmth and discipline, truth and patience.

If you are raising children, aim for four steady practices:

1. **Clear expectations:** children obey better when the goal is plain.
2. **Consistent correction:** correction loses power when it is random.

3. **Quick repair:** when conflict happens, return to peace through confession and forgiveness.

4. **Daily instruction:** not only lectures, but short conversations that connect choices to God's Word.

If you are an adult child, Scripture's call to honor does not end when you leave home. Honor may look different in difficult situations, especially if parents are unsafe or manipulative. Honor can include boundaries. Honor never requires enabling sin. Yet a Christian should resist contempt, bitterness, and public shaming as normal speech.

6) Treat the Church as a Real Family

Scripture describes the church as a household, not a club. That means you belong to people you did not choose, and you learn love that is not based on similarity.

Colossians 3:12–14 (NSV) calls believers to put on compassion, kindness, humility, patience, and forgiveness, and to bind everything together with love. This is relationship language. It assumes friction will happen, and it commands a holy response.

In church history, this "one another" life formed a visible witness. Early Christians cared for widows, orphans, and the sick. Later believers built hospitals, schools, and charitable networks. These works did not replace preaching. They proved that the gospel creates a new kind of community.

The practical point is simple: if your theology is sound but your church life is full of unresolved conflict, your discipleship is incomplete. God intends the church to train believers in forgiveness, truth-telling, service, and patience.

7) Define Neighbor-Love as Action, Not Sentiment

Many people say "love your neighbor" as a slogan. Scripture treats it as a command with substance.

Leviticus 19:18 (NSV) commands love for neighbor and forbids vengeance and grudges. Love is not mainly a feeling. Love is a decision to seek another's good, with integrity and restraint.

Jesus reinforces this in Luke 10:25–37 (NSV) through the parable of the Good Samaritan. The Samaritan does not feel sympathy and move on. He acts. He crosses social hostility, offers practical help, and pays a cost. Jesus presents neighbor-love as tangible mercy.

Is neighbor-love limited to people you like? No. Jesus chose an enemy figure in that story to make the point unavoidable. Neighbor-love reaches across boundaries.

This does not mean you trust every person. Love and trust are not the same. Love seeks good. Trust is earned. You can love wisely while maintaining safety and truth.

8) Practice Forgiveness with Truth and Boundaries

Forgiveness is essential in Christian relationships, but many people misunderstand it.

Biblical forgiveness is not denial. It does not call evil good. It does not erase consequences. It does not require immediate closeness. Forgiveness means you release personal vengeance and entrust justice to God while pursuing wise steps toward peace when possible.

Ephesians 4:31–32 (NSV) calls believers to put away bitterness and malice and to forgive one another as God forgave them in Christ. The model is God's grace. Yet Scripture also calls for protection and accountability. In cases of abuse, ongoing unrepentant harm, or serious danger, love may require distance and the involvement of church leaders and lawful authorities.

Healthy forgiveness has three marks:

- **Truth:** you name what happened without minimizing it.
- **Mercy:** you refuse revenge and pray for God's work in the offender.
- **Wisdom:** you set boundaries that match the situation.

9) Watch the "Relationship Sins" That Grow Quietly

Some sins do not look scandalous, but they destroy relationships over time:

- **Gossip:** it feels social, but it is theft of reputation.
- **Partiality:** it honors the impressive and ignores the weak.
- **Harsh speech:** it claims "truth" while lacking love.

- **Refusal to reconcile:** it keeps peace at a distance but leaves wounds open.

Proverbs 18:21 (NSV) warns that death and life are in the power of the tongue. Words shape atmosphere. Words set direction. Words either build trust or collapse it.

If you want to grow in relationships, begin with speech. Then move to habits. Small changes, practiced consistently, create real stability.

10) Build a Simple Relationship Rule for Daily Life

If you want a practical rule that fits marriage, family, and neighbor-life, use this:

1. **Speak truthfully.**
2. **Act faithfully.**
3. **Repair quickly.**
4. **Serve quietly.**

Truthfully means no double stories.

Faithfully means keep your promises.

Repair quickly means do not let conflict rot in silence.

Serve quietly means do good without needing praise.

This rule does not solve every complex situation. It does shape the kind of person who can handle complex situations with greater wisdom.

Human relationships are where doctrine shows its strength. God made people for covenant life. Sin distorts that life through pride and self-rule. Christ restores it by creating a new heart and a new community. So do not treat relationships as a side topic. They are a primary field for obedience.

CHAPTER 7

ADMIT HUMAN LIMITS: ACCEPT WHY YOU CANNOT SAVE YOURSELF

Most people want a salvation story that keeps them in charge. They want a plan that says, "Try harder, be better, and God will do the rest." Scripture tells a different story. It is more honest, and it is better news. The Bible teaches that humanity's deepest problem is not a lack of effort. It is a lack of life. Sin is not only what we do. Sin is what we are apart from God's grace. That is why salvation must be rescue, not self-repair.

This chapter will show why you cannot save yourself, even with sincere religion and moral discipline. We will also show why that truth is not meant to crush you. It is meant to end false hope so you can receive true hope.

1) Start with God's Standard: "Good Enough" Is Not the Measure

Many people assume God grades on a curve. They picture God as comparing them to worse people, then giving a passing mark. Scripture never speaks that way. God's standard is His own holiness.

Romans 3:10–12 (NSV) gives a sweeping assessment of humanity: none is righteous, no one understands, no one seeks God. The point is not that people are incapable of kindness. The point is that no one meets God's righteous standard, and no one naturally seeks God as God.

This matters because self-salvation always depends on lowering the standard. If the standard becomes "better than others," then pride rises quickly. But God does not ask whether you are better than your neighbor. God asks whether you are righteous before Him.

2) Understand the Problem: Sin Reaches Motives, Not Only Actions

You can change habits and still keep the same heart. That is why Scripture exposes the inner person.

Isaiah 64:6 (NSV) shocks modern ears: even our righteous deeds are like a polluted garment. The prophet is not saying every good act is worthless. He is saying no act can stand as a clean payment before a holy God, because sin contaminates motives and aims.

Here is a common example. A person gives money, but the motive is praise. Another serves, but the motive is control. Another avoids scandal, but the motive is reputation. Outward acts may look clean. The inner life can be ruled by pride.

This is why self-salvation fails. It focuses on behavior while leaving the worship problem untouched. The heart still wants self-rule.

3) See Why Religion Alone Cannot Fix the Heart

Some people respond to guilt and shame by becoming more religious. They assume religious activity can function as a spiritual payment plan. Scripture exposes that as a dead end.

In Luke 18:9–14 (NSV), Jesus tells a story about a Pharisee and a tax collector. The Pharisee lists his religious efforts and thanks God that he is not like other people. The tax collector will not even lift his eyes. He pleads for mercy. Jesus says the tax collector went home justified, not the Pharisee.

The lesson is direct: religious activity can become pride in costume. It can hide self-trust instead of producing repentance. When religion becomes self-salvation, it produces judgment toward others and blindness toward personal sin.

This is also why churches must be careful. A church can train people to look clean while leaving them unconverted. Scripture calls for preaching that exposes self-trust and directs people to Christ.

4) Accept the Bible's Diagnosis:
You Need More Than Guidance—You Need New Life

Many modern messages treat humans as basically healthy but confused. Scripture treats humans as guilty and spiritually helpless apart from God.

Titus 3:3 (NSV) describes life apart from Christ: foolish, disobedient, led astray, enslaved to passions and pleasures, living in malice and envy. That is not a flattering description, but it is honest. It explains why people return to the same bondage even after strong resolutions.

This is not meant to deny human dignity. You still bear God's image. It is meant to state human need. Image-bearers are not autonomous. We were made for God. When we cut ourselves off from God's rule, we do not become free. We become enslaved to lesser masters.

5) Learn the Key Truth: God Must Draw You, or You Will Not Come

One of the clearest statements about human inability is found in Jesus' own words.

John 6:44 (NSV) says no one can come to Christ unless the Father draws him. That is not a statement about intelligence. It is a statement about spiritual ability. Apart from God's drawing grace, people do not come to Christ with faith.

This does not remove responsibility. Scripture still calls people to repent and believe. It does mean that saving faith is not the result of human willpower. It is the result of God's merciful action that changes the heart.

This truth should produce humility. If you believe, you cannot boast as if you were wiser than others. You can only give thanks that God showed mercy.

6) Track the Church's Reflection: Why the Early Debates Still Matter

This doctrine was not invented in later centuries. It was clarified because false teachers kept returning to the same basic claim: "Humans can obey God and secure salvation by their own moral ability."

In the early church, a British monk named Pelagius argued that humans could obey God's commands without needing inward renewing grace. Augustine, a pastor and theologian in North Africa, opposed that claim. Augustine argued that sin damages the will and desires so deeply that people need God's grace not only for forgiveness, but for the ability to believe and obey.

The church addressed these debates in councils and synods. The key concern was pastoral and biblical: if humans can save themselves, then grace becomes a bonus rather than a necessity. The gospel becomes advice rather than rescue.

Later, the Council of Orange (AD 529) strongly affirmed the necessity of grace for the beginning of faith, while also rejecting fatalism. The goal was to preserve biblical balance: God's grace is necessary and effective, and humans remain responsible to respond.

During the Reformation, the same issue returned. Reformers stressed that justification is by grace through faith, apart from works, and that even faith itself is a gift of God's mercy. They were not trying to be difficult. They were trying to protect the gospel from becoming a moral achievement system.

You do not need to memorize the names to benefit from the lesson. The lesson is this: whenever the church forgets human inability, it turns Christianity into self-help with religious vocabulary. Whenever the church remembers human inability, grace becomes central again.

7) Reject False Hope: "I Can Fix Myself" Sounds Strong but Fails

Self-salvation appears in several popular forms.

Form 1: Moral Improvement as the Gospel

This approach says, "Follow Jesus' ethics, and you will be fine." Ethics matter, but ethics are not the gospel. If ethics were enough, the cross would be unnecessary.

Form 2: Identity Repair through Achievement

This approach uses success to silence shame. It says, "If I can prove myself, I will finally feel clean." Achievement can distract you, but it cannot cleanse you. It can even become an idol that deepens anxiety.

Form 3: Religious Performance to Earn Peace

This approach treats prayer, giving, and service as currency. You do them to make God owe you. When pain comes anyway, bitterness grows. The heart says, "I paid, so why did God not deliver?"

All three forms share one assumption: the main problem is outside you, and the main solution is inside you. Scripture says the opposite. The problem is inside, and the solution must come from God.

Admitting you cannot save yourself is not despair. It is the doorway to the gospel.

Psalm 130:3–4 (NSV) asks a question with a clear answer: if the Lord kept a record of sins, who could stand? Then it declares that with the Lord there is forgiveness, so that He may be feared. Forgiveness does not produce casualness. It produces reverence and gratitude.

When God forgives, He does more than erase a record. He restores fellowship and begins real change. That change is not the foundation of acceptance. It is the result of acceptance.

This is where many people breathe again. They have spent years trying to prove they are worthy. Scripture frees them from that burden by saying, in effect, "You are not worthy on your own. That is why God gives mercy."

9) Apply This Doctrine in Three Practical Ways

Application 1: Stop Negotiating with God

If you think you can save yourself, you will bargain: "I will obey if You bless." Scripture calls you to surrender: "You are God, and I need mercy." Surrender is not weakness. It is honesty.

Application 2: Practice Repentance as a Lifestyle

Repentance is not a one-time apology. It is a daily turning from self-rule to God's rule. When you fail, you confess quickly. When you succeed, you give thanks quickly. This keeps pride from regrowing.

Application 3: Treat Others with Patience

When you know you are saved by grace, you become less harsh with sinners and more honest about sin. You do not excuse evil. You do not treat people as projects. You speak truth and offer help with humility, because you remember what you were apart from grace.

10) Keep the Balance Clear: Helpless Does Not Mean Hopeless

Some hear "you cannot save yourself" and assume they are stuck. Scripture does not leave you stuck. It calls you to respond to God's invitation.

The Bible's pattern is consistent: God commands what you cannot produce on your own, then God provides what He commands through grace. He calls you to repent, and He gives mercy. He calls you to believe, and He draws hearts. He calls you to obey, and He supplies strength by His Spirit.

So do not confuse inability with hopelessness. The point is not that you cannot come. The point is that you cannot come on your own terms. You come as a sinner in need of grace, trusting God's promise rather than your performance.

BOOK THREE

SALVATION: RECEIVE GOD'S RESCUE IN CHRIST

A Simple Guide to Grace, Faith, the Cross, and a New Life

CHAPTER 1

TRACE GOD'S RESCUE PLAN: FOLLOW THE COVENANTS FROM PROMISE TO FULFILLMENT

Many people treat the Bible like a stack of disconnected lessons. Scripture presents one unfolding rescue plan with a clear center: God saves sinners by grace through faith in the promised Messiah. The details develop across centuries, but the purpose stays steady. God is not reacting to history. God is accomplishing His plan within history.

This chapter will trace that plan in a structured way. We will look at promise, covenant, sacrifice, kingship, and fulfillment in Christ. We will also note how the church summarized these truths in early creeds, and how major Christian traditions have explained the Bible's unity without denying real differences in the covenants.

1) Define Salvation in Biblical Terms

Salvation includes several connected acts of God:

- **Deliverance from guilt** before a holy Judge.
- **Deliverance from slavery** to sin's rule.
- **Reconciliation with God** through forgiveness and restored fellowship.
- **A new identity** as God's people.
- **A new future** shaped by resurrection hope.

This is why Scripture uses multiple images: courtroom language, family language, liberation language, and covenant language. Salvation is not a single metaphor. It is a full rescue.

Romans 3:23–24 (NSV) states the problem and the gift: all have sinned, and sinners are justified by God's grace as a gift. That one sentence removes boasting and establishes hope.

After humanity's rebellion, God did not abandon His creation. He announced His intent to redeem. You have already seen that Scripture holds judgment and mercy together from the earliest pages. Now notice something else: the rescue plan develops through promises that God keeps, even when people fail.

God's promises are not vague. They take shape through covenants—binding commitments where God establishes a relationship, defines obligations, and gives signs that confirm His word.

A covenant is not merely a contract. A contract is an exchange between equals. A covenant in Scripture is God's gracious commitment that creates a people and binds them to Himself.

3) Track the Covenant with Abraham: Blessing for the Nations

One of the clearest covenant turning points is God's call of Abram. Genesis 12:1–3 (NSV) includes a promise that reaches beyond one family: God will bless Abram, and through him blessing will come to all families of the earth.

That promise accomplishes several things at once:

- It narrows the rescue plan to a particular line.
- It sets a global aim: the nations.
- It shows salvation is God's initiative, not Abram's achievement.

Later, God confirms the promise in covenant form. The Abrahamic covenant becomes a backbone for the Old Testament storyline. It also becomes essential for the New Testament's explanation of the gospel, because the church sees Christ as the promised offspring through whom the nations are blessed.

This is not a new invention. Paul argues this directly in Galatians 3 (you can read the whole chapter in the NSV for the flow). The point is covenant continuity: God's promise stands, and God fulfills it.

4) Understand the Exodus Pattern: Salvation as Deliverance and Belonging

The Exodus is the Bible's great rescue event in the Old Testament. God delivers Israel from slavery and then brings them into covenant life.

Exodus 6:6–7 (NSV) captures the structure: God will deliver, redeem, take them as His people, and be their God. Notice the order. God rescues first, then calls them to obedience as His people.

This pattern matters because it shows how grace and obedience relate. Obedience does not purchase rescue. Obedience follows rescue. God saves, then God teaches His people how to live.

The Exodus also shapes how later prophets describe future salvation. They often portray coming restoration as a new deliverance, a new return, and a deeper cleansing. The New Testament then presents Jesus as the fulfillment of that deliverance pattern in a final, decisive way.

5) Read Sacrifice as Theology: Why Blood and Altars Were Central

Many modern readers struggle with sacrifices. Yet sacrifices were not random rituals. They taught Israel what sin does and what forgiveness requires. They also pointed ahead.

Hebrews 10:1 (NSV) describes the law's sacrificial system as a shadow of good things to come, not the final reality. The sacrifices taught three truths:

1. **Sin brings real guilt** and deserves judgment.
2. **Forgiveness is costly**; it is not cheap denial.
3. **God provides a substitute**, pointing toward a greater provision.

The Old Testament never suggests animals are a final solution. The sacrifices function as a God-given signpost that aims beyond itself. This prepares you to grasp why the New Testament speaks of Christ's death as the climactic sacrifice that truly cleanses.

6) Follow the Covenant with David: A King Who Will Reign Forever

God's rescue plan also includes kingship. The promise of a righteous king becomes a major theme.

2 Samuel 7:12–13 (NSV) records God's commitment to David: God will raise up an offspring and establish his kingdom. This promise is not merely political. It becomes messianic. Israel's hope for a faithful king grows, especially as later kings fail.

Psalm 110:1 (NSV) strengthens this hope by describing a Lord who reigns at God's right hand. Jesus later uses this Psalm to confront shallow views of the Messiah. The early church also used it to explain Jesus' exaltation.

So salvation is not only rescue from guilt. It is the arrival of God's rightful King who rules and restores.

7) Receive the New Covenant Promise: Forgiveness and a Changed Heart

The prophets looked forward to a covenant renewal that would reach deeper than external reform.

Jeremiah 31:31–34 (NSV) announces a new covenant marked by God's law written on the heart and by real forgiveness. This promise is not anti-law. It is anti-stony-heart. It points to inward renewal.

Ezekiel 36:26–27 (NSV) speaks in similar terms: God will give a new heart and put His Spirit within His people so they walk in His ways. This is salvation described as transformation from the inside out.

These promises prepare you for the New Testament's emphasis on regeneration, new birth, and Spirit-given renewal. Salvation is more than a legal declaration. It is also a new life that produces real obedience.

8) See Christ as the Fulfillment of the Whole Story

The New Testament does not treat Jesus as an isolated figure. It presents Him as the fulfillment of the Scriptures.

Luke 24:27 (NSV) describes the risen Jesus explaining Moses and the prophets as pointing to Him. This is a crucial interpretive key. The Bible's storyline has a center.

Galatians 4:4–5 (NSV) adds a second key: when the fullness of time came, God sent His Son to redeem those under the law so they might receive adoption. That sentence ties together promise, timing, redemption, and family belonging.

Then 1 Corinthians 15:3–4 (NSV) gives a simple early summary of the gospel: Christ died for sins according to the Scriptures, He was buried, and He was raised on the third day according to the Scriptures. This is not merely Paul's opinion. It reflects the church's early teaching and public proclamation.

9) Learn from the Creeds: The Church Summarized the Gospel Early

The early church did not create a new gospel. It summarized the apostolic gospel to guard it.

The Apostles' Creed, in its basic form, confesses Christ's incarnation, suffering under Pontius Pilate, death, burial, resurrection, ascension, and coming judgment. That creed is intentionally historical. It anchors faith in real events, not private speculation.

The Nicene Creed deepens the confession of Christ's identity, especially against teachings that reduced the Son to a creature. This matters for salvation because only a true Savior can reconcile sinners to God.

Later, the Definition of Chalcedon (AD 451) clarified that Christ is one person with two natures, fully God and fully man, without confusion or division. That protects the biblical claim that Christ can truly represent humanity and truly reveal God.

These creeds are not Scripture. Yet they show how the church read Scripture and fought to preserve the gospel's meaning.

10) Address a Common Tension: How Can One Plan Include Different Covenants?

As you study covenants, you will notice both continuity and change.

- There is continuity: one God, one moral will, one promise moving toward Christ.
- There is change: new stages, new administrations, new signs, and clearer revelation.

Christians have explained this in different ways.

Covenant theology often emphasizes one overarching covenant purpose, with different covenant administrations across history. It highlights unity and the way earlier covenants prepare for Christ.

Dispensational frameworks often emphasize distinct stages in God's dealings, with careful attention to Israel and the nations. It highlights progression and the specific features of each covenant era.

Faithful Christians hold these frameworks with varying conclusions. Yet both traditions, at their best, affirm the central truth: salvation is fulfilled in Christ, and Scripture's story moves with purpose toward Him.

Your goal as a beginner is not to pick a camp quickly. Your goal is to read Scripture carefully and keep Christ at the center.

11) Apply the Rescue Story to Your Life Now

This storyline is not only for study. It shapes daily faith.

- If God keeps covenant promises across centuries, you can trust Him in your week.
- If God rescues before He commands, you can obey without trying to earn love.
- If God provides the true sacrifice, you can stop using shame as a leash.
- If God gives a true King, you can submit with confidence rather than fear.
- If God promises a new heart, you can seek change with hope, not despair.

The rescue plan is not an abstract chart. It is the reason you can repent, believe, and keep going.

CHAPTER 2

KNOW THE PROMISED SAVIOR: CONFESS JESUS CHRIST AS GOD AND MAN

Salvation rises or falls on one question: **Who is Jesus Christ?** If Jesus is only a teacher, then the cross becomes a tragedy and forgiveness becomes wishful thinking. If Jesus is only a spiritual figure without true humanity, then He cannot stand in for sinners or bear our guilt in our place. Scripture presents Jesus as both fully God and fully man, one Person with a real human life, a real death, and a real resurrection. This is not an academic detail. It is the core of Christian hope.

This chapter will help you confess Christ as the Bible presents Him. We will look at His names and titles, His two natures, His mission, and why the church guarded these truths so carefully. Then we will apply this doctrine to worship, assurance, and daily obedience.

1) Start with Jesus' Main Title: "Christ" Means the Anointed King

"Jesus" is His personal name. "Christ" is His title. "Christ" means "Anointed One," the promised King set apart by God to rule and save.

Peter's confession in Matthew 16:16 (NSV) is a turning point: "You are the Christ, the Son of the living God." Peter is not offering a compliment. He is identifying Jesus as the long-promised Messiah, the King who fulfills God's covenant promises.

This title carries weight. It means Jesus does not merely show a path. He brings a kingdom. He does not simply advise sinners. He has authority to call, forgive, and judge.

Scripture is clear on both truths, and it holds them together without apology.

Jesus is truly God.

John 1:1 (NSV) says, "In the beginning was the Word, and the Word was with God, and the Word was God." A few verses later, John states the Word became flesh (John 1:14, NSV). John ties Jesus to God's eternal identity and then ties Jesus to real human life.

Thomas responds to the risen Christ in worship: "My Lord and my God!" (John 20:28, NSV). Jesus does not correct him. Scripture presents this confession as right.

Jesus is truly man.

Hebrews 2:14 (NSV) says that since the children share in flesh and blood, He Himself likewise shared the same, so that through death He might break the hold of the one who has the power of death. Jesus took a real body and entered real human vulnerability. He hungered, grew tired, and wept. He did not "appear" human; He became human.

You may wonder, *why must both be true?* The answer is simple: **only God can save, and only man can represent mankind.** If Jesus lacks deity, He cannot give a saving sacrifice of infinite worth. If Jesus lacks humanity, He cannot stand in our place as our true substitute.

3) Receive the Meaning of the Incarnation: God Came Near without Changing Who He Is

The incarnation means the Son of God took on human nature and lived among us. He did not stop being God. He took on what He was not: true humanity.

Philippians 2:6–8 (NSV) describes Christ's humility. Though He existed in the form of God, He took the form of a servant and became obedient to the point of death. This is not the story of a creature rising to divinity. It is the story of the eternal Son stooping to save.

The incarnation also answers a common fear: "Can God relate to my weakness?" Hebrews 4:15 (NSV) says we have a high priest who can sympathize with our weaknesses, having been tempted as we are, yet without sin. Jesus meets human life fully, yet without moral failure. That makes Him both compassionate and clean.

Across Scripture, God's people needed three kinds of help: truth from God, cleansing before God, and righteous rule under God. Jesus fulfills all three.

Jesus as Prophet

A prophet speaks God's word with authority. Jesus does more than repeat messages. He reveals the Father. Deuteronomy 18:15 (NSV) promises a prophet like Moses whom God will raise up. The early church understood Jesus as the fulfillment of this prophetic hope because He speaks God's word as God's Son.

When Jesus teaches, He does not merely interpret. He declares: "But I say to you…" He exposes the heart. He calls for repentance. He announces the kingdom.

Jesus as Priest

A priest stands between God and people, offering sacrifice and interceding. Hebrews 7:25 (NSV) says Jesus is able to save completely those who draw near through Him, since He always lives to intercede for them. His priesthood is not temporary. It continues.

Jesus also offers the decisive sacrifice. Hebrews 9:12 (NSV) says He entered the holy place once for all, securing eternal redemption. The focus is finality. His sacrifice is not repeated because it is sufficient.

Jesus as King

A king rules and protects. Revelation 19:16 (NSV) calls Jesus "King of kings and Lord of lords." This kingship is not a political slogan. It is the final reality of history. Jesus reigns now and will bring all things into open submission at the end.

These three offices show why salvation is complete. Jesus teaches truth, cleanses guilt, and rules His people into holiness.

5) Guard One Person, Two Natures: The Church's Clear Summary

The church fought over Christology because false ideas harmed the gospel.

Some claimed Jesus was a great man adopted by God. Others claimed Jesus was a divine being who only seemed human. Both errors break salvation: the first removes true deity; the second removes true humanity.

The Definition of Chalcedon (AD 451) summarized the biblical teaching with careful language: Jesus is one Person, fully God and fully man, without confusion, change, division, or separation. The statement was meant to protect what Scripture teaches, not to replace it.

You do not need to memorize Chalcedon. You do need to keep its aim: **do not split Jesus into two persons, and do not blend His natures into a third thing.** Scripture presents one Savior, truly God and truly man.

6) See Why the Virgin Birth Matters

The virgin birth is not a decorative miracle. It serves the saving purpose.

Matthew 1:21–23 (NSV) ties Jesus' birth to His mission: He will save His people from their sins, and He will be called Immanuel, "God with us." The virgin birth signals that salvation begins with God's initiative. It also highlights the uniqueness of this Son. He is not a mere moral reformer rising from within fallen humanity. He is the holy Savior sent from God, entering humanity in a new way.

This truth does not demand that you understand biology. It calls you to trust God's testimony: God can do what humans cannot do, and He does it for salvation.

7) Receive the Meaning of Jesus' Sinless Life

Many people focus on Jesus' death but forget His obedience. Scripture includes both. Jesus lived a perfectly righteous life, fulfilling God's law in heart and action.

1 Peter 2:22 (NSV) states it plainly: "He committed no sin, and no deceit was found in his mouth." His sinlessness matters because a guilty substitute cannot bear guilt for others. A stained sacrifice cannot cleanse.

Jesus' obedience also matters because salvation includes righteousness credited to believers. Later in this Book we will explore justification more fully. For now, hold this: Jesus saves not only by removing guilt, but also by providing true righteousness.

8) Trust Jesus as the Only Mediator

People often assume they need multiple mediators: saints, rituals, personal merit, or spiritual achievements. Scripture centers salvation in Christ alone.

1 Timothy 2:5 (NSV) says there is one God and one mediator between God and men, the man Christ Jesus. The verse highlights both His unity and His humanity. He stands between God and sinners as the appointed mediator.

This does not make the church useless. It puts the church in its proper role. The church proclaims Christ, teaches His word, and shepherds believers. The church does not replace Christ.

9) Apply Christ's Person to Your Assurance

Assurance becomes unstable when you look first at yourself. Your repentance can feel weak. Your obedience can be uneven. Your emotions can swing. Scripture directs you to look first at Christ.

Because Jesus is God and man, His saving work is reliable. Because He is Priest, He intercedes for you. Because He is King, He will keep you. Because He is Prophet, He will keep teaching and correcting you through His word.

Here is one genuine question: **What do you do when you feel unworthy to come to God?** You come through Christ immediately, because your access is based on His worth, not yours. Hebrews 10:22 (NSV) calls believers to draw near with a true heart in full assurance, with hearts sprinkled clean. The cleansing is God's provision, not your achievement.

10) Respond with Worship and Obedience

Christology is never only a doctrine to recite. It is a truth to live.

If Jesus is truly King, then obedience is not optional. If Jesus is truly Priest, then confession is safe and necessary. If Jesus is truly Prophet, then Scripture must shape your beliefs and choices.

A mature Christian life grows from a clear confession: Jesus Christ is Lord. That confession will cost you at times. It will also steady you. You will stop trying to carry your own salvation. You will stop treating God as distant. You will begin to live under the care of the Savior who became man for your redemption.

In the next chapter we will focus on the cross and resurrection—how Jesus saves by His death and victory. But never forget: the work of salvation rests on the Person of the Savior. The gospel is not a method. The gospel is Christ.

CHAPTER 3

TRUST THE CROSS AND RESURRECTION: RECEIVE ATONEMENT, VICTORY, AND PEACE WITH GOD

If you want clarity about salvation, you must look straight at two events: **the cross** and **the resurrection**. The cross answers the question, "How can God forgive guilty people without denying His justice?" The resurrection answers the question, "How do we know Jesus truly saves, and what future does He secure?"

Christ's death is not a sad ending to a good teacher. It is God's appointed sacrifice for sins. Christ's resurrection is not a comforting symbol. It is God's public declaration that Jesus is Lord, that sin's debt is paid, and that death's authority is broken.

This chapter will explain what the cross accomplished, why it had to be this way, and how the resurrection completes the gospel.

1) Begin with the Problem: Sin Creates Real Debt and Real Judgment

Many people want forgiveness without guilt, acceptance without repentance, and peace without justice. Scripture does not offer that kind of peace. It offers a better peace: peace that comes through a real payment and a real victory.

God's holiness means sin must be judged. God's love means He provides a way for sinners to be forgiven. The cross is where holiness and love meet without compromise.

The Bible uses several connected pictures to explain Christ's death. These are not competing ideas. They are angles on the same saving work.

Substitution: Christ in the place of sinners

Mark 10:45 (NSV) states it with sharp clarity: the Son of Man came not to be served but to serve, and to give His life as a ransom for many. "Ransom" means a price paid to secure release. The verse shows purpose, not accident.

2 Corinthians 5:21 (NSV) gives another angle: God made Him who knew no sin to be sin for us, so that in Him we might become the righteousness of God. This is the heart of substitution. Jesus stands where sinners should stand, so sinners can receive what Jesus deserves.

Sacrifice: Christ as the true offering

In the Old Testament, sacrifices taught that sin brings death and forgiveness is costly. In Christ, that pattern reaches its fulfillment. The cross is not God ignoring sin. It is God dealing with sin through a true sacrifice.

Reconciliation: Christ restores peace with God

Sin breaks fellowship with God. The cross restores that fellowship. Peace with God is not mainly a feeling; it is a changed standing. Christ removes hostility by removing the guilt that created it.

3) See the Cross as God's Plan, Not Human Chaos

Some assume Jesus' death proves history is out of control. Scripture says the opposite.

Acts 2:23–24 (NSV) says Jesus was delivered up according to God's definite plan and foreknowledge, and that God raised Him up, loosening the pangs of death. Human guilt is real in the crucifixion, but God's purpose is also real. The cross is not a surprise to God. It is the center of God's saving plan.

This matters for faith. If the cross happened by accident, your salvation rests on uncertainty. If the cross happened by God's wise purpose, your salvation rests on God's faithfulness.

Justification is a courtroom word. It means God declares a person righteous, not because that person has earned righteousness, but because Christ's righteousness is credited to them.

Romans 4:25 (NSV) summarizes the cross and resurrection together: Jesus was delivered up for our trespasses and raised for our justification. That verse teaches two truths at once:

- The cross addresses real guilt ("trespasses").
- The resurrection confirms God's saving verdict ("justification").

Justification does not mean you are never corrected. It means God's final verdict over you is settled in Christ. That verdict produces peace, not pride.

5) Receive the Cross as Victory, Not Only Payment

Some people understand the cross only as payment for sin. That is true, but Scripture also speaks of victory.

Colossians 2:13–15 (NSV) teaches that God forgave sins, canceled the record of debt that stood against us, and set it aside, nailing it to the cross. Then it adds that God disarmed rulers and authorities and put them to open shame. The cross cancels guilt and defeats hostile powers.

This does not mean Christians live without conflict. It means the decisive battle is won. Satan's accusations lose their legal force because guilt is dealt with in Christ. That is why the gospel brings real freedom to a burdened conscience.

6) Hold Together Two Necessary Truths: God's Love and God's Justice

Some people fear that justice makes God harsh. Others fear that love makes God soft. The cross shows both clearly.

Romans 5:8 (NSV) says God shows His love for us in that while we were still sinners, Christ died for us. God did not wait for you to become worthy. He acted while you were guilty.

At the same time, the cross shows that sin is serious. Forgiveness required blood, not because God is cruel, but because sin is deadly and God is holy. The cross tells you the truth about your sin and the truth about God's mercy in a single event.

7) Understand the Resurrection: God's "Yes" to Jesus and God's "No" to Death

The resurrection is not an extra chapter. It is essential.

1 Corinthians 15:20–22 (NSV) says Christ has been raised from the dead, the firstfruits of those who have fallen asleep; as in Adam all die, so in Christ shall all be made alive. "Firstfruits" means the beginning of a harvest that guarantees the rest. Jesus' resurrection is the start of the future resurrection of His people.

This changes daily life. If Jesus is raised, then:

- The gospel is true history, not a moral story.

- Your sins are truly dealt with, not merely covered by optimism.

- Your future is not decay; it is resurrection life.

8) Apply the Cross and Resurrection to Your Conscience

Many believers struggle with repeated accusations in the mind: "You failed again," "You are dirty," "God is done with you." The cross and resurrection give you a direct answer.

When guilt accuses, you do not argue from your effort. You argue from Christ's finished work: the debt is canceled.

When shame threatens identity, you do not argue from your reputation. You argue from Christ's cleansing: you belong to Him.

When fear of death rises, you do not pretend you are strong. You stand on the resurrection: death will not have the last word.

Here is a sincere question many ask: *What if my faith feels small?* Faith is not powerful because it is intense. Faith is powerful because its object is Christ. A weak hand can still receive a strong gift.

9) Practice Three "Cross-Shaped" Habits This Week

1. **Confess quickly.** Do not let sin rot in secret. Bring it into light before God.

2. **Forgive deliberately.** Release personal vengeance, not because evil is small, but because Christ will judge justly and you are called to mercy.

3. **Serve quietly.** The cross trains you to live for others, not for applause. If Jesus served you at such cost, you can serve others with patience.

These habits do not earn salvation. They express it.

CHAPTER 4

RECEIVE GRACE THROUGH FAITH:
STOP EARNING AND START TRUSTING CHRIST

Many people hear the word *salvation* and assume it works like wages: do enough good, avoid enough bad, and God will accept you. Scripture says the opposite. Salvation is a gift. It is not bought, bargained for, or deserved. God saves by grace, and we receive that grace through faith.

This chapter will clarify three essentials:

1. **Grace**: why salvation starts with God's kindness, not your merit.
2. **Faith**: what it is, what it is not, and how it receives Christ.
3. **Works**: where obedience fits after you are saved.

These truths have strengthened believers for centuries because they steady the conscience and protect the gospel from turning into a performance system.

1) Define Grace: God's Free Favor to the Undeserving

Grace is God's kindness shown to people who have no claim on it. Grace does not mean God ignores sin. Grace means God provides what sinners need through Christ.

Ephesians 2:8–9 (NSV) states it plainly: you are saved by grace through faith, and this is not from yourselves; it is the gift of God, not from works, so no one may boast. That short passage removes every ground for pride. If salvation is a gift, then boasting is excluded.

Grace also explains why Christians can have real peace instead of constant anxiety. If salvation rests on your record, peace disappears the moment you fail. If salvation rests on Christ's work and God's promise, peace becomes possible even while you grow.

A sincere question arises here: *If grace is free, will people abuse it?* Some will try. Scripture addresses that later by teaching that true grace changes the heart and produces new obedience. Grace is not permission to sin. Grace is rescue from sin.

2) Define Faith: Trusting Christ, Not Trusting Yourself

Faith is not positive thinking. Faith is not denying fear. Faith is relying on Christ as Savior and Lord.

Romans 10:9–10 (NSV) says if you confess with your mouth that Jesus is Lord and believe in your heart that God raised Him from the dead, you will be saved. The passage ties faith to Christ's lordship and resurrection. It is not vague belief in "something." It is trust in a specific Person and a specific saving victory.

Faith also includes a personal turning. John 1:12 (NSV) says those who received Christ and believed in His name were given the right to become children of God. Faith receives. It does not achieve.

Here is a helpful sentence: **faith is an empty hand that receives a full Savior.** Faith is not powerful because you feel strong. Faith is powerful because Christ is strong.

3) Distinguish Faith from "Works Faith"

Some people believe facts about Jesus but still trust themselves. They may agree that Jesus died and rose, yet rely on their morality, their church attendance, or their spiritual discipline as the real foundation. That is not saving faith. That is self-trust wearing Christian language.

Philippians 3:8–9 (NSV) shows Paul rejecting that approach. He counts his religious credentials as loss in order to gain Christ and be found in Him, not having a righteousness of his own from the law, but a righteousness through faith in Christ. Paul does not despise obedience. He despises using obedience as a way to secure acceptance.

This matters because many sincere churchgoers remain restless. They think, "I hope God accepts me," because they have not stopped trying to earn acceptance. The gospel offers a better sentence: **"God accepts me in Christ."**

4) Learn Justification's Core: God Declares, Not God Negotiates

Justification means God declares the believer righteous in Christ. God does not negotiate acceptance with you, as if salvation is a shared project where you contribute enough and God meets you halfway. Scripture presents a verdict grounded in Christ's work.

Romans 5:1 (NSV) states the result: since we have been justified by faith, we have peace with God through our Lord Jesus Christ. Peace with God is not first a mood. It is a settled relationship because the guilt problem is solved.

You may ask, *does this mean God stops caring about holiness?* No. Justification changes your standing. Then sanctification changes your life. Confusing them leads to two errors: either you try to justify yourself by improvement, or you treat improvement as optional. Scripture teaches neither.

5) Place Works in the Right Spot: Fruit, Not Root

Works matter, but they belong in the right place. Works do not cause salvation. Works confirm and display salvation.

Ephesians 2:10 (NSV) follows immediately after the grace-and-faith verses: we are God's workmanship, created in Christ Jesus for good works, which God prepared beforehand, that we should walk in them. The order is crucial:

- Saved by grace through faith (gift).
- Then created for good works (purpose).

A healthy Christian life obeys because it is loved, not in order to be loved. That shift changes everything. It produces obedience marked by gratitude rather than panic.

James also insists that genuine faith produces action. James 2:17 (NSV) says faith by itself, if it does not have works, is dead. James is not contradicting Paul. James is confronting empty claims that never produce a changed life. Paul denies that works justify. James denies that living faith remains alone.

Faith is not mere agreement. It includes a turning from sin and self-rule. Repentance does not earn forgiveness. Repentance is how a sinner comes honestly to Christ.

Acts 17:30 (NSV) says God commands all people everywhere to repent. Repentance means you stop defending sin, stop naming rebellion as freedom, and return to God's rightful rule.

A practical way to define repentance is simple:

- **Confession**: "God, You are right about my sin."
- **Turning**: "I will not keep walking that direction."
- **Trust**: "Christ is my only hope."

If someone claims faith yet refuses repentance as a settled posture, they are not trusting Christ. They are trying to keep Christ as a helper while keeping sin as a master.

7) Learn from Church History: Why This Chapter Has Been a Battlefield

The church has repeatedly had to guard the gospel at this exact point: Is salvation a gift received by faith, or a reward earned by performance?

Early teachers fought forms of self-salvation that treated grace as optional. Later, medieval debates often centered on how grace, sacraments, and merit relate. The Reformation sharpened the issue again, insisting that justification is by faith apart from works, because Scripture excludes boasting and locates righteousness in Christ.

Different Christian traditions have nuanced language about how faith, baptism, and ongoing obedience relate. Yet whenever the church blurs the difference between **justification** (God's verdict in Christ) and **sanctification** (God's transforming work in the believer), people lose assurance and drift into either pride or despair.

A steady rule will help you: **anything that makes your performance the basis of God's acceptance is not the gospel.** The gospel makes Christ's performance the basis.

Assurance

Assurance grows when you look to Christ and God's promise, not to your spiritual mood.

John 6:37 (NSV) records Jesus' promise: whoever comes to Me I will never cast out. That promise is not fragile. It does not say, "I will keep you unless you struggle." It says He will not reject those who come.

Growth

Grace also fuels growth. When you are secure in God's acceptance, you can repent honestly without fear of being discarded. You can face hard truths because the foundation is not your pride. It is Christ.

A sincere question appears again: *What if my obedience is inconsistent?* Your inconsistency should drive you to repentance and renewed reliance on Christ, not to self-salvation. Growth is real, and it often is slow. The believer's hope remains Christ, not personal momentum.

9) Practice Receiving the Gift in Daily Life

Here are three simple practices that fit this chapter's teaching.

1. **Preach the gospel to yourself each morning.**

   Say, "I am accepted in Christ because of grace, received by faith." Then thank God.

2. **Confess quickly, without bargaining.**

   When you sin, do not offer God a trade. Confess, turn, and rely on Christ.

3. **Obey one clear command as grateful response.**

   Choose a specific act of obedience—truthful speech, generosity, purity, or forgiveness—and do it as worship, not as payment.

Grace is not a theory. It is the ground you stand on. Faith is not a mood. It is reliance on the Savior who keeps His promise.

CHAPTER 5

BE BORN AGAIN: REPENT, BELIEVE, AND WALK IN NEW LIFE

Many people treat Christianity as behavior improvement with religious language. Scripture describes something far deeper: **new birth**. God does not merely adjust your habits. He gives you new life. That is why the Bible speaks of conversion as being made alive, being renewed, and being transferred into a new kingdom.

New birth does not mean you instantly become mature. It means you become real. You move from spiritual death to spiritual life. You gain new desires, new loyalties, and a new direction. This is also where repentance becomes practical. Repentance is not a single tearful moment. It is a turning that marks a whole life.

This chapter will clarify what it means to be born again, how repentance and faith work together, and what new life looks like in daily practice.

1) Let Jesus Define the New Birth

The clearest place to begin is Jesus' conversation with Nicodemus. Jesus does not flatter him. Nicodemus is religious, educated, and respected, yet Jesus tells him a person must be born again to see the kingdom of God.

John 3:3 (NSV) states it plainly: "Unless one is born again he cannot see the kingdom of God." Jesus is not talking about becoming more religious. He is talking about a new beginning that comes from above.

Nicodemus misunderstands, so Jesus clarifies. John 3:5–6 (NSV) explains that one must be born of water and the Spirit, and that what is born of flesh is flesh, and what is born of the Spirit is spirit. The point is not mystery for mystery's sake. The point is source. Spiritual life comes from the Spirit, not from human effort.

This changes how you think about conversion. Becoming a Christian is not mainly joining a community or adopting rules. It is receiving life from God.

2) Understand Why New Birth Is Necessary

New birth is necessary because the human problem is not only guilt. It is also bondage. People do not merely commit sins; they love sin, defend sin, and return to sin. Without inward change, the heart remains set against God.

Scripture describes this as spiritual deadness and blindness. That is why the gospel is not advice. It is good news with power. When God gives new birth, the heart begins to respond differently to truth. The conscience becomes more sensitive. Sin becomes less comfortable. Christ becomes more precious.

A common question is, "If new birth is necessary, does that mean I am passive?" No. Scripture calls you to repent and believe. Yet it also teaches that God must make you alive to do so. When a dead person rises, they truly stand, walk, and speak. Their actions are real, but the life was given to them.

3) Tie New Birth to the Word of God

God does not usually bring new birth through vague spiritual feelings. He brings it through His Word, proclaimed and received.

1 Peter 1:23 (NSV) says believers are born again, not of perishable seed but of imperishable, through the living and abiding word of God. This does not turn the Bible into a magic object. It shows that God uses truth as His instrument. The gospel message is not optional. It is the seed God plants.

That is why faithful preaching, Scripture reading, and teaching matter. People do not need religious motivation alone. They need the Word that reveals Christ and calls for repentance and faith.

4) Define Repentance: Turn from Sin and Return to God

Repentance is often misunderstood. Some treat it as feeling sorry. Others treat it as self-punishment. Scripture treats repentance as a moral and spiritual turning.

Repentance includes at least three parts:

- **Conviction**: you recognize sin as sin, not as personality or mistake.
- **Confession**: you agree with God's verdict about it.
- **Turning**: you change direction, with practical steps.

Proverbs 28:13 (NSV) captures this: whoever conceals transgressions will not prosper, but whoever confesses and forsakes them will obtain mercy. Notice the movement: confession and forsaking. Repentance does not mean you never struggle again. It means you stop protecting sin. You stop calling it harmless. You stop keeping it as a private right.

Repentance is also God-centered. It is not mainly, "I dislike the consequences." It is, "I have offended God, and I want to return to His ways."

5) Connect Repentance and Faith: Two Sides of One Response

Repentance turns from sin. Faith turns to Christ. They belong together. If you try to repent without faith, you will end in despair or pride. If you try to claim faith without repentance, you will end in self-deception.

Acts 26:20 (NSV) summarizes the apostolic pattern: people should repent and turn to God, performing deeds in keeping with repentance. Notice the order. Turning to God comes first, then deeds that fit the turn. The deeds do not purchase acceptance. They confirm that a real change has begun.

Faith, in this context, is not "I believe God exists." Faith is "I trust Christ to save me, rule me, and keep me."

6) Expect Real Change: New Life Produces New Direction

New birth does not mean instant perfection, but it does mean a new direction. A person who is born again begins to fight sin instead of feeding it. They begin to pursue obedience instead of avoiding it. They begin to love Christ's people instead of treating church as a consumer product.

Galatians 2:20 (NSV) describes the new life in personal terms: "I have been crucified with Christ. It is no longer I who live, but Christ who lives in me." Paul is not saying he lost his personality. He is saying a new center now governs his life. The old self-rule has been judged. A new life is now active.

This is where many people need honesty. If there is no new direction, no new desires, and no new conflict with sin, it is wise to ask whether the person has merely adopted religious habits without receiving new life.

7) Make Peace with the Ongoing Fight

New birth begins a fight that did not exist before. Before conversion, many people can sin with little inner resistance. After conversion, the conscience wakes up, and sin begins to feel heavier. That struggle can surprise new believers.

Do not interpret that struggle as proof you are lost. Often it is proof you are alive.

Romans 6:11–14 (NSV) gives practical instruction: consider yourself dead to sin and alive to God in Christ Jesus, and do not present your members to sin as instruments for unrighteousness. The language is realistic. It assumes temptation remains. It commands decisive choices rooted in a new identity.

The Christian life is not "never tempted again." It is "no longer ruled by sin." You may stumble, but you are not owned.

8) Learn from Church History:
Why the Church Emphasized Regeneration

Across centuries, pastors and theologians stressed new birth because they saw a repeated danger: people can live inside church life without truly knowing Christ.

Augustine emphasized that grace must change the will, not merely inform the mind. During the Reformation era, many teachers stressed that justification is God's verdict, and regeneration is God's inward work. Later, revivals often returned to Jesus' words about being born again, because outward religion was common while transformed life was rare.

The point is not to chase emotional experiences. The point is to seek the reality Scripture describes: a changed heart that turns to Christ and begins a new life.

9) Practice New Life in Simple, Concrete Ways

New birth is God's work, but God calls you to respond with steady obedience. Here are five practices that fit Scripture's pattern:

1. **Speak the truth quickly.** When you sin, confess it without delay. Hiding feeds darkness.

2. **Cut access to common temptations.** Remove the "easy path" to sin—apps, relationships, websites, financial habits, or hidden routines that keep you trapped.

3. **Choose one obedience step each day.** One truthful conversation. One act of generosity. One refusal to gossip. One disciplined hour of work.

4. **Stay close to the Word.** Read Scripture daily, not to earn acceptance, but to keep your mind aligned with God's voice.

5. **Attach to the church.** New life is meant to grow in community through worship, accountability, and service.

These practices do not create new birth. They help new life grow strong.

10) Keep the Main Point Clear: God Gives Life, and You Live It Out

New birth is God's gift. Repentance is your turning. Faith is your reliance on Christ. Together, they form the start of a new life that keeps unfolding.

If you feel weak, do not wait for strength before you come to Christ. Come to Christ for strength. If you fear you have failed too often, do not hide. Confess and return. The mark of new life is not sinlessness. It is repentance and renewed trust.

CHAPTER 6

GROW IN GRACE DAILY: FOLLOW HOW GOD APPLIES SALVATION AND CHANGES YOU

Many Christians can explain the cross, yet feel unsure about daily change. They know Christ saves, but they wonder why progress is slow and why old habits still tug hard. Scripture gives a clear answer: salvation is not only something Christ accomplished in history; it is also something God **applies** to a person over time. God does not merely forgive you and leave you to figure the rest out. He calls you, joins you to Christ, gives you a new standing, brings you into His family, and then shapes you into holiness.

This chapter will explain how God applies salvation in an ordered, wise way. Christians have often called this the "order of salvation." The goal is simple: help you understand what God has done, what God is doing, and what faithful growth looks like in ordinary life.

1) Begin with God's Call: Salvation Starts with God's Voice, Not Your Search

Scripture speaks of God calling people out of darkness into light. This call is more than an invitation you might ignore. In God's mercy, it is also an effective summons that awakens faith.

2 Thessalonians 2:13–14 (NSV) says God chose believers for salvation through sanctification by the Spirit and belief in the truth, and that God called them through the gospel. Notice the link: the gospel is preached, and God calls through that message.

This protects you from pride. If you came to Christ, it was not because you were smarter than others. It was because God was kind. It also strengthens evangelism. God uses the preached gospel to call sinners into life.

A believer's blessings are not scattered gifts. They are joined to one central reality: union with Christ. Scripture often describes Christians as being "in Christ," and Christ living in them.

Colossians 3:1–4 (NSV) ties identity and growth together: if you have been raised with Christ, seek the things above; your life is hidden with Christ in God; Christ is your life. The logic is direct. Your new identity shapes your new direction.

Union with Christ explains why salvation is not only a legal change. It is also a life change. You are joined to a living Savior. That union becomes the source of obedience, endurance, and hope.

3) Separate Two Works without Dividing Them:
Justification and Sanctification

Many believers either confuse justification and sanctification or split them apart. Scripture keeps them distinct while holding them together.

Justification is God's verdict. God declares you righteous in Christ. This is your standing.

Sanctification is God's transforming work in you. God makes you holy in practice. This is your growth.

Romans 8:33–34 (NSV) anchors justification with courtroom clarity: who will bring a charge against God's elect? It is God who justifies. Christ Jesus died, was raised, and intercedes. That passage settles the courtroom issue. The believer's standing does not swing daily with emotions.

Sanctification, however, is a process. It includes growth, setbacks, learning, and daily warfare against sin. A justified believer can still be immature. Yet a justified believer will not remain unchanged.

4) Receive Adoption:
God Brings You into His Family, Not Only His Courtroom

Some Christians know they are forgiven but still live like unwanted servants. Scripture gives a stronger reality: adoption.

1 John 3:1 (NSV) calls believers to see the love the Father has given,

that we should be called children of God—and so we are. Adoption means you belong. You are not on probation. You are not tolerated. You are received.

Adoption does not erase discipline. Fathers correct children. Yet discipline is not rejection. Discipline confirms belonging. This changes how you repent. You confess as a child returning to a Father, not as a criminal trying to bargain with a judge.

5) Define Sanctification: God Trains You for Holiness in Real Life

Sanctification is not vague spirituality. Scripture defines it as growth in holiness through the Spirit, shaped by the Word, practiced in obedience, and expressed in love.

1 Thessalonians 4:3 (NSV) states it plainly: this is the will of God, your sanctification. God's will for your life is not hidden. It is holiness.

2 Corinthians 3:18 (NSV) describes how this happens: believers behold the Lord's glory and are transformed into the same image from one degree of glory to another, and this comes from the Lord who is the Spirit. Growth is gradual, real, and Spirit-driven.

This keeps you from despair when change is slow. Scripture expects "degrees." It also keeps you from complacency. God's will is not stagnation. It is steady transformation.

6) Expect the Fight: The Old Patterns Resist the New Life

A believer has a new identity, yet the believer still lives in a world shaped by sin, with habits formed over years. Sanctification includes conflict.

This conflict shows up in three places:

- **The mind**: old thought patterns, fears, and false beliefs.
- **The desires**: cravings that once ruled you now demand attention.
- **The habits**: routines and relationships that pull you back.

Scripture does not treat temptation as strange. It treats it as part of the Christian life. The goal is not to pretend you are beyond struggle. The goal is to learn faithful resistance with repentance when you fall.

One genuine question is common here: *If I am truly saved, why do I still feel pulled toward sin?* The answer is straightforward: salvation is real, and so is remaining corruption. God does not deny the fight; He supplies grace within it, and He teaches you to walk in new patterns.

7) Use the Means God Provides: Word, Prayer, Church, and the Lord's Table

God does not call you to holiness and then leave you with empty hands. He gives "means of grace," ordinary channels through which He strengthens faith.

The Word

God's Word renews the mind and corrects self-deception. Regular Scripture intake trains you to recognize lies and respond with truth.

Prayer

Prayer is dependence practiced. Prayer does not earn change. Prayer receives help. It also exposes motives. People often discover what they worship by noticing what they pray about most.

The Church

Sanctification is personal, but it is not private. God uses pastors, teachers, and fellow believers to encourage, correct, and protect.

The Lord's Table

Across church history, many traditions have treated the Lord's Table as a steady reminder and seal of gospel reality. You do not come because you are worthy. You come because Christ is worthy, and because you need grace. The Table trains humility, gratitude, and unity.

The early church emphasized these practices because believers needed steady formation, not occasional inspiration. Later, the Reformers stressed the same point: God shapes His people through Word and sacrament, within a real church community.

8) Practice "Put Off / Put On" in Sanctification

Sanctification becomes practical when you replace sin, not merely resist it. Scripture teaches this replacement pattern.

A useful approach is:

1. **Put off** the old pattern (name it clearly).
2. **Renew** the mind with Scripture (replace the lie).
3. **Put on** the new practice (choose an action).

Example:

- Put off harsh speech.
- Renew the mind: God hears my words and calls for patience.
- Put on: speak fewer words, speak honest words, speak gentle words.

This is not behavior control alone. It is worship. You are learning to live under God's rule in ordinary situations.

9) Learn Assurance Wisely: Look First to Christ, Then to Fruit

Assurance is not arrogance. It is settled trust in God's promise.

Scripture gives two main supports for assurance:

- **Christ's finished work**: God justifies, Christ intercedes, and accusations cannot overturn God's verdict (Romans 8:33–34, NSV).
- **The Spirit's fruit**: real change shows that new life is present. Growth may be slow, but direction matters.

If you look only at fruit, you may panic on hard days. If you look only at claims without fruit, you may drift into self-deception. Scripture gives a balanced path: rest first in Christ, then examine your life with honesty and hope.

10) Keep the End in View: God Will Finish What He Starts

Salvation applied is not a fragile project. God completes what He begins. This is where many believers gain steadiness. Sanctification is hard, but it is not uncertain.

The same God who called you through the gospel, joined you to Christ, justified you, and adopted you is the God who will keep shaping you. That truth does not produce laziness. It produces confidence for daily obedience.

BOOK FOUR

THE SPIRIT: LIVE BY GOD'S PRESENCE AND POWER

A Simple Guide to the Holy Spirit's Person, Work, Gifts, and Guidance

CHAPTER 1

MEET THE HOLY SPIRIT AS GOD: TRUST HIS PRESENCE AND FOLLOW HIS LEADING

Some Christians speak about the Holy Spirit with uncertainty. Others speak with confidence but little biblical precision. Scripture calls for something better: reverent clarity. The Holy Spirit is not an "it." He is not a mood. He is not a mere influence. He is **God**, and He relates to God's people personally.

If you misunderstand the Spirit, you will misunderstand salvation applied, prayer, growth, guidance, assurance, and the church's unity. If you know the Spirit as Scripture presents Him, you will gain steadiness. You will stop trying to live the Christian life by human energy alone.

This chapter will establish three foundations: the Spirit's **personhood**, the Spirit's **deity**, and the Spirit's **core works** in the life of believers.

1) Start with a Clear Question: Is the Spirit a Person or a Power?

Scripture answers with repeated personal actions. The Spirit speaks. The Spirit teaches. The Spirit can be grieved. The Spirit distributes gifts as He wills. These are not traits of an impersonal force.

Jesus speaks of the Spirit as "He," not "it." In John 14:16–17 (NSV), Jesus promises "another Helper" who will be with His disciples and in them. The word "Helper" points to personal support, counsel, and presence. Jesus presents the Spirit as someone who comes alongside God's people.

Paul also speaks of the Spirit in personal terms. Ephesians 4:30 (NSV) warns believers not to grieve the Holy Spirit of God. You cannot grieve electricity. You can grieve a person. This verse also links the Spirit to God's saving mark: believers are sealed for the day of redemption.

If the Spirit is a person, then Christian life includes relationship: dependence, listening, obedience, and comfort—not mere technique.

2) Confess the Spirit as God, Not a Lesser Being

Scripture does not present the Spirit as a created messenger. It presents Him as divine.

A direct passage appears in Acts 5:3–4 (NSV). Peter confronts Ananias for lying to the Holy Spirit, then says he has not lied to man but to God. The logic is unavoidable: lying to the Spirit is lying to God. The Spirit is not merely representing God; He is God.

The Spirit also displays divine attributes. In 1 Corinthians 2:10–11 (NSV), Paul says the Spirit searches everything, even the depths of God, and that no one comprehends God's thoughts except the Spirit of God. This is not creaturely guesswork. It is divine knowledge.

The Spirit is also included in the church's Trinitarian language of blessing and worship. 2 Corinthians 13:14 (NSV) places the Spirit alongside the Father and the Son: the grace of the Lord Jesus Christ, the love of God, and the fellowship of the Holy Spirit. Scripture does not place creatures inside this kind of sacred, covenant blessing.

So the Spirit is a person, and the Spirit is God. This matters because the Christian life is not powered by self-effort. It is powered by God's own presence.

3) Hold to the Trinity: One God, Three Persons, One Saving Work

Christians did not invent the Trinity to complicate faith. The church confessed the Trinity because Scripture revealed the Father, the Son, and the Spirit as distinct and divine, yet one God.

For the Spirit, this confession protects two truths at once:

- The Spirit is not a replacement for Christ; He glorifies Christ and applies Christ's work.
- The Spirit is not a lesser helper; He is God present with God's people.

This also protects your worship. If the Spirit is God, then His work in you deserves reverence and gratitude, not casual talk or fear-driven speculation.

4) Understand the Spirit's Core Work: He Makes Salvation Real in You

Book 3 focused on what Christ accomplished. Now we focus on how God brings that saving work into a person's life.

Scripture describes the Spirit's work in several key actions:

The Spirit gives new life

Jesus connects new birth to the Spirit's work (John 3:5–6, NSV). We have already covered that earlier, so here is the same truth from another angle: the Spirit does not merely influence; He gives life. Without the Spirit's renewing work, people remain spiritually dead.

The Spirit unites believers to Christ

Union with Christ is not a human achievement. It is Spirit-wrought reality. The Spirit joins believers to Christ so Christ's benefits become theirs: forgiveness, righteousness, adoption, and a new direction.

The Spirit assures believers of belonging

Romans 8:15–16 (NSV) taught that the Spirit bears witness that believers are God's children. We used that earlier; the point here is simple: assurance is not created by self-talk alone. The Spirit strengthens confidence in God's Fatherly love.

The Spirit empowers holiness

The Christian life is not powered by guilt. It is powered by grace applied through the Spirit. Without the Spirit, commands become crushing weight. With the Spirit, commands become a path you can actually walk.

5) Learn How the Spirit Works with the Word

Some people separate the Spirit from Scripture, as if the Spirit leads mainly through impressions. Others treat Scripture as a textbook and neglect the Spirit's living ministry. Scripture holds Word and Spirit together.

The Spirit inspired Scripture, and the Spirit uses Scripture to shape believers. When you read, hear, and submit to God's Word, you are not merely collecting information. You are placing yourself under the Spirit's instrument for renewal.

A reliable rule will protect you: the Spirit will never lead you to contradict what He has already spoken in Scripture. True guidance will align with God's revealed character and commands.

This also protects the church from chaos. When "the Spirit told me" becomes a way to bypass Scripture, correction becomes impossible and pride grows. The Spirit does not lead God's people into confusion. He leads them into truth and holiness.

6) Recognize the Spirit's Leading Without Treating It Like Fortune-Telling

Many believers want guidance about jobs, relationships, and decisions. Scripture does teach that God leads. Yet it rarely encourages you to seek secret messages. It encourages you to seek wisdom.

The Spirit's leading is often ordinary:

- He renews your mind through Scripture so you can judge wisely.
- He shapes your desires so you want what honors Christ.
- He uses counsel from mature believers to correct blind spots.
- He opens and closes doors through providence.

That means you can make decisions without superstition. You pray, search Scripture, seek counsel, and act with integrity. If you want a simple definition: the Spirit's leading is God's faithful direction that produces obedience, not anxiety.

7) Address Two Common Errors About the Spirit

Error 1: Treating the Spirit as optional

Some believers focus so heavily on doctrine that they live as if the Spirit's presence were irrelevant. The result is dry faith and self-powered effort.

Error 2: Treating the Spirit as unpredictable energy

Others chase experiences, unusual claims, and constant novelty. The result can be instability, confusion, and spiritual pride.

Scripture calls for a steady middle: honor the Spirit as God, receive His gifts with gratitude, and test everything by Scripture in the life of the church.

8) Learn from Church History:
Why the Spirit's Deity Had to Be Defended

In the fourth century, some groups treated the Spirit as a high creature. The church responded by confessing the Spirit's full deity in the Nicene tradition. The Nicene-Constantinopolitan Creed (381) speaks of the Spirit as "the Lord" and "giver of life," worshiped and glorified with the Father and the Son.

This was not political maneuvering. It was pastoral necessity. If the Spirit is not God, then God is not truly present with His people in the way Scripture promises. And if the Spirit is not God, then the Christian life becomes human moral effort rather than Spirit-powered renewal.

9) Make This Personal:
What Changes When You Know the Spirit Is God?

Three changes should follow.

You stop treating growth like self-improvement

You still work, but you work in dependence. You ask for help. You trust God to supply what He commands.

You treat sin more seriously and repentance more hopefully

The Spirit convicts, but He also comforts. He exposes sin to heal it, not to destroy you.

You value the church more deeply

The Spirit does not create isolated spiritual heroes. He forms one body. He builds unity through shared truth, shared worship, and shared mission.

10) Take One Concrete Step: Practice Daily Reliance

If you want an action step that fits this chapter, begin your day with three short prayers:

1. "Holy Spirit, help me see Christ clearly today."
2. "Holy Spirit, show me any sin I am excusing."
3. "Holy Spirit, strengthen me to obey in one specific area."

Then open Scripture and read a short passage with attention. Do not rush. Ask what it requires. Ask what it reveals about God. Then obey one clear instruction before the day ends.

Meeting the Holy Spirit as God is not mainly about having unusual experiences. It is about living with steady dependence on God's presence.

CHAPTER 2

TRACE THE SPIRIT'S WORK IN THE OLD TESTAMENT: SEE GOD'S PRESENCE BEFORE PENTECOST

Many Christians assume the Holy Spirit appears only in the New Testament. Scripture does not support that idea. The Spirit is active from the opening lines of Genesis, and His work runs through Israel's history in ways that prepare you to understand Pentecost, the church, and the Christian life.

At the same time, the Old Testament and New Testament describe the Spirit's work with different emphases. In the Old Testament, the Spirit is often shown empowering particular people for particular tasks at particular times—kingship, craftsmanship, prophecy, leadership, and deliverance. In the New Testament, following Christ's finished work, the Spirit is poured out broadly on God's people in a fuller covenant sense. If you miss the Old Testament foundation, you may either downplay the Spirit's work or speak about it without biblical structure.

This chapter will trace the Spirit's work in the Old Testament under four headings: **creation, covenant life, empowerment for service, and promise of future outpouring**. Along the way, we will note how careful Christian teaching has drawn these themes together.

1) See the Spirit at Creation: God Brings Order and Life

The first time you meet the Spirit in Scripture is not in Acts. It is in Genesis.

Genesis 1:2 (NSV) describes the Spirit of God present over the waters as God prepares to bring order, beauty, and life. This verse teaches a basic truth: the Spirit is not a late addition to God's work. He is present at the beginning, active in creation.

The Bible reinforces this later. Job 33:4 (NSV) states, "The Spirit of God has made me, and the breath of the Almighty gives me life." Scripture connects the Spirit with life-giving power. He is not a distant concept. He is the divine giver of life and order.

This matters for theology and for daily faith. If the Spirit gives life in creation, then the Spirit giving life in salvation is consistent with who He is. New birth is not strange. It is God acting according to His nature.

2) Understand "Spirit" Language: Breath, Wind, and Presence

Old Testament language often uses words that carry the sense of breath or wind. The point is not poetic fog. The point is power and presence that cannot be controlled by human hands.

Wind is real, strong, and unseen. Breath is invisible yet essential for life. These images teach reverence. The Spirit is not a tool you can manage. He is God present and active.

This also protects you from treating spiritual life as technique. If the Spirit is God's living presence, then the right posture is dependence, prayer, obedience, and humility.

3) Trace the Spirit in Israel's Covenant Life: Guidance and Instruction

The Spirit is not only about extraordinary moments. The Old Testament shows the Spirit sustaining God's people through guidance and instruction.

Nehemiah 9:20 (NSV) praises God's mercy: God gave His good Spirit to instruct His people. That is striking. The Spirit is connected with teaching and formation, not only dramatic deliverances. God shepherds His people by His Spirit.

This also explains why Scripture and Spirit belong together. God's Spirit instructs in truth. He does not lead God's people into moral confusion. He forms them through God's Word, God's commands, and God's covenant purposes.

One of the most visible Old Testament themes is the Spirit empowering leaders for rescue and righteous action.

In the time of the judges, Scripture repeatedly states that the Spirit came upon a deliverer to rescue Israel from oppression. Judges 3:10 (NSV) says the Spirit of the Lord came upon Othniel, and he judged Israel and went out to war, and the Lord gave victory. The pattern repeats in the book: God raises a deliverer, empowers him, and rescues His people.

Two points matter here:

1. **The Spirit empowers for service, not self-display.** The goal is deliverance and protection of God's people, not personal fame.

2. **The Spirit's empowerment does not equal moral maturity.** Some judges were courageous yet deeply flawed. This warns you against equating visible gifting with holiness. God can empower a task without endorsing a person's character.

This is a practical lesson for today. A gifted leader may still require accountability. Spiritual power does not excuse sin. The Old Testament already teaches you to separate gifting from godliness.

5) See the Spirit Equip Craftsmanship: Skill for God's House

Many people think the Spirit only empowers "spiritual" activities like preaching. The Old Testament widens your view.

Exodus 31:2–5 (NSV) describes Bezalel being filled with the Spirit of God with ability, intelligence, knowledge, and craftsmanship to build for the tabernacle. That is Spirit-given skill in design, artistry, and construction for holy worship.

This expands your theology of vocation. The Spirit's work includes wisdom and skill used for God's glory. In modern terms, God can strengthen faithful work in teaching, administration, music, care, building, and problem-solving—especially when that work serves worship and the good of God's people.

This does not mean every talent is automatically spiritual. It means God is free to supply real ability for His purposes, and believers should honor skilled work as meaningful service.

The Spirit's relationship to kingship in the Old Testament is central for understanding Jesus as the anointed Messiah.

1 Samuel 16:13 (NSV) describes Samuel anointing David, and the Spirit of the Lord rushing upon him from that day forward. The Spirit's empowerment for David connects to leadership under God's authority. Israel's king was meant to rule in obedience to God, guarding justice and honoring the covenant.

Yet the Old Testament also warns that the Spirit's empowering presence in leadership could be forfeited in a covenantal sense through hardened rebellion. This is why David prays in Psalm 51:11 (NSV), "Do not cast me away from Your presence, and do not take Your Holy Spirit from me." David is not describing ordinary Christian experience after Pentecost in the same way. He is pleading as a covenant king who knows his sin threatens the stability of his calling and the wellbeing of the people he leads.

This is a key interpretive lesson: **Old Testament Spirit language often relates to roles—king, prophet, leader—within the covenant administration.** That prepares you to see why the New Testament later stresses the Spirit's indwelling of all believers as a shared covenant blessing.

7) See the Spirit in Prophecy: God Speaks Through His Servants

The prophets did not speak as private thinkers offering religious opinions. They spoke as God's messengers.

2 Peter 1:21 (NSV) states a New Testament summary of the Old Testament prophetic pattern: men spoke from God as they were carried along by the Holy Spirit. The Spirit is tied to revelation. God's Word comes by God's Spirit.

This is why the church has always treated Scripture as Spirit-given. It also explains why prophecy in Scripture is not merely encouragement. It includes rebuke, warning, and covenant instruction. The Spirit's work is not only comfort; it is truth.

8) Grasp a Major Old Testament Tension: Presence with Limits, Promise of More

The Old Testament shows God's real presence and real power, yet it also builds anticipation. Several passages look forward to a day when the Spirit's work would be more widespread and more inward.

Zechariah 4:6 (NSV) gives a famous principle: "Not by might, nor by power, but by My Spirit, says the Lord." This line addresses human weakness and God's sufficiency. It also points forward. God's work will not be secured by human strength. It will be secured by divine action.

The prophets also speak about a future era marked by deeper internal renewal. The Old Testament repeatedly connects hope with a change of heart and a greater work of God among His people. This prepares you for the New Testament's language about new birth, indwelling, and Spirit-given transformation across the whole church.

9) Learn from Israel's Failure: The Spirit Can Be Resisted and Grieved

The Old Testament is candid about rebellion. God's people often received mercy and still resisted God.

Isaiah 63:10 (NSV) says they rebelled and grieved His Holy Spirit. That verse is important because it holds two truths together: the Spirit is personal, and resistance is real. People can oppose God's leading. They can harden their hearts. They can reject instruction.

This prepares you to understand why the New Testament includes both comfort and warning. The Spirit strengthens believers, and believers are also commanded not to resist, quench, or ignore His work. The covenant story teaches that spiritual privilege never justifies spiritual carelessness.

10) Connect Old Testament Themes to Christ: The Spirit Prepares the Way

The Old Testament's Spirit-work is not isolated. It is preparation for Christ.

- The Spirit gives life in creation, preparing you to see the Spirit give life in regeneration.
- The Spirit empowers leaders and kings, preparing you for the Messiah, the true anointed King.

- The Spirit speaks through prophets, preparing you for Christ, the final Word and faithful Prophet.

- The Spirit instructs and guides the people, preparing you for a fuller covenant community shaped from within.

In church history, this is one reason theologians spoke about the unity of God's saving work: the Spirit's presence is consistent, yet His covenant administration unfolds with the storyline. The Old Testament is not "Spirit-less." It is "promise-shaped." It creates categories that become clearer after Christ's death, resurrection, and ascension.

11) Apply This Chapter: Live with Reverence, Gratitude, and Wise Expectations

Here are three practical ways this Old Testament view helps you today.

First, it keeps you from treating the Spirit as novelty.

The Spirit has been active from the beginning. You do not need constant new claims to take Him seriously.

Second, it teaches you to value character above gifting.

Judges and kings show that empowerment for a task does not guarantee holiness. Do not confuse visible ability with spiritual maturity.

Third, it teaches you to seek the Spirit's help in ordinary work.

The Spirit equipped Bezalel for craftsmanship. Pray for wisdom, skill, patience, and faithfulness in the work God has given you.

The Old Testament teaches that God's Spirit is real, personal, and powerful—present in creation, guiding covenant life, empowering service, and promising deeper renewal. In the next chapter, we will move into the life and ministry of Jesus to see how the Spirit's work is displayed in the Messiah Himself, preparing for the Spirit's outpouring on the church.

CHAPTER 3

FOLLOW THE SPIRIT IN JESUS' LIFE: SEE THE MESSIAH ANOINTED FOR HIS MISSION

If you want to understand the Holy Spirit, do not begin with debates or unusual claims. Begin with Jesus. The Spirit's work in Christ's life shows what true anointing looks like: it produces holiness, truth, compassion, and faithful obedience to the Father. It also shows that salvation is not only about what Jesus did *for* you on the cross, but also about what He did *as* the obedient Messiah—living, resisting temptation, proclaiming the kingdom, and carrying out His mission by the Spirit's power.

This chapter will trace the Spirit's role in Jesus' life from conception to ministry to sacrifice. The goal is to help you see the Spirit's work with biblical clarity and to apply it wisely to Christian life today.

1) Start at the Beginning: The Spirit's Work in the Incarnation

Jesus did not begin His existence in Bethlehem. He is the eternal Son who took on human nature. Yet the incarnation enters history through the Spirit's work.

Luke 1:35 (NSV) explains to Mary that the Holy Spirit will come upon her, and the power of the Most High will overshadow her. This is not an abstract miracle. It is God preparing a true human nature for the Son, in a holy and unique way. The Spirit's work here guards two truths: Jesus is truly human, and He is holy from the start.

This matters for salvation because a Savior who shares our humanity can represent us, and a Savior who is sinless can save us.

2) Notice the Pattern: The Spirit Marks Jesus as the Promised Messiah

In the Old Testament, kings were anointed as a sign of divine appointment. Jesus is "the Christ," the Anointed One, and the Spirit's presence marks His identity and mission.

At Jesus' baptism, the Spirit descends on Him. Luke 3:21–22 (NSV) describes the Spirit coming in bodily form like a dove, and the Father's voice declaring Jesus as His beloved Son. This event is Trinitarian, public, and decisive. It shows that Jesus' mission begins with divine confirmation.

The Spirit's descent does not mean Jesus lacked deity before baptism. Jesus is eternally the Son. Rather, it shows Jesus beginning His public ministry as the Messiah, equipped for His role as the obedient servant-king.

3) See the Spirit Lead Jesus into Testing: Holiness Before Public Power

Many people chase public power while neglecting holiness. Jesus' path is the reverse. The Spirit leads Him into testing before public ministry.

Luke 4:1–2 (NSV) says Jesus, full of the Holy Spirit, was led by the Spirit in the wilderness. This is important. Temptation is not always a sign God is absent. Sometimes it is part of God's shaping work. Jesus faces real temptation, not as a sinner, but as the righteous Messiah who must succeed where Adam and Israel failed.

He resists by Scripture. He does not argue with clever philosophy. He stands on God's Word. This teaches you that the Spirit's leading will not separate you from Scripture. The Spirit strengthens obedience, and Scripture provides the clear line.

4) Hear Jesus Describe His Ministry: The Spirit Anoints for Good News and Mercy

Jesus does not leave you guessing about the Spirit's role in His mission. He explains it openly.

Luke 4:18–19 (NSV) records Jesus reading from Isaiah: the Spirit of the Lord is upon Me because He has anointed Me to preach good news to the poor, proclaim liberty to captives, recovery of sight to the blind, and freedom to the oppressed. Then Jesus says this Scripture is fulfilled in their hearing.

This is one of the most important Spirit passages in the Gospels. It shows the Spirit's anointing leads to:

- proclamation of good news,
- mercy to the weak,

- liberation from bondage,
- visible signs that confirm the kingdom's arrival.

The focus is not spectacle. The focus is the kingdom of God advancing through truth and compassion.

5) Understand Miracles as Signs of the Kingdom, Not Performances

Jesus' miracles are not random displays of ability. They are signs that God's reign has arrived and that the curse is being reversed.

When Jesus heals, restores, and delivers, He is showing what God's kingdom does. In doing so, He also shows that spiritual power is meant for service. Jesus' miracles do not create ego. They create worship, gratitude, and amazement at God's mercy.

This corrects a modern temptation: to treat spiritual power as status. In Christ, power serves love. Any claim of Spirit-power that produces pride, manipulation, or harm is already out of step with Jesus.

6) See the Spirit and the Father's Will Working Together

In Jesus' life, the Spirit's power never competes with the Father's will. The Spirit leads Jesus into obedience, suffering, and faithful endurance.

Jesus' ministry includes joy and compassion, but it also includes conflict, rejection, and ultimately the cross. The Spirit's presence does not guarantee an easy path. It guarantees faithful obedience and divine strength to complete the mission.

This matters for believers. If you assume the Spirit's presence means life will be simple, you will become confused when hardship comes. Jesus' Spirit-filled life included suffering with purpose.

7) Understand Christ's Obedience as Representative: He Succeeds Where We Failed

Jesus lived in full obedience not only as an example, but also as the representative Messiah. He stands in the place of His people. His obedience fulfills righteousness.

This connects the Spirit's work to salvation directly. The Spirit empowered Jesus' human life for obedient service. Then Jesus offers His obedient life and atoning death as the ground of salvation.

This is not a small detail. If Jesus is only an example, you are left trying to imitate Him without hope. If Jesus is Savior and representative, you can imitate Him from a secure position, not to earn acceptance.

8) Learn What True Anointing Produces: Fruit Before Gifts

If you want a simple test of Spirit-work, look at Jesus:

- humility instead of self-promotion,
- truth instead of manipulation,
- compassion instead of contempt,
- purity instead of compromise,
- endurance instead of quitting.

This does not mean gifts are unimportant. It means fruit is the first evidence of the Spirit's work. Gifts can be counterfeited or misused. Christlike character cannot be faked for long.

A church that seeks gifts without seeking Christlike character will eventually drift into confusion. A believer who seeks experiences without seeking holiness will eventually be disappointed.

9) Connect Jesus' Ministry to the Promise of the Spirit for Believers

Jesus' Spirit-anointed life is not meant to remain unique and distant. It prepares for the Spirit's outpouring on the church.

Jesus promises that His followers will receive the Spirit in a new covenant fullness after His work is finished. The Gospels present Jesus as the one who baptizes with the Holy Spirit, bringing God's presence to His people in a deeper way.

So the Spirit's work in Jesus is both model and foundation: it shows what Spirit-empowered faithfulness looks like, and it prepares the way for believers to live by the Spirit as those united to Christ.

10) Apply This Chapter: Follow Christ's Pattern in Three Ways

First, pursue holiness before influence.

The Spirit led Jesus into the wilderness before the crowds. Do not rush past hidden obedience.

Second, tie guidance to Scripture.

Jesus resisted temptation with God's Word. Do not treat impressions as higher than Scripture.

Third, serve with compassion.

Jesus' Spirit-anointed ministry brought good news to the poor and help to the afflicted. Measure your "spiritual life" by whether it produces patient love.

When you study the Spirit in Jesus' life, you gain a stable picture of true Spirit-work. It is not chaotic. It is not self-centered. It is Christ-centered and Father-pleasing. In the next chapter, we will move from Jesus' ministry to the Spirit's arrival in the early church, especially at Pentecost, and we will see what changed and what remained consistent with the Old Testament foundation.

CHAPTER 4

RECEIVE THE SPIRIT'S PROMISE: UNDERSTAND PENTECOST AND THE CHURCH'S NEW COVENANT STRENGTH

Pentecost can sound like a single striking day with unusual sounds and foreign languages. Scripture presents it as far more than a memorable moment. Pentecost is the public launch of the new covenant era, when the risen Jesus pours out the Holy Spirit on His people. It confirms that Jesus reigns, that the gospel will go to the nations, and that ordinary believers will be equipped for witness, holiness, prayer, and unity.

This chapter will explain what happened at Pentecost, why it mattered, how it connects to Old Testament promises, and how the Spirit's work spread from Jerusalem outward.

1) Place Pentecost in the Story: From Feast to Fulfillment

Pentecost was already a major Jewish feast, celebrated fifty days after Passover. Israel gathered to give thanks for God's provision. In God's timing, that feast became the stage for a greater gift: not grain, but God's own Spirit given to God's people. The timing matters. The cross occurred at Passover, the resurrection followed, and the Spirit's outpouring came at Pentecost. God was teaching the church to read redemption as a connected whole.

2) Observe the Event: The Spirit Comes with Clear Signs

Acts 2:1–4 (NSV) describes the disciples gathered together when a sound like a mighty wind filled the house, tongues as of fire appeared, and they were filled with the Holy Spirit and began to speak in other tongues as the Spirit gave them utterance. These signs were not

146

entertainment. They were signals. Wind and fire echo God's presence in Scripture, and the tongues served a mission purpose: the gospel would cross language barriers.

It is also important to notice what the passage emphasizes: the Spirit fills, the people speak, and God is making a public statement. Pentecost is not mainly about private spirituality. It is about God equipping public testimony to Christ.

3) Connect Pentecost to Prophecy: God Keeps His Word

Peter explains the event by appealing to prophecy. He cites Joel to show that God had promised an outpouring of the Spirit on "all flesh," including sons and daughters, young and old, servants and handmaids. Acts 2:16–18 (NSV) presents this as fulfillment, not novelty. The point is breadth: the Spirit will not be limited to a small group of leaders. In the new covenant era, God gives His Spirit broadly to His people.

This does not erase roles in the church. Pastors, teachers, and elders still matter. Yet Pentecost signals that every believer is personally involved in the life of the Spirit, the confession of Christ, and the mission of witness.

4) Hear the Main Message: The Spirit Exalts the Risen Jesus

Pentecost is not a Spirit-centered celebration that forgets Christ. Peter's sermon centers on Jesus' death, resurrection, and exaltation. The Spirit's arrival is presented as evidence that Jesus is enthroned and active.

John 16:14 (NSV) captures the same principle from Jesus' teaching: the Spirit will glorify Christ. If the Spirit's work in a church or in a life does not draw attention to Christ's lordship, Christ's gospel, and Christ's commands, something is out of alignment. The Spirit does not compete with Jesus. He makes Jesus known and trusted.

5) Track the Immediate Fruit: Conviction, Repentance, and a New Community

Acts 2 records that the crowd is cut to the heart and asks what to do. Peter calls them to repent, and the passage describes many being added to the church. Then the text highlights ordinary church life: teaching, fellowship, breaking bread, and prayers (Acts 2:42, NSV). The Spirit's strength shows itself in a new community with new priorities.

This guards you from a common error: treating the Spirit's work as only the spectacular. Pentecost includes signs, but it produces steady practices. A Spirit-filled church is never merely loud; it is devoted, generous, prayerful, and anchored in apostolic teaching.

6) Understand Languages as Mission: God Opens the Nations

The tongues at Pentecost were understood languages, heard by people from many regions. The message was not secret. It was public and intelligible. God was reversing Babel's scattering for gospel purposes, not by erasing languages, but by enabling the message to cross them.

This matters for the church's calling. The Spirit is the engine of global mission. He pushes the church outward, beyond comfort, beyond cultural walls, and beyond fear. A church that claims to be Spirit-led yet avoids witness and mercy is resisting the Spirit's purpose.

7) Follow the Expansion: From Jerusalem to the Ends of the Earth

Acts continues the Pentecost pattern as the gospel spreads. When the believers pray under pressure, the Spirit strengthens them for bold speech. Acts 4:31 (NSV) says they were filled with the Holy Spirit and continued to speak the word of God with boldness. Again, the emphasis is witness, not self-display.

Later, the Spirit's gift reaches Gentiles in a decisive way. Acts 10:44–48 (NSV) describes the Holy Spirit falling on those who heard the word, leading the Jewish believers to recognize that God grants the same gift to the nations. This moment shows Pentecost's reach. The Spirit unites Jews and Gentiles in one gospel.

8) Learn from Early Church Teaching: Guard Unity, Test Claims

Because the Spirit is active, the church had to learn discernment. The apostles insisted that the Spirit's work be tested by the apostolic gospel and by the confession of Jesus as Lord. As the church grew, it also had to reject teachings that reduced the Spirit to a creature or treated Him as an impersonal energy.

In the fourth century, the church clarified in its creedal language that the Spirit is "Lord" and "giver of life," worthy of worship with the Father and the Son. This was not an attempt to add to Scripture. It was an attempt to protect what Scripture already taught, so churches would pray, worship, and live with correct reverence.

9) Apply Pentecost Today: Seek the Spirit's Aims, Not Mere Sensations

Pentecost teaches you what to pray for. Ask for courage to witness, strength to obey, and love that builds the church. Ask for conviction that leads to repentance, and comfort that leads to endurance. Ask for unity that crosses social and cultural lines.

Also learn this: the Spirit often works through ordinary means. He uses Scripture preached and read. He uses prayer in the gathered church. He uses repentance practiced quickly. He uses faithful service that gets little notice. If you measure the Spirit's work only by what feels unusual, you will miss much of what He is doing.

10) Keep the Center: The Spirit Brings Christ's Presence to Christ's People

Pentecost does not replace Jesus. It makes Jesus' saving reign personally present to His people. The Spirit unites believers to Christ, equips witness to Christ, and forms a community that obeys Christ. When you keep that center, Pentecost becomes steady ground, not confusion.

In the next chapter, we will study the Spirit's indwelling and filling in daily Christian life, including how to pursue holiness without fear and how to discern true guidance with clarity.

CHAPTER 5

LIVE FILLED WITH THE SPIRIT: PRACTICE DAILY DEPENDENCE, HOLINESS, AND WISDOM

After Pentecost, many believers ask a practical question: what does it mean to live "filled with the Spirit" on an ordinary Tuesday? Scripture does not present Spirit-filled life as rare or unpredictable. It presents it as steady dependence on God, expressed through prayer, obedience, love, and courage. The Spirit's presence is God's gift to every believer, and Scripture also commands believers to be filled and to walk by the Spirit. That means God supplies real help, and believers respond with real choices each day.

This chapter explains the difference between the Spirit's indwelling and the Spirit's filling, how to pursue holiness without fear, and how to seek guidance without superstition. The aim is a stable practical Christian life that honors Christ in speech, desires, decisions, and relationships.

1) Distinguish Indwelling and Filling

The Spirit's indwelling is God's abiding presence in the believer. Filling is the Spirit's active influence and strengthening that shapes behavior and witness in a given moment.

Paul's command in Ephesians 5:18 (NSV) is direct: do not get drunk with wine, but be filled with the Spirit. Drunkenness is an image of control. Wine controls the mind and actions. Paul contrasts that with the Spirit's control, which leads to worship, gratitude, and love. The command is given to the church, which implies this is normal Christian life, not a special tier.

Indwelling is not lost every time you sin. Believers may grieve the Spirit, but God does not treat His children as temporary guests. Filling,

150

however, can be resisted. You can live in ways that dull the conscience and weaken prayer. That is why Scripture calls you to seek the Spirit's filling as an ongoing pattern.

2) Look for the First Evidence: Christlike Character

The Spirit's work is seen first in character, not in visibility. Galatians 5:22–23 (NSV) lists the fruit of the Spirit: love, joy, peace, patience, kindness, goodness, faithfulness, gentleness, and self-control. Fruit grows over time. It shows a living root. It also gives you a simple test: is my life becoming more like Christ?

These traits are not personality types. They are moral qualities produced as the Spirit shapes the heart. A believer may have gifts and still lack gentleness. Scripture does not treat that as a minor issue. The Spirit forms Christlike people.

3) Learn the Battle Plan: Walk by the Spirit

Galatians 5:16 (NSV) gives a daily instruction: walk by the Spirit, and you will not gratify the desires of the flesh. "Flesh" means the old patterns of self-rule. Walking is steady. It is step after step. That is the right image for sanctification.

Walking by the Spirit includes decisions. You do not drift into holiness. You choose it with help. A useful pattern is: name the temptation, reject the lie behind it, and replace it with obedience. If the temptation is anger, reject the lie that you must defend your pride, and replace it with patient speech. If the temptation is lust, reject the lie that pleasure is your right, and replace it with guarded eyes and honest confession.

4) Use the Means God Gives: Word, Prayer, and the Church

The Spirit can act in any way He chooses. Yet Scripture shows He commonly works through ordinary means.

First, the Word. The Spirit inspired Scripture, and He uses it to correct and renew the mind. If you starve Scripture, you will be driven by impulse. If you feed on Scripture, your mind gains clarity.

Second, prayer. Prayer is dependence in action. Ask for wisdom before decisions. Ask for strength in temptation. Ask for love when you feel cold. The Spirit helps believers pray in weakness, shaping requests that fit God's will.

Third, the church. The Spirit unites believers into one body, and He uses other Christians to encourage, correct, and support. Isolation makes temptation louder and shame stronger. A faithful church life gives protection and perspective.

5) Seek Guidance Wisely: Replace Superstition with Wisdom

Believers often want guidance in big choices: marriage, work, moving, conflict, and money. Scripture does teach God leads His people. Yet it rarely tells you to hunt for secret signs. It calls you to pursue wisdom.

James 1:5 (NSV) says if any of you lacks wisdom, let him ask God, who gives generously. Wisdom is the skill of living faithfully. The Spirit's guidance often looks like a renewed mind, sober evaluation of options, godly counsel, and a conscience shaped by Scripture.

Ask three grounding questions:

1. Does this choice align with God's commands?
2. Does it reflect love for neighbor and integrity?
3. Is my motive clean, or am I protecting an idol?

When you cannot see a single "perfect" option, choose the wisest option you can, then act in faith and humility. God can redirect you. His leading is not fragile.

6) Address Spiritual Dryness: What to Do When You Feel Nothing

Many believers assume the Spirit's work must always be felt. Scripture teaches that faith rests on God's promise, not on constant emotional warmth. Dryness can come from fatigue, stress, unconfessed sin, neglected prayer, or seasons of testing.

Return to basic obedience. Confess what you know is wrong. Read Scripture even when you feel dull. Pray short, honest prayers. Serve someone quietly. Meet with believers. Over time, the Spirit often restores joy through ordinary faithfulness.

Psalm 143:10 (NSV) models a wise request: teach me to do Your will, for You are my God; let Your good Spirit lead me on level ground. The prayer is not about excitement. It is about obedience.

7) Avoid Two Ditches: Quenching and Controlling

Scripture warns against quenching the Spirit, which includes resisting conviction, despising true teaching, and clinging to sin. A quenched life often looks busy but cold, informed but proud, religious but unchanged.

Scripture also warns against trying to control the Spirit, as if God exists to validate our plans. This posture appears when someone uses "God told me" to end a conversation and avoid correction. The Spirit does not make you unaccountable. He makes you teachable.

8) Practice Filling in Daily Life: Five Habits

1. Begin the day with surrender: "Lord, rule my thoughts and words today."
2. Read a short passage of Scripture and obey one clear instruction from it.
3. Confess quickly when you sin; do not rehearse excuses.
4. Choose one act of love that costs you time, comfort, or pride.
5. End the day with gratitude, naming three specific mercies.

These habits do not earn the Spirit's presence. They place you where His work is welcomed rather than resisted.

9) Keep the Main Point Clear

The Spirit's filling is not mainly about unusual experiences. It is about daily Christlike life. He forms a believer who speaks truthfully, loves steadily, repents quickly, and serves faithfully. As you pursue that aim, you will grow in stability and usefulness in the church's mission, because the Spirit's strength produces humble courage.

In the next chapter, we will examine spiritual gifts and their purpose in the church, including how to value gifts without making them the measure of maturity.

CHAPTER 6

ENDURE WITH THE SPIRIT'S COMFORT: FACE SUFFERING, STAND FIRM, AND KEEP HOPE

Sooner or later every believer discovers a hard truth: knowing sound doctrine does not remove pain. Illness still comes. Betrayal still cuts. Work can fail. Loved ones die. Fear can rise in the night even when the mind knows the gospel. In those moments, Christians need more than information. They need God's presence. Scripture teaches that God provides that presence through the Holy Spirit, who comforts, strengthens, and steadies believers for endurance.

This chapter explains how the Spirit supports Christians in suffering. We will address why suffering does not mean abandonment, how the Spirit helps in weakness, how to pray when words fail, and how hope grows in the middle of grief. The aim is not to give neat answers. The aim is to help you stand with faith when life is heavy.

1) Reject a Common Lie: Suffering Does Not Prove God Is Absent

Many believers assume that if they were truly walking with God, life would become easier. Scripture corrects that assumption. Jesus warned His disciples that trouble would come and that persecution would come. The Spirit's presence is not a guarantee of comfort. It is a guarantee of help.

John 14:26–27 (NSV) includes Jesus' promise that the Helper will teach and remind, and Jesus gives peace that is not like the world's peace. This peace is not the absence of problems. It is a settled confidence in the Father's care, even when circumstances remain painful.

This matters because suffering often tempts you to interpret God's love by your circumstances. Scripture calls you to interpret your circumstances by God's love revealed in Christ.

154

2) Receive the Spirit as Helper: God Comes Near to the Weak

Jesus calls the Spirit "Helper." That is not weak language. It means God gives active support to believers who cannot carry life by themselves.

Suffering exposes limits. It forces you to admit you cannot control outcomes. The Spirit meets you there. He does not merely observe. He helps.

The Spirit's help often looks ordinary: strength to get out of bed, clarity to speak one truthful sentence, patience to endure a long hospital wait, restraint when anger rises, courage to ask for prayer, humility to receive help. These may look small to outsiders, but they are often evidence of real grace.

3) Learn How the Spirit Helps You Pray When You Are Worn Down

In suffering, prayer can feel impossible. Words can dry up. The mind can race. Shame can silence you. Scripture addresses that reality with direct comfort.

Romans 8:26–27 (NSV) says the Spirit helps our weakness. We do not know what to pray for as we ought, but the Spirit Himself intercedes for us with groanings too deep for words. The passage does not romanticize pain. It speaks of groaning. Yet it anchors hope: the Spirit intercedes according to God's will.

This means your prayer life does not collapse when your emotions collapse. Even when you cannot form polished sentences, you can still come. A short prayer like "Lord, help" can be sincere faith. The Spirit is not waiting for eloquence. He helps weakness.

4) Hold on to Adoption: The Spirit Teaches You to Cry "Father"

Suffering can make you feel like an outsider. It can make you think, "God must be punishing me," or "God must love others more." Scripture counters that with adoption.

Romans 8:15 (NSV) says believers received the Spirit of adoption by whom we cry, "Abba, Father." That word "cry" matters. It suggests urgency and emotion. In suffering, the Spirit presses you toward God rather than away from God. He trains you to pray like a child, not like a worker begging for wages.

This does not remove discipline when believers sin. Yet discipline is not rejection. A Father corrects children because they belong. In suffering, do not assume God's nearness is measured by comfort. God's nearness is measured by covenant promise, and the Spirit confirms that promise in the believer's heart.

5) Understand Weakness as a Place Where God Shows Strength

Many Christians only accept weakness in theory. In practice, they treat weakness as failure. Scripture treats weakness as an arena where God's strength becomes visible.

The Spirit's comfort does not always remove the thorn. Often it supplies endurance. The Spirit teaches believers to rely on God's strength rather than their own. This reliance is not passive resignation. It is active trust: "I cannot carry this, but God will."

This is why some believers grow in humility and kindness through suffering. Suffering strips away self-sufficiency. The Spirit replaces it with dependence that is steady and realistic.

6) Receive Hope as a Present Anchor, Not a Future Escape

Christian hope is not fantasy. It is rooted in God's promises, Christ's resurrection, and the Spirit's pledge.

Ephesians 1:13–14 (NSV) says believers were sealed with the promised Holy Spirit, who is the guarantee of our inheritance until we acquire possession of it. The Spirit is not only comfort for the moment. He is God's pledge that the future is real.

This matters because suffering often narrows your vision to the next hour. The Spirit widens your vision to the full story: God will finish what He began. The believer's future is not endless loss. It is resurrection life with God.

Hope does not deny grief. Hope gives grief a boundary. Grief is real, but it is not ultimate.

7) Learn How the Spirit Builds Endurance Through the Church

The Spirit rarely comforts in isolation. He comforts through the body of Christ. Many believers try to suffer alone, thinking that asking for help is weakness. Scripture treats shared burdens as normal Christian life.

When believers pray for one another, speak Scripture to one another, and show practical care, the Spirit is at work. Comfort is often delivered through meals, visits, truthful words, and steady presence. This is why detachment from the church is so dangerous in suffering. Isolation makes fear louder and hope quieter.

A practical step is simple: name your need to mature believers and ask for prayer. Not as a performance. As a child asking family for help.

8) Guard Your Mind: The Spirit Uses Truth to Resist Despair

Suffering can magnify lies: "Nothing will change," "God does not care," "I am alone," "This proves I am cursed." The Spirit combats these lies with truth. He reminds believers of Christ, of God's promises, and of the church's hope.

This does not always feel dramatic. Often it is slow: returning to Scripture, repeating promises, rejecting hopeless self-talk, choosing worship when you do not feel like worshiping. These choices are not hypocrisy. They are faith.

This is also why the Spirit's comfort should never be separated from Scripture. Comfort without truth becomes empty reassurance. Truth without comfort becomes cold. The Spirit provides both.

9) Practice Lament: Honest Prayer Without Accusation

Scripture includes lament because believers need words for sorrow. Lament is not rebellion. It is faithful honesty that brings pain to God rather than turning pain into unbelief.

Lament includes three movements:

1. Tell God what hurts.
2. Ask God for help.
3. Reaffirm trust in God's character.

The Spirit helps believers lament. He does not demand fake cheerfulness. He leads believers to bring grief into God's presence with reverence and hope.

A short lament can be as simple as: "Father, this hurts. I am afraid. Help me trust You and do what is right today." That is not sophisticated. It is faithful.

10) Endure with a Clear Focus:
The Spirit Shapes You for Witness in Pain

Suffering often places you in front of people who are watching. They may not listen to sermons, but they will watch how you carry grief. The Spirit can use your endurance as witness, not because you are impressive, but because Christ is sustaining you.

This does not mean you must always look strong. A humble confession—"I am struggling, but God is helping me"—often carries more weight than polished speech.

The Spirit comforts so believers endure. The Spirit strengthens so believers obey. The Spirit gives hope so believers do not quit.

CHAPTER 7

GUARD UNITY BY THE SPIRIT: BUILD PEACE, PRACTICE TRUTH, AND KEEP THE CHURCH STRONG

A church can confess right doctrine and still fracture. Personal offense, rivalry, fear, and careless speech can pull believers apart faster than a false teacher. Scripture treats unity as a spiritual matter, not a social preference. Unity is the Spirit's work, and it is also the believer's responsibility. The Spirit creates one people in Christ, and believers are commanded to protect that unity through humility, patience, and truth.

This chapter shows how the Spirit produces unity, what threatens unity, and what ordinary practices keep a church steady. The goal is not shallow agreement. The goal is peace rooted in the gospel, where believers can disagree on lesser matters without breaking fellowship, and where sin is confronted without cruelty.

1) Begin with Jesus' Prayer: Unity Is a Gospel Witness

Before the cross, Jesus prayed for His people. John 17:21 (NSV) records Jesus asking that believers may all be one, so that the world may believe that the Father sent the Son. Unity is connected to the credibility of the church's witness. When believers live in constant hostility, they announce a different message than the one they preach.

This does not mean unity requires pretending. It means unity requires shared center. The center is Christ: His gospel, His lordship, His commands, and His love.

Unity is not built by clever programs. Unity is a spiritual reality created by God when He joins believers to Christ.

Romans 12:5 (NSV) says that though many, we are one body in Christ, and individually members of one another. The church is not a crowd of customers. It is a body with shared life. This changes how you treat other believers. You treat them as family you are responsible to love.

Psalm 133:1 (NSV) celebrates this: how good and pleasant it is when brothers dwell in unity. The Psalm does not claim unity is effortless. It claims unity is worth protecting because it reflects God's own goodness.

3) Learn the Spirit's Method: Unity Grows Through Humility

Pride is the quickest path to division. Pride turns every disagreement into a threat, every correction into an insult, and every preference into a demand. The Spirit produces humility, which makes unity possible.

1 Peter 3:8 (NSV) calls believers to be harmonious, sympathetic, brotherly, tenderhearted, and humble-minded. These are not optional virtues for "nice" Christians. They are survival skills for church life.

Humility does not mean weakness. It means you can say, "I might be wrong," and "Your good matters to me," and "I will not treat my preference as a law."

4) Name the Main Threats: What Breaks Unity in Real Churches

Most church divisions do not begin with major doctrine. They begin with ordinary sins that are tolerated.

- Gossip: it spreads suspicion while hiding behind "concern."
- Rivalry: it treats ministry as competition.
- Partiality: it honors the impressive and ignores the quiet.
- Unresolved offense: it turns pain into distance instead of conversation.
- Harsh certainty: it speaks truth without love and calls it courage.

The Spirit does not bless these patterns. They grieve the church and weaken witness. If a church wants unity, it must treat these sins as serious.

5) Practice Truth-Telling: Unity Without Truth Is Fragile

Some churches fear conflict so much that they avoid truth. That kind of unity is thin. It breaks under pressure.

1 Corinthians 1:10 (NSV) urges believers to agree and that there be no divisions, but that they be united in the same mind and judgment. Paul writes this to a church filled with party spirit. His solution is not silence. His solution is shared commitment to Christ and to clear teaching.

Truth-telling includes doctrinal clarity, but it also includes honest conversation. It means you do not weaponize silence. You speak, but you speak for the good of the other.

6) Handle Conflict with a Spirit-Guided Process

Conflict is unavoidable where sinners gather. The difference between a healthy church and an unhealthy church is not the presence of conflict, but the way conflict is handled.

A Spirit-guided process is simple and demanding:

1. Go directly. Do not recruit allies first.
2. Speak specifically. Vague accusations multiply resentment.
3. Listen carefully. You may have misunderstood.
4. Confess what is yours. Repentance disarms pride.
5. Seek a clear next step.

Galatians 6:1–2 (NSV) gives the church a tone for restoration: if someone is caught in a trespass, those who are spiritual should restore him in a spirit of gentleness, watching themselves, and bearing one another's burdens. Restoration requires truth. Gentleness requires humility.

7) Make Room for Differences: Wisdom on "Disputable Matters"

Unity does not require uniformity. Churches include different backgrounds, cultures, and temperaments. Wise Christians learn to distinguish between core gospel truths and secondary questions.

Core truths are non-negotiable: the person of Christ, the gospel of grace, the authority of Scripture, the call to holiness. Secondary matters include many preferences and some theological questions that faithful believers have debated without breaking the faith.

The Spirit helps believers hold convictions without contempt. He trains you to say, "I have a view, and I can still honor you," and "I can disagree without questioning your faith."

One practical safeguard is shared confession. When a church regularly admits sin, asks forgiveness, and extends forgiveness, pride loses oxygen. Corporate prayer also knits hearts together, because believers hear one another's needs and learn compassion again.

8) Protect Unity through Shared Worship and Shared Service

Unity grows when believers share a life, not only a meeting.

Shared worship centers hearts on God rather than on the self. Shared service reduces rivalry because you begin to see each other as fellow workers, not obstacles. When believers serve together, resentments often shrink because mission becomes larger than personality.

9) Strengthen Unity through Wise Leadership and Clear Commitment

Unity needs structure. The Spirit uses ordered leadership and clear commitments to protect the church.

Leaders must model humility and courage. They must correct false teaching, confront persistent sin, and refuse favoritism. They must also listen and treat members as people, not as problems.

Members must commit to the church's life. When people drift without real belonging, conflicts linger because there is no shared commitment to repair.

10) End with a Practical Rule: "Speak for Peace, Act for Peace"

If you want one rule that protects unity, use this: speak for peace and act for peace.

Speak for peace means your words aim at building, not scoring. It means you refuse gossip. It means you ask questions before you assume motives.

Act for peace means you take the first step when offense arises. It means you forgive quickly when repentance is real. It means you keep serving even when your feelings are mixed.

Unity is not a mood. It is a Spirit-produced life that believers protect through humility, truth, and patient love. When a church guards unity this way, it becomes a stable home for discipleship and a clear witness to Christ's reign.

BOOK FIVE

THE FUTURE: LIVE READY FOR CHRIST'S RETURN

A Simple Guide to Hope, Judgment, Resurrection, and the New Creation

CHAPTER 1

FIX YOUR HOPE ON CHRIST'S RETURN: LIVE WATCHFUL, FAITHFUL, AND UNAFRAID

Many people avoid end-times teaching because they have seen it misused. Some have heard predictions that failed. Others have watched believers argue about timelines with more heat than humility. Scripture calls you to a better approach: learn what God has clearly revealed, refuse speculation, and let hope shape how you live today.

The Christian future is not built on guesses. It is built on Christ's promise. The center is not a chart. The center is a Person who will return. When Scripture speaks about the end, it presses two truths at once: Christ's return is certain, and the timing is not for us to control. That combination is meant to produce readiness without panic.

1) Start with the Main Promise: Jesus Will Return

The New Testament treats Christ's return as normal Christian expectation. The church is not waiting for an idea. The church is waiting for its King.

Acts 1:11 (NSV) records the angels' words after Jesus ascended: this Jesus, who was taken up from you into heaven, will come in the same way as you saw Him go. The promise is direct. Jesus' return will be real, personal, and public.

That promise matters because it anchors hope in history. Christians are not trusting their ability to improve the world. Christians are trusting that Christ will finish what He began.

2) Know What "Return" Means: Christ Comes as Judge and Savior

Some people hear "judgment" and only think of terror. Scripture presents judgment as both sobering and good. It is good because evil will not rule forever. It is sobering because every person will answer to God.

2 Timothy 4:1 (NSV) says Christ Jesus will judge the living and the dead, and Paul charges Timothy to preach the word in light of that coming reality. Judgment is not a side doctrine. It shapes faithful ministry and holy living.

Yet the return is also salvation for God's people. Christ returns to complete rescue, not to restart it. Believers are not waiting to see if God will accept them. Believers are waiting to see the fullness of what God has promised.

3) Refuse Date-Setting: Read the Bible's Warnings About Speculation

Scripture tells you to be ready, not to be a predictor.

Matthew 24:36 (NSV) teaches that concerning that day and hour no one knows, not even angels in heaven, nor the Son, but the Father only. The point is not to make you indifferent. The point is to end the pride of secret knowledge.

Across church history, believers have repeatedly tried to fix dates, and those attempts have repeatedly failed. Wise teachers learned to emphasize what Scripture emphasizes: certainty of return, uncertainty of timing, and responsibility in the present.

4) Practice Readiness: Watchfulness Is a Lifestyle

If you cannot know the time, what should you do? Jesus answers: be ready.

1 Thessalonians 5:6 (NSV) calls believers to not sleep as others do, but to keep awake and be sober. The language is moral and spiritual, not literal insomnia. Watchfulness means you do not drift. You do not treat sin as harmless. You do not treat prayer as optional. You stay alert because you belong to Christ.

Watchfulness is also calm. A sober person is steady, not frantic. Christians should not live in constant alarm. They should live in daily faithfulness.

5) Hold a Clear Expectation: The Return Will Be Public and Final

Scripture does not describe Christ's return as a hidden event that only a few notice. It describes a decisive arrival that ends this present age.

Revelation 1:7 (NSV) says He is coming with the clouds, and every eye will see Him. The verse also reminds you that the return will confront rebellion. Christ's coming is comfort for believers and exposure for those who reject Him.

This public finality protects you from unhealthy fascination with rumors. The Bible directs you away from endless speculation and toward a simple readiness rooted in the gospel.

6) Learn How Christians Have Differed: Three Major Approaches

Faithful believers agree on the core: Christ will return, the dead will be raised, judgment will come, and God will make a new creation. Believers have differed on how to understand the timing of certain events, especially the "millennium" of Revelation 20. Here are three common views, stated fairly.

Amillennial view: Many believe the "millennium" describes Christ's present reign from heaven, with the church living between His first coming and His return. In this view, the focus is not on a future earthly thousand-year reign, but on Christ reigning now and returning once to judge and renew all things.

Postmillennial view: Some believe the gospel will advance broadly in history so that a long era of widespread Christian influence and peace occurs before Christ's return. In this view, Christ returns after that gospel-shaped era.

Premillennial view: Many believe Christ will return before a future millennium, understood as a distinct reign on earth. Within premillennial thought there are differences about how to read tribulation and the relationship between Israel and the church.

You do not need to choose a view quickly to live faithfully. Begin with what Scripture makes plain: Christ will return, and your task is readiness, not rivalry.

A major purpose of end-times teaching is moral formation. Scripture links future hope with present purity.

1 John 3:2–3 (NSV) says that when Christ appears we shall be like Him, and everyone who hopes in Him purifies himself as He is pure. That is simple and strong. Hope is not passive. Hope trains the believer to resist sin because the believer belongs to a coming kingdom.

This also corrects a common excuse: "Since the end is coming, nothing matters." Scripture says the opposite. Since Christ is coming, everything matters. Your choices are training for eternity.

8) Let the Return Strengthen Endurance and Courage

Believers suffer in the present age, and Scripture does not hide it. The return of Christ means suffering is not the final chapter.

James 5:7–8 (NSV) tells believers to be patient until the coming of the Lord, establishing their hearts because the Lord's coming is near. "Near" here means certain and approaching, not a calendar prediction. The command is to establish your heart: plant your courage in God's promise.

This helps in ordinary trials. When life is unfair, you can endure without bitterness. When obedience costs you, you can persist without regret. Christ's return means faithfulness is never wasted.

9) Keep Your Focus: Readiness Is Ordinary Faithfulness

End-times readiness is not mainly about collecting information. It is about living clean, serving others, and staying close to Christ.

Readiness looks like this:

- Repent quickly when you sin.
- Forgive when you are wronged.
- Speak truth without cruelty.
- Work honestly.
- Pray steadily.
- Serve in the church.
- Share the gospel without shame.

This is how the early church lived. They confessed, "He will come again," and then they preached, endured persecution, cared for the needy, and worshiped with seriousness and joy.

10) End with the Future's Bright Center: God Will Make All Things New

The Bible's future is not endless clouds and vague spiritual existence. It is renewal.

Revelation 21:5 (NSV) records God's declaration: "Behold, I am making all things new." That promise does not minimize grief. It answers it. God does not discard His creation. He redeems it. The final hope is not escape from physical reality. It is the healing of reality under God's reign.

As we continue in Book 5, we will look closely at resurrection, judgment, and the new creation. For now, hold this as your daily anchor: Christ will return, and His return makes watchfulness wise, holiness necessary, and hope steady.

CHAPTER 2

TRACE THE SPIRIT'S WORK IN THE OLD TESTAMENT: SEE GOD'S PRESENCE BEFORE PENTECOST

Many Christians assume the Holy Spirit appears only in the New Testament. Scripture does not support that idea. The Spirit is active from the opening lines of Genesis, and His work runs through Israel's history in ways that prepare you to understand Pentecost, the church, and the Christian life.

At the same time, the Old Testament and New Testament describe the Spirit's work with different emphases. In the Old Testament, the Spirit is often shown empowering particular people for particular tasks at particular times—kingship, craftsmanship, prophecy, leadership, and deliverance. In the New Testament, following Christ's finished work, the Spirit is poured out broadly on God's people in a fuller covenant sense. If you miss the Old Testament foundation, you may either downplay the Spirit's work or speak about it without biblical structure.

This chapter will trace the Spirit's work in the Old Testament under four headings: **creation, covenant life, empowerment for service, and promise of future outpouring**. Along the way, we will note how careful Christian teaching has drawn these themes together.

1) See the Spirit at Creation: God Brings Order and Life

The first time you meet the Spirit in Scripture is not in Acts. It is in Genesis.

Genesis 1:2 (NSV) describes the Spirit of God present over the waters as God prepares to bring order, beauty, and life. This verse teaches a basic truth: the Spirit is not a late addition to God's work. He is present at the beginning, active in creation.

The Bible reinforces this later. Job 33:4 (NSV) states, "The Spirit of God has made me, and the breath of the Almighty gives me life." Scripture connects the Spirit with life-giving power. He is not a distant concept. He is the divine giver of life and order.

This matters for theology and for daily faith. If the Spirit gives life in creation, then the Spirit giving life in salvation is consistent with who He is. New birth is not strange. It is God acting according to His nature.

2) Understand "Spirit" Language: Breath, Wind, and Presence

Old Testament language often uses words that carry the sense of breath or wind. The point is not poetic fog. The point is power and presence that cannot be controlled by human hands.

Wind is real, strong, and unseen. Breath is invisible yet essential for life. These images teach reverence. The Spirit is not a tool you can manage. He is God present and active.

This also protects you from treating spiritual life as technique. If the Spirit is God's living presence, then the right posture is dependence, prayer, obedience, and humility.

3) Trace the Spirit in Israel's Covenant Life: Guidance and Instruction

The Spirit is not only about extraordinary moments. The Old Testament shows the Spirit sustaining God's people through guidance and instruction.

Nehemiah 9:20 (NSV) praises God's mercy: God gave His good Spirit to instruct His people. That is striking. The Spirit is connected with teaching and formation, not only dramatic deliverances. God shepherds His people by His Spirit.

This also explains why Scripture and Spirit belong together. God's Spirit instructs in truth. He does not lead God's people into moral confusion. He forms them through God's Word, God's commands, and God's covenant purposes.

One of the most visible Old Testament themes is the Spirit empowering leaders for rescue and righteous action.

In the time of the judges, Scripture repeatedly states that the Spirit came upon a deliverer to rescue Israel from oppression. Judges 3:10 (NSV) says the Spirit of the Lord came upon Othniel, and he judged Israel and went out to war, and the Lord gave victory. The pattern repeats in the book: God raises a deliverer, empowers him, and rescues His people.

Two points matter here:

1. **The Spirit empowers for service, not self-display.** The goal is deliverance and protection of God's people, not personal fame.

2. **The Spirit's empowerment does not equal moral maturity.** Some judges were courageous yet deeply flawed. This warns you against equating visible gifting with holiness. God can empower a task without endorsing a person's character.

This is a practical lesson for today. A gifted leader may still require accountability. Spiritual power does not excuse sin. The Old Testament already teaches you to separate gifting from godliness.

5) See the Spirit Equip Craftsmanship: Skill for God's House

Many people think the Spirit only empowers "spiritual" activities like preaching. The Old Testament widens your view.

Exodus 31:2–5 (NSV) describes Bezalel being filled with the Spirit of God with ability, intelligence, knowledge, and craftsmanship to build for the tabernacle. That is Spirit-given skill in design, artistry, and construction for holy worship.

This expands your theology of vocation. The Spirit's work includes wisdom and skill used for God's glory. In modern terms, God can strengthen faithful work in teaching, administration, music, care, building, and problem-solving—especially when that work serves worship and the good of God's people.

This does not mean every talent is automatically spiritual. It means God is free to supply real ability for His purposes, and believers should honor skilled work as meaningful service.

6) Trace the Spirit in Kingship: Anointing, Rule, and Responsibility

The Spirit's relationship to kingship in the Old Testament is central for understanding Jesus as the anointed Messiah.

1 Samuel 16:13 (NSV) describes Samuel anointing David, and the Spirit of the Lord rushing upon him from that day forward. The Spirit's empowerment for David connects to leadership under God's authority. Israel's king was meant to rule in obedience to God, guarding justice and honoring the covenant.

Yet the Old Testament also warns that the Spirit's empowering presence in leadership could be forfeited in a covenantal sense through hardened rebellion. This is why David prays in Psalm 51:11 (NSV), "Do not cast me away from Your presence, and do not take Your Holy Spirit from me." David is not describing ordinary Christian experience after Pentecost in the same way. He is pleading as a covenant king who knows his sin threatens the stability of his calling and the wellbeing of the people he leads.

This is a key interpretive lesson: **Old Testament Spirit language often relates to roles—king, prophet, leader—within the covenant administration.** That prepares you to see why the New Testament later stresses the Spirit's indwelling of all believers as a shared covenant blessing.

7) See the Spirit in Prophecy: God Speaks Through His Servants

The prophets did not speak as private thinkers offering religious opinions. They spoke as God's messengers.

2 Peter 1:21 (NSV) states a New Testament summary of the Old Testament prophetic pattern: men spoke from God as they were carried along by the Holy Spirit. The Spirit is tied to revelation. God's Word comes by God's Spirit.

This is why the church has always treated Scripture as Spirit-given. It also explains why prophecy in Scripture is not merely encouragement. It includes rebuke, warning, and covenant instruction. The Spirit's work is not only comfort; it is truth.

The Old Testament shows God's real presence and real power, yet it also builds anticipation. Several passages look forward to a day when the Spirit's work would be more widespread and more inward.

Zechariah 4:6 (NSV) gives a famous principle: "Not by might, nor by power, but by My Spirit, says the Lord." This line addresses human weakness and God's sufficiency. It also points forward. God's work will not be secured by human strength. It will be secured by divine action.

The prophets also speak about a future era marked by deeper internal renewal. The Old Testament repeatedly connects hope with a change of heart and a greater work of God among His people. This prepares you for the New Testament's language about new birth, indwelling, and Spirit-given transformation across the whole church.

9) Learn from Israel's Failure: The Spirit Can Be Resisted and Grieved

The Old Testament is candid about rebellion. God's people often received mercy and still resisted God.

Isaiah 63:10 (NSV) says they rebelled and grieved His Holy Spirit. That verse is important because it holds two truths together: the Spirit is personal, and resistance is real. People can oppose God's leading. They can harden their hearts. They can reject instruction.

This prepares you to understand why the New Testament includes both comfort and warning. The Spirit strengthens believers, and believers are also commanded not to resist, quench, or ignore His work. The covenant story teaches that spiritual privilege never justifies spiritual carelessness.

10) Connect Old Testament Themes to Christ: The Spirit Prepares the Way

The Old Testament's Spirit-work is not isolated. It is preparation for Christ.

- The Spirit gives life in creation, preparing you to see the Spirit give life in regeneration.
- The Spirit empowers leaders and kings, preparing you for the Messiah, the true anointed King.

- The Spirit speaks through prophets, preparing you for Christ, the final Word and faithful Prophet.
- The Spirit instructs and guides the people, preparing you for a fuller covenant community shaped from within.

In church history, this is one reason theologians spoke about the unity of God's saving work: the Spirit's presence is consistent, yet His covenant administration unfolds with the storyline. The Old Testament is not "Spirit-less." It is "promise-shaped." It creates categories that become clearer after Christ's death, resurrection, and ascension.

11) Apply This Chapter: Live with Reverence, Gratitude, and Wise Expectations

Here are three practical ways this Old Testament view helps you today.

First, it keeps you from treating the Spirit as novelty.

The Spirit has been active from the beginning. You do not need constant new claims to take Him seriously.

Second, it teaches you to value character above gifting.

Judges and kings show that empowerment for a task does not guarantee holiness. Do not confuse visible ability with spiritual maturity.

Third, it teaches you to seek the Spirit's help in ordinary work.

The Spirit equipped Bezalel for craftsmanship. Pray for wisdom, skill, patience, and faithfulness in the work God has given you.

The Old Testament teaches that God's Spirit is real, personal, and powerful: present in creation, guiding covenant life, empowering service, and promising deeper renewal.

CHAPTER 3

FOLLOW THE SPIRIT IN JESUS' LIFE:
SEE THE MESSIAH ANOINTED FOR HIS MISSION

If you want to understand the Holy Spirit, do not begin with debates or unusual claims. Begin with Jesus. The Spirit's work in Christ's life shows what true anointing looks like: it produces holiness, truth, compassion, and faithful obedience to the Father. It also shows that salvation is not only about what Jesus did *for* you on the cross, but also about what He did *as* the obedient Messiah—living, resisting temptation, proclaiming the kingdom, and carrying out His mission by the Spirit's power.

This chapter will trace the Spirit's role in Jesus' life from conception to ministry to sacrifice. The goal is to help you see the Spirit's work with biblical clarity and to apply it wisely to Christian life today.

1) Start at the Beginning: The Spirit's Work in the Incarnation

Jesus did not begin His existence in Bethlehem. He is the eternal Son who took on human nature. Yet the incarnation enters history through the Spirit's work.

Luke 1:35 (NSV) explains to Mary that the Holy Spirit will come upon her, and the power of the Most High will overshadow her. This is not an abstract miracle. It is God preparing a true human nature for the Son, in a holy and unique way. The Spirit's work here guards two truths: Jesus is truly human, and He is holy from the start.

This matters for salvation because a Savior who shares our humanity can represent us, and a Savior who is sinless can save us.

2) Notice the Pattern: The Spirit Marks Jesus as the Promised Messiah

In the Old Testament, kings were anointed as a sign of divine appointment. Jesus is "the Christ," the Anointed One, and the Spirit's presence marks His identity and mission.

At Jesus' baptism, the Spirit descends on Him. Luke 3:21–22 (NSV) describes the Spirit coming in bodily form like a dove, and the Father's voice declaring Jesus as His beloved Son. This event is Trinitarian, public, and decisive. It shows that Jesus' mission begins with divine confirmation.

The Spirit's descent does not mean Jesus lacked deity before baptism. Jesus is eternally the Son. Rather, it shows Jesus beginning His public ministry as the Messiah, equipped for His role as the obedient servant-king.

3) See the Spirit Lead Jesus into Testing: Holiness Before Public Power

Many people chase public power while neglecting holiness. Jesus' path is the reverse. The Spirit leads Him into testing before public ministry.

Luke 4:1–2 (NSV) says Jesus, full of the Holy Spirit, was led by the Spirit in the wilderness. This is important. Temptation is not always a sign God is absent. Sometimes it is part of God's shaping work. Jesus faces real temptation, not as a sinner, but as the righteous Messiah who must succeed where Adam and Israel failed.

He resists by Scripture. He does not argue with clever philosophy. He stands on God's Word. This teaches you that the Spirit's leading will not separate you from Scripture. The Spirit strengthens obedience, and Scripture provides the clear line.

4) Hear Jesus Describe His Ministry: The Spirit Anoints for Good News and Mercy

Jesus does not leave you guessing about the Spirit's role in His mission. He explains it openly.

Luke 4:18–19 (NSV) records Jesus reading from Isaiah: the Spirit of the Lord is upon Me because He has anointed Me to preach good news to the poor, proclaim liberty to captives, recovery of sight to the blind, and freedom to the oppressed. Then Jesus says this Scripture is fulfilled in their hearing.

This is one of the most important Spirit passages in the Gospels. It shows the Spirit's anointing leads to:

- proclamation of good news,
- mercy to the weak,

- liberation from bondage,
- visible signs that confirm the kingdom's arrival.

The focus is not spectacle. The focus is the kingdom of God advancing through truth and compassion.

5) Understand Miracles as Signs of the Kingdom, Not Performances

Jesus' miracles are not random displays of ability. They are signs that God's reign has arrived and that the curse is being reversed.

When Jesus heals, restores, and delivers, He is showing what God's kingdom does. In doing so, He also shows that spiritual power is meant for service. Jesus' miracles do not create ego. They create worship, gratitude, and amazement at God's mercy.

This corrects a modern temptation: to treat spiritual power as status. In Christ, power serves love. Any claim of Spirit-power that produces pride, manipulation, or harm is already out of step with Jesus.

6) See the Spirit and the Father's Will Working Together

In Jesus' life, the Spirit's power never competes with the Father's will. The Spirit leads Jesus into obedience, suffering, and faithful endurance.

Jesus' ministry includes joy and compassion, but it also includes conflict, rejection, and ultimately the cross. The Spirit's presence does not guarantee an easy path. It guarantees faithful obedience and divine strength to complete the mission.

This matters for believers. If you assume the Spirit's presence means life will be simple, you will become confused when hardship comes. Jesus' Spirit-filled life included suffering with purpose.

7) Understand Christ's Obedience as Representative: He Succeeds Where We Failed

Jesus lived in full obedience not only as an example, but also as the representative Messiah. He stands in the place of His people. His obedience fulfills righteousness.

This connects the Spirit's work to salvation directly. The Spirit empowered Jesus' human life for obedient service. Then Jesus offers His obedient life and atoning death as the ground of salvation.

This is not a small detail. If Jesus is only an example, you are left trying to imitate Him without hope. If Jesus is Savior and representative, you can imitate Him from a secure position, not to earn acceptance.

8) Learn What True Anointing Produces: Fruit Before Gifts

If you want a simple test of Spirit-work, look at Jesus:

- humility instead of self-promotion,
- truth instead of manipulation,
- compassion instead of contempt,
- purity instead of compromise,
- endurance instead of quitting.

This does not mean gifts are unimportant. It means fruit is the first evidence of the Spirit's work. Gifts can be counterfeited or misused. Christlike character cannot be faked for long.

A church that seeks gifts without seeking Christlike character will eventually drift into confusion. A believer who seeks experiences without seeking holiness will eventually be disappointed.

9) Connect Jesus' Ministry to the Promise of the Spirit for Believers

Jesus' Spirit-anointed life is not meant to remain unique and distant. It prepares for the Spirit's outpouring on the church.

Jesus promises that His followers will receive the Spirit in a new covenant fullness after His work is finished. The Gospels present Jesus as the one who baptizes with the Holy Spirit, bringing God's presence to His people in a deeper way.

So the Spirit's work in Jesus is both model and foundation: it shows what Spirit-empowered faithfulness looks like, and it prepares the way for believers to live by the Spirit as those united to Christ.

10) Apply This Chapter: Follow Christ's Pattern in Three Ways

First, pursue holiness before influence.

The Spirit led Jesus into the wilderness before the crowds. Do not rush past hidden obedience.

Second, tie guidance to Scripture.

Jesus resisted temptation with God's Word. Do not treat impressions as higher than Scripture.

Third, serve with compassion.

Jesus' Spirit-anointed ministry brought good news to the poor and help to the afflicted. Measure your "spiritual life" by whether it produces patient love.

When you study the Spirit in Jesus' life, you gain a stable picture of true Spirit-work. It is not chaotic. It is not self-centered. It is Christ-centered and Father-pleasing. In the next chapter, we will move from Jesus' ministry to the Spirit's arrival in the early church, especially at Pentecost, and we will see what changed and what remained consistent with the Old Testament foundation.

CHAPTER 4

STUDY VIEWS WITH CHARITY: COMPARE MAJOR END-TIMES FRAMEWORKS FAIRLY

Christians who love Scripture have not always agreed on how to arrange end-times details. That fact should not surprise you. Some passages are direct and simple. Others are symbolic and require careful reading. The church's best teachers have urged believers to hold tight to what is clear, and to handle debated points with humility.

Here is the baseline every faithful framework must keep:

- Jesus will return bodily and publicly.
- The dead will be raised.
- Final judgment will come.
- God will renew creation and dwell with His people.
- The gospel must be preached to the nations, and believers must endure.

Within that shared center, Christians differ mainly on how they interpret **Revelation 20** (the "thousand years"), the relationship between Christ's return and that millennium, and how to understand tribulation language.

1) Begin with the "Clear Core" Before the "Complex Map"

When believers argue, it is often because they start with disputed details instead of shared truths. Scripture gives you a better order. Start with what the whole Bible repeats often, then work outward.

A helpful anchor is **2 Peter 3:10–13 (NSV)**, which describes the day of the Lord, God's judgment, and the promise of "new heavens and a new earth." Whatever your end-times view, it must fit that movement: Christ returns, evil is judged, and creation is renewed.

Revelation 20:1–6 (NSV) is the key text that drives the big differences. Christians ask: Is this "thousand years" a present reality, a future era, or a symbolic description of a long period?

A. Amillennial view

- "Millennium" is understood as the present reign of Christ from heaven during the church age.

- Satan is restrained in a real sense, so the gospel can go to the nations.

- Christ returns once, bringing resurrection and judgment, followed by the new creation.

Why many find it persuasive: it ties Revelation 20 tightly to the New Testament theme of Christ reigning now and returning in a single climactic event.

B. Postmillennial view

- The "millennium" is often understood as a long era (not necessarily exactly 1,000 years) in which the gospel's influence expands widely.

- Christ returns after that era, followed by final judgment and renewal.

Why many find it persuasive: it emphasizes the power of the gospel to spread and shape nations over time, and it reads certain kingdom promises with strong historical optimism.

C. Premillennial view

- Christ returns before a future millennium, understood as a distinct reign.

- After the millennium comes a final judgment and then the new creation.

Why many find it persuasive: it reads Revelation 20's sequence more straightforwardly and often links it to Old Testament kingdom promises.

3) Recognize Two Major Premillennial Families

Premillennialism is not one uniform view.

Historic premillennialism often emphasizes continuity between Israel and the church and reads tribulation as a reality the church may face.

Dispensational premillennialism more sharply distinguishes Israel and the church and often includes a framework for tribulation and end-times events that differs from historic premillennialism.

Faithful believers exist in both groups. The practical takeaway is to listen carefully before assuming what someone means by "premillennial."

4) Handle the Tribulation with Care

Scripture speaks plainly about suffering and pressure for believers. The question is how to place certain "tribulation" texts in a timeline.

A responsible approach does three things:

- It refuses panic.
- It prepares believers for endurance and faithfulness.
- It resists turning every headline into a prophecy key.

John 16:33 (NSV) keeps a steady tone: in the world you will have tribulation, but take heart; Christ has overcome the world. That is not a timeline. It is an endurance promise.

5) Avoid Two Common Mistakes

Mistake 1: Treating a framework as the gospel.

Your framework must serve Scripture, not replace it. The gospel is Christ crucified and risen, calling sinners to repent and believe.

Mistake 2: Treating disagreements as disloyalty to Christ.

Many differences are real, but they are not always worth breaking fellowship. A church should have clarity, but believers should also show restraint and honor.

Charity does not mean "anything goes." It means you speak fairly, you summarize opposing views accurately, and you do not assign motives. You can say, "I disagree," without saying, "You reject Scripture."

If you want a simple rule:

Be firm about Christ's return and careful about disputed sequences.

CHAPTER 5

LONG FOR THE NEW CREATION:

SEE HEAVEN AND EARTH MADE NEW

Many people picture the Christian future as floating souls, endless clouds, and a vague spiritual calm. Scripture offers something better: **new creation**. God will renew heaven and earth, remove the curse, and dwell with His people in open fellowship.

The Bible's final hope is not escape from physical reality. It is the healing of reality under Christ's reign.

1) Start with God's Promise: Renewal, Not Disposal

Isaiah spoke of a future where God creates "new heavens and a new earth." **Isaiah 65:17 (NSV)** presents that promise in direct terms. The language is not about God abandoning His world. It is about God restoring it.

This changes how you live now. What God plans to renew, you must not despise. Creation matters. Bodies matter. Work matters. Justice matters. These things are not ultimate, but they are meaningful.

2) Understand "Heaven" as God's Dwelling, Then God's Dwelling With Us

Scripture often uses "heaven" to refer to God's realm and presence. The Bible's end is not believers going up forever while earth is discarded. The end is God's dwelling with His people in renewed creation.

Revelation 21:1–4 (NSV) describes a new heaven and new earth, the holy city coming down, and God dwelling with His people. It also states that God will wipe away every tear, and death will be no more. The future is personal: comfort, healing, and removal of the curse.

3) Take Comfort in What Will Be Removed

New creation is not only about what you gain. It is about what God removes:

- death
- mourning
- crying
- pain
- corruption
- injustice

That removal matters because many believers carry grief that does not resolve in this life. Scripture does not insult that grief. It answers it with promise.

4) See Holiness as Home, Not Burden

Some people fear eternity because they imagine it as endless rules. Scripture presents it as holy joy. In the new creation, holiness will not feel like strain, because sin will no longer pull the heart in competing directions.

Revelation 22:3–5 (NSV) describes the removal of the curse, worship, and God's people reigning forever. That is not boredom. It is life finally ordered as it should be: worship, purpose, and peace.

5) Let New Creation Reshape Suffering

If the end is renewal, then suffering is not meaningless. It is real, and it hurts, but it is not the final word.

Romans 8:18–23 (NSV) describes creation's groaning and the believer's longing for redemption. Scripture gives language for waiting without pretending. The future does not erase present pain, but it does keep pain from becoming your master.

6) Live with "Future-Faithfulness"

The hope of new creation does not make Christians passive. It makes them steady. You can endure hardship without despair, because you are headed toward restoration. You can serve without needing applause, because your labor is not wasted. You can forgive, because justice will be done.

New creation hope forms a people who are difficult to corrupt, because they are not desperate to squeeze heaven out of the present age.

CHAPTER 6

LIVE READY NOW: PRACTICE FAITHFULNESS, WATCHFULNESS, AND JOY

The New Testament does not teach readiness as fear-driven survival. It teaches readiness as steady faithfulness. You live ready by staying close to Christ, turning from sin quickly, serving your neighbors, and doing your daily work with integrity.

Readiness is not mainly about knowing more information. It is about living with the return of Christ in view.

1) Choose Watchfulness Over Speculation

Jesus calls His people to be ready, not to predict.

Luke 12:35–37 (NSV) pictures servants dressed for action, lamps burning, awaiting their master. The emphasis is simple: live in a state of spiritual readiness. Do not drift into carelessness.

Watchfulness means:

- you keep repentance close,
- you keep prayer regular,
- you keep conscience tender,
- you keep Christ's commands in view.

2) Practice Faithfulness in Ordinary Work

Many believers think readiness means doing "religious" tasks only. Scripture teaches readiness in daily labor and daily responsibilities.

Colossians 3:23–24 (NSV) calls believers to work heartily, as for the Lord and not for men, knowing they will receive an inheritance from the Lord. That passage turns ordinary work into worship. Faithfulness is not glamorous, but it is deeply Christian.

190

3) Hold Joy as a Duty and a Gift

Christian joy is not denial. It is confidence in Christ's reign and promise. Joy grows when you stop demanding that this present age provide what only the new creation will provide.

Titus 2:11–13 (NSV) ties daily life to future hope: grace trains believers to live self-controlled, upright, and godly lives while waiting for the blessed hope—the appearing of Jesus Christ. Notice the structure: grace trains, and hope steadies.

4) Refuse the Two Readiness Traps

Trap 1: Alarm.

Alarm reads every event as a secret sign and produces anxiety. Scripture calls for sobriety, not panic.

Trap 2: Sleep.

Sleep treats sin lightly, prayer lightly, and church life lightly. Scripture calls for alertness.

Readiness is neither frantic nor careless. It is steady.

5) Invest in What Will Last

A ready life puts energy into what endures:

- truth
- love
- holiness
- mercy
- gospel witness
- church faithfulness
- generosity

1 Corinthians 15:58 (NSV) calls believers to be steadfast and always abounding in the work of the Lord, knowing their labor is not in vain. That verse is grounded in resurrection hope. It is not motivational talk. It is a future-based promise.

If you want a practical readiness plan, use this daily rule:

- **Confess**: ask God to expose sin quickly.
- **Trust**: rehearse one clear gospel truth about Christ.
- **Obey**: do one specific act of obedience before the day ends.
- **Serve**: do one act of love that costs time or pride.
- **Hope**: end the day remembering Christ will return.

OVERALL CONCLUSION

HOLD TO CHRIST, LIVE WITH CLARITY, AND FINISH WELL

Systematic theology is not a shelf item for scholars. It is a steady guide for ordinary believers who want to know God, love Him, and follow Him with confidence. Over these five Books, you have traced the central truths of the Christian faith: God's character and works, humanity's dignity and fall, salvation in Christ, the Holy Spirit's presence and ministry, and the future God has promised.

These doctrines belong together. When you separate them, faith becomes unstable. When you hold them together, faith becomes grounded. You learn to worship God as He truly is, not as culture imagines Him to be. You learn to see yourself honestly—created in God's image, yet in need of grace. You learn to trust Christ as the only Savior whose life, death, and resurrection secure real forgiveness and real peace with God. You learn to reflect on the Holy Spirit not as a vague influence, but as God who applies salvation, strengthens holiness, equips the church, and comforts believers in suffering. And you learn to look to the future without fear, because Christ will return, judgment will be just, resurrection will be real, and God will renew all things.

The aim of this book has never been information alone. The aim is transformation that rests on truth. Sound doctrine produces humble worship, clear repentance, steady obedience, and resilient hope. It trains you to live in the present age without being ruled by it. It helps you love the church with patience, serve others with integrity, and face hardship without surrendering to despair. Above all, it keeps your eyes on Christ—the center of Scripture, the head of the church, and the Lord of history.

As you close this volume, do not treat it as finished work that belongs behind you. Treat it as a framework you return to. Revisit the chapters. Open your Bible. Pray with purpose. Practice what you have learned. The Christian life is not sustained by intensity, but by daily faithfulness. God is faithful, and He will keep His people.

May the Lord strengthen you to think clearly, love deeply, and live ready—until the day you see Christ face to face.

PART 2: SYSTEMATIC THEOLOGY WORKBOOK 5-IN-1

Guided Exercises, Reflections, and Study Questions on God, Humanity, Salvation, the Spirit, and the Future

INTRODUCTION

This 5-in-1 workbook is for Christians who want a steady, Bible-shaped faith. It is for people who want to know what they believe, why they believe it, and how to live it out with a clear mind and a faithful heart. Many believers love God, yet feel unsure when hard questions come. Some have pieces of truth, but the pieces do not connect. This collection helps you put those pieces together, using Scripture as the foundation.

Systematic theology means gathering what the whole Bible teaches about key topics and holding those truths side by side. It is not about winning arguments. It is about learning to think God's thoughts after Him, as best we can, with humility. Clear doctrine protects your joy. It guards you from errors that sound kind but pull you away from truth. It also strengthens your worship, because you praise God more truly when you see Him more clearly.

This series is a workbook on purpose. Many books explain ideas but never help you practice them. Here, each chapter gives a short teaching section in plain language. Then it gives guided exercises that help the truth move from your head to your life. You will read, write, reflect, and pray. You will also be asked to connect doctrine to daily choices, relationships, and habits. That is where growth becomes real.

You can expect a steady pattern in every chapter. First, you will get a focused lesson that stays on one theme. It will not wander. It will use Scripture carefully and avoid filler. Then you will move into a workbook section. That section includes study questions, space for your own words, and prompts that call for honest self-examination. You will also find short prayer starters. These are meant to help you respond to God with reverence and trust.

This collection is arranged as five short books, each with six chapters. Each book covers one major area of Christian doctrine.

Book One helps you know God as He has revealed Himself. You will study His self-revelation, the Trinity, His rule over all things, His moral goodness, His relationship with time, and the call to worship Him in truth.

Book Two focuses on humanity. You will study what it means to be made in God's image, why human life has worth, what sin is, what the fall has done to us, and how we should live as image-bearers in a broken world.

Book Three focuses on salvation. You will study God's grace, the work of Christ, the call to faith and repentance, justification, growth in holiness, and the steady hope God gives to those who belong to Him.

Book Four focuses on the Holy Spirit. You will study who the Spirit is, how He gives life, how He unites believers to Christ, how He shapes character, how He works in the church, and what it looks like to walk in daily dependence on Him.

Book Five focuses on the future. You will study the return of Christ, resurrection, judgment, the final state, and how Christian hope shapes faithful living right now.

Each book builds on the last. You will see how the doctrines connect. What you learn about God shapes how you understand yourself. What you learn about humanity shapes why salvation is needed. What you learn about salvation shapes how you depend on the Spirit. What you learn about the Spirit shapes how you wait for the future with steady hope.

What will you gain if you work through this collection with care?

You can gain a clearer view of God's character. Many fears shrink when God's greatness becomes more real to you. You can gain stronger confidence in Scripture, because you will practice handling key passages with attention and respect. You can gain better discernment, because you will learn to test ideas against biblical truth. You can gain a steadier prayer life, because your prayers will be shaped by what God has revealed. You can gain greater humility, because theology done well reminds us we are creatures, not the Creator. You can also gain a stronger sense of purpose, because doctrine connects belief to obedience.

You can also expect to grow in your ability to explain your faith with clarity. Some believers want to share Christ but feel stuck when questions come. Others have the right words but struggle to speak with gentleness. This workbook helps you practice simple explanations, using careful language. Scripture calls believers to be ready to give a reason for the hope within them, with gentleness and respect (1 Peter 3:15, NSV). This study helps you move in that direction.

This workbook is also meant to help you notice what you already assume. Everyone has beliefs, even if they have never written them down. Some beliefs came from family. Some came from church culture. Some came from pain. Some came from social media. Over time, people can collect ideas that do not fit together. This can cause confusion and doubt. When you study doctrine in an ordered way, you begin to see what is true, what is uncertain, and what needs to change. That is a gift from God.

Here is how to use this workbook well

First, take it slow. The goal is not speed. The goal is depth and obedience. Plan a steady pace you can keep. Many people do well with one chapter per week. That gives time to read, write, pray, and revisit key ideas.

Second, keep your Bible open. Do not treat the teaching section as the final word. It is a guide, not a replacement for Scripture. Look up each passage. Read the surrounding verses when you can. Note repeated words. Note what the text says and what it does not say. A wise habit is to write the main point of each passage in one sentence, using your own words.

Third, write your answers. You may feel tempted to think through the questions without writing. Writing slows you down in a good way. It helps you notice what you really believe. It also gives you a record you can review later. Over time, you will see growth. You will also see patterns in your struggles and prayers. Those patterns can help you seek counsel and make changes.

Fourth, be honest. Some questions will reveal fears, doubts, or sins you would rather avoid. Do not hide from those moments. Bring them into the light before God. He already knows your heart. The goal is not to look strong. The goal is to become steady in faith.

Fifth, use this with others if you can. You can work through it with a friend, a spouse, a small group, or a class. When believers study together, they often see things they would miss alone. You can also sharpen one another through respectful conversation. If you do it as a group, set a simple plan. Read the teaching section beforehand. Then discuss the questions and share what you learned. Keep the tone humble. Stay close to Scripture. Pray at the end.

You may wonder if theology will make your faith dry. It does not have to. Theology becomes dry when it is separated from worship and obedience. But when theology is rooted in Scripture and applied to life, it becomes a source of strength. It helps you endure suffering. It helps you resist temptation. It helps you forgive others. It helps you face death with hope. It helps you worship with understanding.

Many people feel tossed around by constant opinions. One week they feel sure. The next week they feel lost. The Bible calls believers to maturity, so they are not carried by every changing wind of teaching. A steady grasp of core doctrine is part of that maturity.

You will also notice that this workbook avoids unnecessary arguments. Christians do not agree on every detail in every area. Some topics have faithful believers on more than one side. When that happens, this workbook will focus on what Scripture clearly teaches, and it will keep the main things central. The goal is not to start fights. The goal is to build faithfulness.

You will see that each chapter includes application. Doctrine without application becomes pride. Application without doctrine becomes confusion. God gives truth so we can live in truth. This workbook presses that connection again and again. If you learn a truth about God, you will be asked how it changes your worship. If you learn a truth about sin, you will be asked how it changes your confession and choices. If you learn a truth about salvation, you will be asked how it changes your gratitude and obedience.

Expect some conviction. That is normal. Expect some comfort too. God's truth both exposes and heals. It calls you to repent, and it calls you to trust God's grace. It also gives you language for prayer when your own words feel small.

This collection is also meant to be revisited. You might work through it once, then return later at a slower pace. Or you might use one book during a season of study, then use a different book when new questions arise. Each section stands on its own, but the whole set works best when read in order.

One last encouragement

Ask God to teach you as you study. If you belong to Christ, you are not alone in this work. God uses His Word to shape His people. As you read and write, you are practicing listening. You are training your mind and heart to submit to truth. Over time, that kind of practice bears fruit.

As you begin, keep your aim simple. Know God more truly. Trust Him more deeply. Obey Him more fully. Then teach others what you learn, with patience and love. This workbook is here to help you do just that.

BOOK ONE
KNOW GOD AS HE HAS REVEALED HIMSELF

We do not make guesses about who God is. We listen to what He has said. God reveals Himself through His Word, and that is where we begin. This book focuses on how God has made Himself known: His name, His character, His rule, and His call to worship Him in truth. Each chapter gives Scripture-based teaching and space to reflect and respond. These truths are not for head knowledge alone. They shape how we live, pray, and worship. The goal is simple: to know the true God and respond to Him with faith.

CHAPTER 1

START WITH GOD'S SELF-DISCLOSURE

If we want to know God, we must start with how He has spoken. God is not silent. He has shown who He is through creation, through Scripture, and most clearly through His Son. We do not define Him. He defines Himself.

God told Moses His name at the burning bush: **"I AM WHO I AM"** (Exodus 3:14, NSV). This simple phrase speaks volumes. God depends on no one. He has no beginning or end. He exists in Himself. He is not like us. He does not change. He does not grow. He is always present, always holy, always true.

In the Bible, names often show character. God gives Himself many names, each revealing part of who He is. He is **El Elyon** (God Most High), **El Shaddai** (God Almighty), **Yahweh** (the LORD), and **Jehovah-Jireh** (the LORD Will Provide). These are not just titles. They are truths about His nature and how He acts.

Psalm 19:1 says, **"The heavens declare the glory of God"**. Nature shows His greatness, but nature cannot tell us everything. To know God's heart, His will, and His plan for us, we need His Word. Scripture is not just information. It is revelation. It tells us what He wants us to know. And it does not change with time or culture.

Hebrews 1:1–2 says God once spoke through the prophets, but now speaks through His Son. Jesus is the perfect image of God. When we see Christ, we see God with skin on. He shows us God's mercy, power, and truth in human form.

God's self-disclosure is always clear, but we often don't want to hear it. Romans 1:19–21 says that people suppress the truth. Even though God has made Himself known, many reject Him. They trade His glory for empty idols. But those who listen, believe, and submit find life.

Knowing God is not like reading a textbook. It is personal. It calls for humility. We don't come with answers. We come to receive. And what we receive is truth that brings light. We do not figure God out. He makes Himself known, and we respond in worship.

Here is the main idea: God wants to be known. That is why He speaks. That is why He gave us His Word. That is why He sent His Son. And that is why we begin this study not by asking who we think God is, but by asking: What has God said about Himself?

Workbook Section

Read and Reflect

Read these Scriptures carefully. What do they say about how God reveals Himself?

- Exodus 3:13–15

  ____

  ____

- Psalm 19:1–4

  ____

  ____

- Romans 1:18–23

  ____

  ____

- Hebrews 1:1–3

  ____

  ____

Write down one phrase from each passage that stood out to you:

1. Exodus 3: ____

   ____

2. Psalm 19: ____

   ____

3. Romans 1: ____

   ____

4. Hebrews 1: ______________________________________

____

Now answer these reflection questions:

1. In what ways has God already made Himself known to you through Scripture or life experience?

____

____

____

2. Why do you think people often ignore or reject what God has revealed?

____

____

____

3. Which of God's names means the most to you right now, and why?

____

____

____

____

Personal Application

1. God has revealed Himself in specific ways. Which one (creation, Scripture, or Christ) do you want to focus on more in your life this week?

____

____

____

____

2. How can you build a habit of listening to God's Word instead of
    your own ideas about Him?

    ____

    ____

    ____

    ____

    ____

3. Write out a short response to God, based on what you learned.

    ____

    ____

    ____

    ____

    ____

Prayer Response

"Father, thank You for speaking. Thank You for showing who You are.
Help me to trust what You say. Teach me to listen. Teach me to worship
You for who You are, not who I imagine. Amen."

Key Takeaway

God does not leave us guessing. He speaks. His Word tells us who He is.
Our job is to listen and believe.

CHAPTER 2

SEE GOD AS TRINITY: ONE IN THREE

God is one. This is clear from Scripture. But within that oneness, He has revealed Himself as three persons: the Father, the Son, and the Holy Spirit. Each is fully God. Each is distinct. Yet there is only one God.

This is not a human idea. It is not a problem to solve. It is a truth to receive. God shows this clearly in His Word, beginning in the Old Testament. In Genesis 1:26, God says, **"Let us make man in our image."** He speaks as more than one, yet He acts as one. Later, in Isaiah 48:16, the speaker says, **"The Lord GOD has sent Me, and His Spirit."** One sentence. Three persons.

In the New Testament, the Trinity is even clearer. At Jesus' baptism in Matthew 3:16–17, the Son is baptized, the Spirit descends like a dove, and the Father speaks from heaven. All three are present. All three are active.

Jesus also speaks of the Trinity when He tells His disciples to baptize **"in the name of the Father and of the Son and of the Holy Spirit"** (Matthew 28:19). Notice that the word "name" is singular. One name. Three persons.

The Father is not the Son. The Son is not the Spirit. The Spirit is not the Father. But each is fully God. They are equal in power and nature, but they relate to each other in order. The Father sends the Son. The Son sends the Spirit. They work in unity and never oppose each other.

Some try to explain the Trinity using images like water, clover, or an egg. These are all limited and often lead to wrong ideas. God is not like anything else. He is unique. We must let Scripture lead, even when our minds feel stretched.

The Trinity is not a side point. It is central. Salvation, prayer, and worship all involve the whole Trinity. The Father planned salvation. The Son accomplished it. The Spirit applies it to our hearts. We pray to the Father, through the Son, by the Spirit. We worship one God who is Father, Son, and Spirit.

Why does this matter? Because it shows us that God is complete in Himself. Before the world was made, the Father loved the Son through the Spirit. God did not create us because He was lonely. He created us to reflect His joy and love.

The Trinity also shows how unity and difference can exist together in perfect peace. In a world filled with division, God shows us what perfect love and unity look like. This shapes how we live, how we treat others, and how we serve in the church.

God is not like us. But He has shown enough of Himself that we can know Him truly, even if not fully. We cannot explain the Trinity in full, but we can believe it, because this is what God has said.

Workbook Section

Read and Reflect

Read each passage and write a short summary of what it reveals about the Trinity.

1. Genesis 1:26

    ____

    ____

2. Isaiah 48:16

    ____

    ____

3. Matthew 3:16–17

    ____

    ____

4. Matthew 28:19

    ____

    ____

5. John 14:26

What do these verses teach you about the relationship between the Father, Son, and Spirit?

Why is it important that each person of the Trinity is fully God?

How does the truth of the Trinity affect how you think about God's love?

----

1. In prayer, we often focus on one person of the Trinity. How can you begin to speak to the Father, thank the Son, and depend on the Spirit in your prayers?

----

2. How can the unity within the Trinity shape how you treat others in your family, church, or work?

----

3. Do you struggle with this truth? If so, what holds you back? If not, what helps you rest in it?

Key Takeaway

God is one in nature, three in person. The Father, Son, and Spirit are not separate gods. They are one God. This truth leads us to worship with awe and humility.

Prayer Response

Father, thank You for revealing Yourself as one God in three persons. Thank You for sending the Son to save me and the Spirit to live in me. Help me to trust what You have said, even when I do not fully understand. Help me live in unity with others as You live in perfect unity forever. Amen.

CHAPTER 3

RECOGNIZE GOD'S SOVEREIGNTY IN ALL THINGS

Teaching Section

God is sovereign. This means He reigns over everything, everywhere, all the time. His rule is not limited to certain places or moments. He is never caught off guard, never confused, never overruled. There is no one higher than God, no one stronger, no one wiser.

Psalm 103:19 says, **"The Lord has established His throne in the heavens, and His kingdom rules over all."** His rule is not just a claim—it is a fact. Everything that exists is under His authority, including time, space, nature, rulers, angels, and every human life.

When we say God is sovereign, we mean three things:

1. **God has the right to rule all things.** He made everything. He owns everything. As Creator, He alone has full authority.

2. **God has the power to rule all things.** Nothing can stop Him. He does not need help or permission.

3. **God is actively ruling all things.** He is not passive. He is not distant. He is involved at every level: personal, global, and eternal.

We see God's sovereignty clearly in creation. Genesis 1 shows that He speaks and things happen. Light appears. Land separates from sea. Stars fill the sky. Living creatures fill the earth. Nothing resists Him. Nature listens.

God's rule is not only over nature but also over history. He guided Israel out of Egypt. He chose leaders. He removed kings. He used both faithful and wicked people to accomplish His plans. Proverbs 21:1 says, **"The king's heart is a stream of water in the hand of the Lord; He turns it wherever He will."**

God's rule also extends to nations. Daniel 2:21 says He **"changes times and seasons; He removes kings and sets up kings."** Nations rise and fall, not by chance, but by His hand.

But God's sovereignty is not just big, it is also close. Jesus said that not even a sparrow falls to the ground apart from God, and that every hair on your head is numbered (Matthew 10:29–30). This means God is deeply aware and involved in the smallest parts of your life. He knows your steps. He knows your needs. He knows your tears.

Still, many people struggle with this truth. They ask, "If God is in control, why is the world so broken?" That's an honest question. The Bible gives us a full view: God is not the author of evil, but He is never overpowered by it. He allows sin for a time, but He limits it. And He uses even pain and loss for good in the lives of those who love Him (Romans 8:28). Evil never gets the final word, God does.

This is also true in salvation. God is sovereign in choosing, calling, and saving His people. Ephesians 1:4–5 says God chose us in Christ before the world began. He planned to adopt us through Jesus Christ. He is not waiting to see who will come to Him. He draws people to Himself by grace.

Romans 8:30 says, **"Those whom He predestined He also called, and those whom He called He also justified, and those whom He justified He also glorified."** From beginning to end, salvation is God's work. This does not cancel our responsibility. We must believe and repent. But even our faith is a gift He gives.

Some people fear this truth. But if God were not in control, we could not trust Him. If He had limits, He would not be worthy of worship. God's control is not meant to scare us; it is meant to settle us. He is not reckless. He is wise, good, and just in all He does.

When we truly believe God is sovereign, we can rest. We do not have to carry every burden or solve every problem. We can trust that His plans are better than our own, even when we do not see the full picture.

This also affects how we respond to suffering. Pain is real. Loss is hard. But nothing is wasted in God's hands. Joseph told his brothers in Genesis 50:20, **"You meant evil against me, but God meant it for good."** That's not a weak hope. It's a strong truth. God rules over both joy and sorrow, and He brings good even from what others mean for harm.

So how do we live under God's rule?

- We trust Him when life is uncertain.
- We obey Him, knowing He sees everything.
- We pray to Him, because He has the power to act.
- We worship Him, because He deserves all glory.

God's sovereignty is not cold. It is personal. He is not only in charge, He is present. He is not only strong, He is good. And He is not only above all—He is near to all who call on Him.

Workbook Section

Read and Reflect

Read the verses below. Write one truth you see in each:

1. Psalm 103:19

   ____

   ____

2. Proverbs 21:1

   ____

   ____

3. Daniel 2:21

   ____

   ____

4. Matthew 10:29–30

   ____

   ____

5. Romans 8:28–30

   ____

   ____

6. Genesis 50:20

   ____

   ____

1. How does knowing God rules all things change how you view your current season of life?

   ____

   ____

   ____

   ____

   ____

2. Think of a time when a plan you made did not work out. Looking back, how might God have used that for your growth?

   ____

   ____

   ____

   ____

3. Do you struggle with trusting God's control over your future? Why or why not?

   ____

   ____

   ____

   ____

A. Resting in God's Rule

Write down one area of your life where you tend to take control or feel anxious. What would it look like to trust God's rule in that area?

____

____

____

____

____

B. Praying Under God's Sovereignty

When you pray, do you truly believe God has the power to act? Why does trusting His rule change the way you pray?

C. Living with Purpose

If God is in control of every part of life, how does that give meaning to even the small tasks in your day?

Key Takeaway

God is not just in control of the universe, He is in control of your life. He does not forget, overlook, or lose sight of anything. His rule brings peace, purpose, and hope.

Prayer Response

Father, You are Lord over all things, past, present, and future. I praise You for ruling with wisdom, not confusion. With purpose, not chance. With love, not distance. Help me surrender my fear, my plans, and my will. Teach me to rest in Your rule and trust that You never fail. In Jesus' name, Amen.

CHAPTER 4

TRUST GOD'S MORAL GOODNESS

Many people believe God is powerful. Fewer believe He is good. Some carry fears about God that come from pain, harsh leaders, or broken homes. Others assume God is like a stricter version of themselves. Scripture corrects all of that. God is morally perfect. He is pure. He is just. He is faithful. And He never acts with sin or blame.

Deuteronomy 32:4 says, "All his ways are justice." That means God never does wrong. He never bends truth. He never takes a bribe. He never plays favorites. He never lies to get His way. His goodness is not a mood. It is part of who He is.

God's goodness includes His holiness. Holiness means God is set apart from all evil. He is completely clean. Isaiah 6:3 calls Him holy. This is not a small detail. If God were not holy, He could not be trusted. A god who can tolerate sin without care is not good. He is unsafe.

God's goodness also includes His justice. Psalm 89:14 says righteousness and justice are the foundation of His throne. God's rule is not random. He does not judge based on opinions. He judges based on truth. He calls sin what it is. He hates what destroys His creation and harms His people. His justice is good news because it means evil will not last forever.

But God's moral goodness is not only justice. It also includes mercy. Mercy means God shows compassion to people who deserve judgment. He does not ignore sin, but He is patient with sinners. Romans 2:4 speaks of God's kindness and patience leading people to repentance. God is not eager to crush. He is eager to save. His patience is not weakness. It is strength under control.

Some people struggle to hold these truths together. They think God must be either loving or just. Scripture says He is both. He does not choose between them. He is not split inside. He is one God, with one perfect character.

Here is a simple way to think about it. God's love means He does good to others. God's justice means He does what is right. God's mercy means He helps the helpless. God's wrath means He opposes evil. Wrath is not God losing control. Wrath is His settled opposition to sin. A good judge must hate what is evil. If God did not oppose sin, He would not be morally good.

James 1:17 says every good gift is from God. This shows another part of His goodness. God is generous. He gives life, breath, daily bread, strength, and help. Many of His gifts come to people who do not thank Him. That is kindness. It is also a call to repentance.

So what does it mean to trust God's moral goodness?

First, it means you let God define good and evil. We live in a time when people rename sin as freedom and call selfishness a right. Scripture calls us to submit our moral judgment to God's Word. Micah 6:8 says God has told us what is good. God does not hide His standards. He makes them known.

Second, trusting God's goodness means you stop measuring God by your comfort. God may lead you through hard days. Hard does not mean evil. Discipline does not mean hate. Correction does not mean rejection. God can be good and still allow hardship for a wise purpose.

Third, trusting God's goodness means you obey even when it costs you. Many sins look pleasant for a moment. Many acts of obedience feel costly at first. But God's commands are not traps. They are good paths. They protect you, shape you, and point you toward life.

Fourth, trusting God's goodness means you repent with hope. When God exposes sin, He is not trying to destroy you. He is calling you back. His goodness invites you to return to Him. His mercy gives room to confess. His justice makes forgiveness meaningful. His holiness makes change possible.

If you want a steady faith, you must settle this truth in your heart. God is morally good. He is never cruel. He is never unfair. He is never careless. When you do not understand His ways, you can still trust His character. That trust becomes a strong anchor in both joy and suffering.

Scripture Study

Read each passage. Then write one sentence that explains what it shows about God's moral goodness.

1. Deuteronomy 32:4

    ____

    ____

2. Psalm 89:14

    ____

    ____

3. Romans 2:4

    ____

    ____

4. James 1:17

    ____

    ____

5. Micah 6:8

    ____

    ____

6. Isaiah 6:3

    ____

    ____

Clear Thinking Exercise

Write short answers. Use your own words.

1. What is the difference between God's justice and God's mercy?

    ____

    ____

    ____

    ____

2. Why is God's holiness good news, not bad news?

----

3. What is one common lie people believe about God's goodness?

Choose one area. Be honest and specific.

1. Where do you most doubt God's goodness right now?

    Examples: your past, your health, your finances, your family, your unanswered prayers.

----

2. What have you been tempted to believe about God because of that struggle?

----

3. Based on the passages you read, what is true about God's character in this area?

Pick one command of God that you find hard to follow. Keep it concrete.

1. The command I struggle with is:

    ----

2. Why it feels hard:

    ----

3. One small act of obedience I will do in the next 48 hours:

    ----

4. One person who can support me in this:

Prayer Response

Write a short prayer of trust. Use your own words. If you get stuck, start with these lines and finish them.

Father, You are holy and You do what is right.

I confess that I have doubted Your goodness when ____.

Help me believe what Your Word says about You.

Teach me to obey You in ____.

Thank You for Your kindness that leads me to repentance.

Amen.

Key Takeaway

God's moral goodness is steady. He is holy, just, and merciful. When you cannot trace His plan, you can trust His character.

CHAPTER 5

UNDERSTAND GOD'S RELATIONSHIP WITH TIME

People live inside time. We count minutes. We feel hurry. We regret the past and worry about the future. God is not like that. He made time, so He is not trapped by it. Scripture shows that God is eternal. He has no beginning and no end. He does not learn new facts. He does not get older. He does not run out of time.

Psalm 90:2 says, "From everlasting to everlasting you are God." God's life has no edges. He is not a long-lived creature. He is the Creator who always is.

God's relationship with time helps us trust Him. We change. Our feelings shift. Our plans fail. God does not change. Malachi 3:6 says, "I the Lord do not change." His promises stay sure. His character stays clean. His purpose stays steady.

God also sees the full story at once. We see one page. God sees the whole book. Isaiah 46:10 says God declares the end from the beginning. This does not mean God guesses well. It means He knows and rules over what will happen. Nothing takes Him by surprise.

This truth is meant to calm us, not confuse us. God is not rushed. He is never late. He is never early. He works with perfect wisdom. 2 Peter 3:8 reminds us that God's sense of time is not like ours. What feels slow to us is not slow to Him. He is patient and purposeful.

God's eternal nature also means He is always faithful in every season. When you feel stuck, God is not stuck. When you feel like time is running out, God is not anxious. When you feel like your past has ruined you, God is still able to redeem. When you fear the future, God is already there.

Still, God works within time. He acts in real history. He gives days and years. He sets seasons. Ecclesiastes 3:1 says there is a time for every matter under heaven. That verse does not mean every moment is pleasant. It means life has rhythms, and God is not absent from them.

God gives time as a gift and a responsibility. Ephesians 5:15–16 tells believers to walk wisely and make the best use of time. That means time matters. We cannot get it back. God calls us to use it well.

So how should we live in light of God's relationship with time?

First, live with steady trust. If God is eternal and unchanging, you do not need to panic when life shifts. You can make plans, but you do not need to cling to them. Proverbs 16:9 says a person plans his way, but the Lord directs his steps. You can hold your plans with open hands.

Second, practice patient obedience. Many people want fast answers. But God often grows His people slowly. Waiting is not wasted time when it is done with faith. God uses waiting to shape character, deepen prayer, and expose idols.

Third, repent quickly. Time is limited for us. James 4:14 says our life is like a mist. That is not meant to scare you. It is meant to wake you up. Do not delay obedience. Do not delay confession. Do not delay seeking peace with others.

Fourth, live with hope. Because God is Lord of time, history is going somewhere. God is not reacting to events. He is carrying out His purpose. The future is not empty. It is held by God.

When you understand God's relationship with time, you can rest. You can also work. You rest because God is steady. You work because your days matter. The goal is not to control time. The goal is to trust the One who holds it.

Workbook Section

Scripture Study

Read each passage. Then write one sentence about what it teaches about God and time.

1. Psalm 90:2

----

2. Malachi 3:6

---

3. Isaiah 46:10

---

4. 2 Peter 3:8

---

5. Ecclesiastes 3:1

---

6. James 4:14

Connect the Truth

Answer in your own words.

1. What is the difference between God being eternal and God being simply "very old"?

---

2. Why does God's unchanging nature matter for His promises?

---

3. What happens to your faith when you measure God's work by
    your timeline?

Write down how you used your time yesterday. Keep it simple and
honest.

Morning: ____

____

Midday: ____

____

Evening: ____

____

Now answer:

1. What part of your day showed wise use of time?

    ----

2. What part of your day felt wasted or careless?

    ----

3. What is one change you can make this week that would honor
    God?

Think of one area where you are waiting on God.

I am waiting for:

What I fear while waiting:

What I can do while waiting:

Now write one sentence of trust based on Isaiah 46:10.

Repent and Act

Choose one area where you have delayed obedience.

The obedience I have delayed is:

Why I have delayed it:

One step I will take in the next 24 hours:

Write a short prayer. If you need help, begin with these lines and finish them.

Lord, You are eternal and You never change.

Help me stop rushing and start trusting You in ____________________ .

Teach me to use my time wisely by ______________________________ .

Give me patience to obey while I wait for ____________________________ .

Thank You that You hold my past, my present, and my future.

Amen.

Key Takeaway

God is eternal and unchanging. He is never rushed and never late. Your time is limited, so use it wisely and trust the God who holds every day.

CHAPTER 6

WORSHIP GOD IN TRUTH

Worship is not a style. Worship is a response to God. It is giving Him the honor He deserves because of who He is and what He has done. True worship begins with truth, not preference. If we worship a version of God we made up, we are not worshiping God. We are worshiping an idea.

Jesus said, "The true worshipers will worship the Father in spirit and truth" (John 4:23, NSV). Truth matters because God is real. He has revealed Himself. He tells us what pleases Him. Worship is not a place you go once a week. It is a life of reverence and obedience that flows from a heart made alive by God.

Worship includes singing, prayer, and hearing Scripture, but it does not stop there. Romans 12:1 calls believers to present their bodies as a living sacrifice. That is worship. When you obey God in private, that is worship. When you forgive, speak truth, and turn from sin, that is worship. When you serve others with love, that is worship.

Truth-shaped worship also means we approach God the way He tells us to. Nadab and Abihu offered unauthorized fire and faced judgment (Leviticus 10:1–3). That account is sobering, but it teaches a lasting lesson. God is not to be treated lightly. He is holy. We do not set the terms. He does.

That does not mean worship should be joyless. God is worthy of gladness and gratitude. Psalm 100:2 calls people to serve the Lord with gladness. But gladness must be guided by truth. Real joy grows when we see God clearly, not when we chase a feeling.

Worship in truth also requires right thinking about God. If you think God is small, your worship will be small. If you think God is harsh, you will either hide from Him or try to earn His favor. If you think God does not care about sin, you will treat sin as a minor issue. But when you see God as He is, worship becomes steady and sincere.

God also cares about the heart. Isaiah 29:13 warns about honoring God with lips while the heart is far away. God does not want empty words. He wants a real response. This is why confession matters. You cannot cling to sin and worship God in truth at the same time. Psalm 24:3-4 asks who may stand in God's holy place. The answer includes clean hands and a pure heart. This is not perfection. It is honesty, repentance, and a desire to obey.

Worship in truth shapes how we live together as the church. Scripture calls believers to build one another up, to let the Word of Christ dwell richly, and to sing with gratitude. In true worship, God stays central. The focus is not the crowd, the mood, or the platform. The focus is God's glory and the good of His people.

So how do you worship God in truth?

Start with Scripture. Let God's Word set your view of Him. Then respond with prayer and praise. Confess sin quickly. Give thanks for real gifts. Obey what God has said. Serve others in love. These things are not separate from worship. They are worship.

Worship in truth also prepares you for hard days. When life is painful, feelings can swing. But truth does not move. If your worship is built on truth, you can keep honoring God even when you are tired, confused, or sad. You may not feel strong, but you can still be faithful.

God is worthy of worship in every season. He is worthy when you understand and when you do not. He is worthy when life is full and when life is empty. Worship in truth is a steady offering of trust, reverence, and obedience to the living God.

Scripture Study

Read each passage. Then write one sentence about what it teaches you about worship.

1. John 4:23

    ----

2. Romans 12:1

    ----

3. Leviticus 10:1–3

    ----

4. Psalm 100:2

    ----

5. Isaiah 29:13

    ----

6. Psalm 24:3–4

Worship Check

Answer honestly.

1. When you think of worship, what do you usually picture?

    ----

2. Which is harder for you, worshiping with joy or worshiping with reverence? Why?

____

____

____

____

3. What tends to distract your heart during worship gatherings or private prayer?

____

____

____

____

Truth Before Feeling

Write a short list of true statements about God that can guide your worship even when feelings are low.

1. God is:

____

____

2. God has:

____

____

3. God will:

____

____

Now write one sentence explaining how these truths help you worship when life is hard.

____

____

____

____

____

Living Worship Plan

Pick one action you will take this week to worship God in truth.

Choose one:

- Daily Scripture reading for 10 minutes

- Confession and repentance in one specific area

- Serving someone quietly without being noticed

- Giving thanks for three specific gifts each day

- Setting aside one hour for prayer and reflection

My choice:

My plan for when and how I will do it:

Repair the Heart

Isaiah 29:13 warns about worship with words but not the heart. Write a short confession if your heart has been distant.

What has pulled my heart away:

What I need to repent of:

What I will change this week:

Prayer Response

Write a prayer in your own words. If you need help, start here and finish it.

Father, You are worthy of honor and praise.

Forgive me for treating worship as _______________________________ .

Teach me to worship You in spirit and truth by _______________

--- .

Help my life match my words.

Thank You for meeting with Your people and shaping us by Your Word.

Amen.

Key Takeaway

True worship is a whole-life response to God, guided by Scripture. It is marked by reverence, gratitude, repentance, and obedience.

BOOK TWO

UNDERSTAND WHAT IT MEANS TO BE HUMAN

To understand yourself and others, you must start where the Bible starts. God made people with purpose, dignity, and responsibility. Even after sin entered the world, human life still matters because it is God's work. This book will help you see what it means to bear God's image, how sin has affected every part of us, and why we still have real worth. Each chapter includes clear teaching and guided exercises that connect Scripture to daily life. The goal is simple: to think rightly about humanity so you can live wisely before God and love people well.

CHAPTER 1

CREATED IN GOD'S IMAGE

The Bible says humans are made in God's image. This is one of the most important truths you can learn about yourself and every other person. It explains why human life has value, why sin is so serious, and why redemption matters.

Genesis 1:27 says God created mankind in His own image, male and female. This verse gives two clear facts. First, our value is not earned. It is given by God. Second, every human being shares this dignity. Image of God is not reserved for the strong, the healthy, the educated, or the successful. It applies to the unborn child, the elderly, the disabled, the poor, the prisoner, and the stranger. It applies to your neighbor and your enemy.

The image of God does not mean we are divine. We are not little gods. We do not share God's power or His authority as Creator. We are still creatures. We need food, rest, and help. We get sick and we die. We can be wrong. We can be foolish. God is not like that. He is perfect. We are not.

So what does it mean to bear God's image?

At a basic level, it means we were made to reflect Him. A mirror does not create light. It reflects light. In a similar way, humans were made to show something true about God in the world God made.

Scripture points to several ways we reflect God.

First, we reflect God through moral awareness. Humans have a sense that some things are right and others are wrong. That sense can be damaged, ignored, or twisted, but it is still there. We are not driven by instinct alone. We can judge our own choices. We can feel guilt. We can confess. We can seek forgiveness. That moral awareness points to a holy and righteous God.

Second, we reflect God through reason and speech. We can think, plan, and learn. We can speak words that carry meaning. James 3:9 says we bless God and then use the same tongue to curse people made in God's likeness. The verse assumes something important: the way we treat people is tied to the fact that they bear God's image. It also shows that our words matter. Speech can build or destroy. God speaks truth. We should aim to do the same.

Third, we reflect God through relationships. God made us for life with others. From the beginning, human life includes family and community. This does not mean every person must marry. It means no one was made to live as an island. We need friendship, counsel, accountability, and care. We also need to learn patience, kindness, and forgiveness. Those are relational virtues.

Fourth, we reflect God through work and stewardship. God entrusted the earth to human care. We are called to cultivate, protect, and use creation wisely. Work is not a curse by itself. Work existed before sin entered the world. Work became painful after sin, but work itself is still part of God's design. When we do honest work with skill and integrity, we show something of God's order and goodness.

Fifth, we reflect God through creativity. Humans make songs, stories, tools, homes, gardens, and systems. We do not create from nothing like God does. But we do create within what He made. This is one reason art can be beautiful and also why it can be misused. Creativity can be used to serve others or to feed pride.

The image of God also explains why violence and abuse are evil. Genesis 9:6 ties the seriousness of murder to the image of God. Taking a human life is not only harming a body. It is attacking a person who bears God's mark. The same logic applies to cruelty, racism, exploitation, and hatred. These sins treat image-bearers like objects.

At the same time, Scripture is honest about what sin has done to us. The image of God in humans has been damaged by the fall, but it has not been erased. People still have dignity, but we do not reflect God perfectly. Our minds can become dark. Our desires can become disordered. Our relationships can become selfish. Our work can become greedy. We can use our gifts to harm instead of help.

This is why we must be careful with two mistakes.

One mistake is to deny human worth because of sin. Some people look at the brokenness of the world and decide humans are worthless. That is not biblical. People are fallen, but still valuable.

The other mistake is to praise human goodness in a way that ignores sin. Some people speak as if humans are naturally fine and just need better education or better systems. Scripture does not allow that either. Sin is real and deep. We need more than improvement. We need rescue.

So how does the image of God connect to Christ?

Colossians 3:10 says believers put on the new self, which is being renewed in knowledge after the image of its Creator. This is hope. God does not only forgive. He also restores. In Christ, God is repairing what sin has damaged. This renewal is real, but it is also a process. It grows over time as believers learn truth, repent of sin, and walk in obedience.

Ephesians 4:24 speaks of the new self, created after the likeness of God in true righteousness and holiness. This tells us what restoration looks like. God is forming His people to reflect His character again. He shapes how we think, what we love, and how we live.

This chapter gives you a starting point for the rest of this book. If you want to understand humanity, start here: every person is made by God, marked by God, and meant to reflect God. That truth should shape how you view yourself. It should also shape how you treat others, even when they are difficult, even when they sin, even when they disagree with you.

Workbook Section

1) Scripture Reading and Notes

Read each passage. Write one short observation from each. Keep it concrete.

1. Genesis 1:27 (NSV)

----

2. Psalm 8:4–6 (NSV)

----

3. Genesis 9:6 (NSV)

----

4. James 3:9 (NSV)

----

5. Colossians 3:10 (NSV)

----

6. Ephesians 4:24 (NSV)

----

2) Define It in Your Own Words

Write a simple definition.

The image of God means:

Now write one sentence that says what it does not mean.

The image of God does not mean:

----

3) Self-View Check

Answer with honesty. Use full sentences.

1. When do you most forget your God-given value?

    ----

2. What do you usually base your value on instead?
    Examples: approval, success, appearance, performance, control.

    ----

3. How does Genesis 1:27 correct that pattern?

    ----

4) Neighbor-View Check

Pick one person you find hard to love. Do not write their name if you do not want to.

This person is hard for me because:

Now connect the truth.

Because this person bears God's image, I should treat them by:

____

____

____

____

Write one specific action you will take this week that shows respect and restraint.

____

____

____

____

My action step:

____

____

____

____

5) Words and the Image of God

James 3:9 connects the tongue to the image of God.

List three kinds of speech that dishonor image-bearers.

1. ____________________________________

2. ____________________________________

3. ____________________________________

List three kinds of speech that honor image-bearers.

1. ____________________________________

2. ____________________________________

3. ____________________________________

Now write one sentence you need to stop saying, or stop implying, about yourself or others.

Sentence to put away:

____

____

Write one sentence you will practice instead.

Sentence to practice:

----

6) Work and Stewardship

Write answers that fit your real life.

1. What is one part of your work or daily responsibility that feels small?

   ----

2. How could you do that task in a way that reflects God's order and care?

   ----

3. What is one resource God has placed in your hands that you can steward better?

   Examples: time, money, attention, health, skills.

   ----

7) Renewal Plan

Colossians 3:10 speaks of renewal. Choose one area where you want God to restore your reflection of Him.

Area for renewal:

Write one habit that supports that renewal.

Habit to begin:

____

____

Write one habit that fights against it.

____

____

Habit to remove:

____

____

Prayer Response

Write a short prayer in your own words. If you need a start, use these lines and complete them.

Father, You made me in Your image.

____

____

Forgive me for treating myself or others like ___________________ .

____

Help me reflect You today through my words, choices, and work.

____

____

Renew me in true righteousness and holiness.

____

____

Amen.

Key Takeaway

Every person is made in God's image. Sin damages us, but it does not erase our worth. In Christ, God restores His people so they reflect Him with growing truth and love.

CHAPTER 2

HUMAN PURPOSE AND GOD'S DESIGN

People often ask why they are here. Some ask it in quiet moments. Others feel it through stress, boredom, or regret. The Bible does not leave us guessing. God made people with purpose, and His design is good. Purpose is not something we invent. It is something we receive from the One who made us.

From the beginning, God created humans to live under His authority and enjoy His care. Genesis 2:15 says the Lord God placed the man in the garden "to work it and keep it" (NSV). This shows that purpose includes responsibility. God made us to build, tend, guard, and serve. Work is part of God's good plan. It existed before sin entered the world. That means work is not a punishment. It is a gift that gives structure and meaning to life.

Work does not only mean a job. Work includes caring for children, cleaning a home, studying, farming, leading, crafting, and serving neighbors. It includes tasks people notice and tasks nobody sees. God values faithfulness in both. The size of the task does not determine its worth. What matters is how we do it and why we do it.

God's design also includes rest. Humans are not machines. We have limits because we are creatures. God alone has no limits. The pattern of work and rest teaches us humility. It reminds us that the world does not depend on us. Rest is not laziness. It is a way of trusting God. When we rest, we admit we are not in control.

God also designed humans for relationships. Genesis 2:18 says, "It is not good that the man should be alone" (NSV). God made people to live in community. We need others to help us, correct us, encourage us, and share life with us. This does not mean every person must marry. It means no person is meant to live cut off from meaningful relationships.

Human purpose includes family life, friendship, and life among God's people. Relationships are part of how we reflect God's care. In healthy relationships, people practice love, patience, truth, and forgiveness. This is part of God's design for human life.

Most of all, God designed humans to know Him and honor Him. Ecclesiastes 12:13 says, "Fear God and keep his commandments" (NSV). To fear God means to treat Him as God. It means we honor His Word and submit to His will. This is the center of human purpose. Work and relationships matter, but they are not the highest goal. They are meant to be lived under God.

The Bible also teaches stewardship. Stewardship means managing what belongs to someone else. God owns all things. He gives people time, skills, money, opportunities, and responsibilities. We will answer to Him for how we use what He gives. This truth shapes daily life. It shapes how we spend time. It shapes how we treat our bodies. It shapes how we handle money. It shapes how we use words.

Sin has twisted human purpose. Many people live as if they belong to themselves. They chase pleasure, power, approval, or comfort as if those things can carry the weight of meaning. But these things cannot hold the human heart. They may satisfy for a moment, then they fade. This is why people can have full schedules and still feel empty.

God's design offers a better way. The greatest commands are to love God and love neighbor (Mark 12:30–31, NSV). This gives purpose in two directions. Love toward God means worship, trust, obedience, gratitude, and prayer. Love toward neighbor means seeking another person's good with truth and kindness. This kind of love does not depend on mood. It is a choice rooted in God's Word.

When you understand human purpose, you gain clarity. You stop trying to build identity from performance. You stop chasing meaning in things that cannot save. You begin to live with steady direction. You work with integrity. You rest with trust. You pursue relationships with patience. You worship God with reverence. You steward your life as a gift.

God's design does not remove hardship. But it gives a path that makes sense. It gives a reason to keep going. It gives a foundation that does not shift with feelings or trends. You were made by God, for God, and under God. That truth is not a cage. It is freedom.

1) Scripture Reading and Notes

Read each passage. Write one clear observation from each.

1. Genesis 2:15 (NSV)

    ----

2. Genesis 2:18 (NSV)

    ----

3. Ecclesiastes 12:13 (NSV)

    ----

4. Mark 12:30–31 (NSV)

    ----

5. Colossians 3:23 (NSV)

    ----

6. Psalm 90:12 (NSV)

    ----

2) Purpose in Plain Words

Finish the sentence using simple language.

God made me to:

Now write one sentence that describes a purpose you have chased that did not satisfy.

I have chased:

----

3) Work as Part of God's Design

Answer with honesty.

1. What kind of work fills most of your week right now?

    ----

2. What part of your work feels most draining?

    ----

3. What would it look like to do that part "as for the Lord" this week?

    ----

4. What is one attitude you need to repent of in your work?

    Examples: complaining, laziness, harshness, pride, cutting corners.

    ----

4) Rest and Limits

Write answers that match your real life.

1. Where do you ignore your limits?

    ----

2. What is one sign you are running on empty?

    ----

3. What is one boundary you can set this week to protect time with God and healthy rest?

    ----

5) Relationships in God's Design

1. Name one relationship you want to strengthen.

    ----

2. What is one step you can take this week to strengthen it?

    ----

3. What is one habit that harms your relationships?
    Examples: interrupting, sarcasm, cold silence, gossip, anger.

    ----

4. What is one habit you want to replace it with?

    ----

6) Stewardship Check

Write short answers.

1. One gift God has given me is:

    ----

2. One resource God has placed in my care is:

    ----

3. One area where I often waste what God gives is:

Now write one action step you will take in the next 48 hours.

My action step:

----

7) Love God and Love Neighbor

Use Mark 12:30–31.

1. One way I will love God this week is:

    ----

2. One way I will love my neighbor this week is:

    ----

3. One barrier that gets in the way is:

    ----

4. One change I will make is:

Prayer Response

Write a short prayer of direction. If you need help, begin here and finish it.

Father, You made me for Your purpose.

Forgive me for chasing meaning in ____________________________ .

Help me honor You in my work, my rest, and my relationships.

Teach me to fear You and keep Your commandments with a willing heart.

Amen.

Key Takeaway

Human purpose is received, not invented. God designed people to worship Him, steward what He gives, and love others with faithful action.

CHAPTER 3

THE FALL: WHAT BROKE IN US

The Bible teaches that God made the world good. He made humans good. But something happened that changed everything. Scripture calls it "the fall." The fall is not a small mistake. It is the entry of sin into human life and into the human heart. It explains why the world is so beautiful and so broken at the same time.

Genesis 3 tells the account. God gave Adam and Eve a clear command. They were free to enjoy God's gifts, but they were not free to define good and evil for themselves. The serpent tempted Eve by questioning God's Word and God's goodness. The temptation was not only about fruit. It was about authority. Would they trust God's command, or would they make themselves the final judge?

They chose rebellion. Eve took and ate. Adam ate too. At that moment, sin entered human life. Their relationship with God changed. Their relationship with each other changed. Their relationship with creation changed. The fall broke what was whole.

The first thing that broke was trust. Sin is not just breaking rules. It is distrusting God's character. It is believing that God is holding back something good. That lie still drives many sins today. People sin because they believe God's way will not satisfy them. They think they must take what they want, their way, in their time.

The second thing that broke was innocence. After they sinned, Adam and Eve felt shame. Genesis 3 says they knew they were naked and they hid. This is important. Before sin, they had nothing to hide. After sin, they felt exposed. Shame entered the human story. Shame is the sense of being unclean, not just guilty. It pushes people to cover up and to pretend.

The third thing that broke was openness with God. Adam and Eve hid from the Lord. They feared His presence. That is what sin does. It makes people run from the One they need most. Instead of confession, they chose hiding. Instead of trust, they chose fear.

The fourth thing that broke was human relationships. When God confronted Adam, Adam blamed Eve. Eve blamed the serpent. Sin produces excuses. It trains the heart to protect itself. It also produces conflict. Genesis 3 shows that harmony was replaced by tension, mistrust, and selfishness.

The fifth thing that broke was creation itself. God pronounced judgment, and the ground was cursed. Work became painful. Life became marked by toil, thorns, and frustration. Pain in childbirth and hardship in labor became part of human life. Death also entered the world. God had warned that the wages of sin would be death. The fall brought separation, decay, and loss.

The fall also explains the spread of sin. Adam was the head of the human race. When he sinned, sin did not stay with him alone. Romans 5:12 teaches that sin came into the world through one man, and death through sin, and so death spread to all people (NSV). This is why every person is born with a sinful nature. We do not become sinners only by copying others. We sin because we are sinners by nature. We inherit a heart bent away from God.

This is hard truth, but it is also honest truth. Many people want to believe humans are basically good and just need better teaching. But Scripture says the problem goes deeper. The heart is corrupted. The will is twisted. Desires are disordered. This is why rules alone cannot fix us. Better habits alone cannot rescue us. We need a new heart.

At the same time, the fall does not erase the image of God. Humans still have dignity. We still have moral awareness. We can still do acts of kindness. But even our "good" acts can be mixed with pride or selfish motives. The fall touched every part of us. It did not destroy us completely, but it damaged us deeply.

Genesis 3 also gives a small beam of hope. God did not destroy Adam and Eve on the spot. He pursued them. He spoke to them. He covered them. And He promised that a descendant would come who would crush the serpent (Genesis 3:15). This is the first promise of a Savior. It shows that God's response to human sin included judgment, but also mercy and a plan of rescue.

Understanding the fall helps you understand yourself. It explains why you struggle with sin even when you know better. It explains why relationships are hard. It explains why work can feel heavy. It explains why suffering exists. It also helps you stop being surprised by human evil. You still grieve it, but you understand its root.

Most of all, the fall prepares you to understand salvation. If the problem is only surface-level, then salvation would only be self-improvement. But if the problem is heart-level, then salvation must be deeper. God must forgive sin and also restore what broke inside us. That is what He does through Christ.

Workbook Section

1) Scripture Reading and Notes

Read each passage. Write one clear observation.

1. Genesis 3:1–7 (NSV)

    ____

    ____

2. Genesis 3:8–13 (NSV)

    ____

    ____

3. Genesis 3:16–19 (NSV)

    ____

    ____

4. Romans 5:12 (NSV)

    ____

    ____

5. James 1:14–15 (NSV)

    ____

    ____

6. Genesis 3:15 (NSV)

    ____

    ____

2) What Broke First?

In Genesis 3, several things break. Write short answers.

1. What lie does the serpent use to tempt?

    ----

2. What emotion shows up right after sin?

    ----

3. What is the first thing Adam and Eve do when they hear God?

    ----

4. How do they respond when confronted?

    ----

3) Trace a Pattern

James 1:14–15 describes how sin grows. Think of a recent temptation you faced. Do not write details that feel unsafe to share. Keep it general.

1. The desire or pull I felt was:

    ----

2. The lie I was tempted to believe was:

    ----

3. The choice I made, or almost made, was:

----

4. The result in my thoughts or relationships was:

Now write one sentence about what you would do differently next time.

Next time I will:

----

4) Shame and Hiding

Answer honestly.

1. What do you tend to hide when you feel shame?
    Examples: feelings, failures, anger, fear, habits.

----

2. What does hiding do to your relationship with God?

----

3. What does hiding do to your relationships with others?

----

4. What is one step of honesty you can take this week?

----

5) The Spread of Sin

Romans 5:12 shows sin spread to all.

1. How does this truth help you understand the world's brokenness?

----

2. How does it help you understand your own struggles?

----

3. What is the danger of blaming only "society" for sin?

----

6) Hope in the Middle of Judgment

Genesis 3:15 is a promise of rescue.

1. What does it tell you about God's response to sin?

----

2. What does it tell you about God's plan?

----

3. How does this give you hope today?

Prayer Response

Write a prayer of confession and hope. If you need help, begin here and finish it.

Lord, You made the world good, but sin has broken us.

I confess that I have believed lies about Your Word and Your goodness.

Forgive me for ____ .

Help me stop hiding and walk in the light.

Thank You that You promised a Savior and that Your mercy is real.

Amen.

Key Takeaway

The fall explains what broke in us. Sin damaged our trust, brought shame, fractured relationships, and brought death into the human story. Yet God pursued sinners and promised rescue.

CHAPTER 4

HOW SIN AFFECTS OUR THINKING AND DESIRES

Sin does more than break rules. Sin bends the inside of a person. It twists how we think and what we want. This is why sin can feel normal, even when it is deadly. It is also why people can know the truth and still choose lies.

Jeremiah 17:9 says the heart is deceitful above all things and sick. That does not mean every thought you have is false. It means your inner life is not a safe guide by itself. Your heart can excuse sin. Your mind can rewrite wrong as right. Your desires can push you toward what harms you.

Sin affects our thinking in several ways.

First, sin darkens the mind. It makes spiritual truth seem foolish. 2 Corinthians 4:4 says the god of this world has blinded the minds of unbelievers. A blind mind cannot see the beauty of Christ. It cannot see sin as sin. It cannot see God as good. This blindness does not mean people lack intelligence. It means the deepest problem is spiritual, not academic.

Second, sin trains us to suppress truth. People can push truth down so they do not have to obey it. They may avoid Scripture. They may avoid godly counsel. They may stay busy so they do not have to think. Over time, the conscience can grow dull. A dull conscience feels less. It warns less. It stops sounding the alarm.

Third, sin distorts our view of God. Many sins begin with a false picture of God. Some think God is distant, so prayer feels useless. Some think God is harsh, so they hide. Some think God is weak, so they take control. But wrong thoughts about God lead to wrong choices. What you believe about God shapes what you do when you are tempted.

Sin also affects our desires.

Desires are not evil by themselves. Hunger is a desire. Rest is a desire. Friendship is a desire. The problem is that sin disorders desire. It takes good things and makes them ruling things. It takes a gift and turns it into a god. It makes the heart say, "I must have this," even when God says no.

James 4:1 says conflicts come from passions at war within us. That verse ties outward trouble to inward desire. When desires rule, people will lie, lash out, and manipulate. They will also envy and resent. They will demand their way. This is not just a personality issue. It is a heart issue.

Sin also makes desire loud. It makes it feel urgent. It tells you, "Do it now," and "You deserve it." Proverbs 14:12 says there is a way that seems right to a man, but its end is the way to death. Temptation often looks right at first. It looks fair. It looks harmless. But it leads to damage.

Here is another way sin harms desire. It teaches us to love the wrong things. Titus 3:3 says people were once foolish, disobedient, led astray, slaves to various passions and pleasures. That word slaves matters. A slave does not feel free. A slave serves a master. Sin makes passions act like a master. It commands. It promises comfort. Then it takes more than it gives.

This is why "follow your heart" is poor advice. Your heart needs guidance. Your heart needs correction. Your heart needs renewal. Proverbs 4:23 says to guard your heart, for from it flow the springs of life. If the spring is polluted, the stream will be polluted too.

So what is the answer?

The Bible does not tell you to trust your thoughts and feelings. It tells you to test them. It tells you to listen to God's Word. It tells you to seek wisdom. It tells you to walk by the Spirit so you do not carry out sinful desires. Galatians 5:16 says, "Walk by the Spirit, and you will not gratify the desires of the flesh" (NSV). This is hope. You are not trapped. God gives help that is stronger than temptation.

Galatians 5:17 explains that the flesh desires what is against the Spirit, and the Spirit desires what is against the flesh. That means there is a real fight inside believers. If you feel that fight, it does not prove you are lost. It may show you are alive. A dead heart does not fight sin. A living heart does.

Sin affects thinking and desire, but God can renew both. Colossians 1:21 says people were once alienated and hostile in mind, doing evil deeds. Then the passage moves toward reconciliation through Christ. God changes the mind and the heart. He does not only forgive the past. He reshapes the present.

How does God reshape us?

First, He gives truth. Truth exposes lies. Psalm 119:105 says God's word is a lamp to your feet and a light to your path. When truth shines, temptation loses some of its pull. You can see the end of the road, not just the first step.

Second, God calls us to repentance. Repentance is a change of mind that leads to a change of direction. It is not self-hate. It is turning from sin because you trust God is better.

Third, God trains desire. This takes time. You may still feel wrong cravings. But you can learn to say no. You can learn to replace lies with truth. You can learn to seek what pleases God. Philippians 2:13 says God works in you, both to will and to work for His good pleasure. God does not only command. He also gives strength.

Fourth, God uses practices that reshape the heart. Scripture reading, prayer, confession, fellowship, and wise boundaries all matter. They are not ways to earn God's love. They are ways to walk in God's help.

This chapter matters because you cannot fight what you do not name. If you think sin is only "bad behavior," you will focus on image. You will try to look good. But if you see sin as an inner problem, you will seek inner change. You will ask God to renew your mind and reorder your desires.

Here is the steady truth to hold. Sin bends what you think and want. God can straighten what sin has bent. He does it through His Word, His Spirit, and a life of humble obedience.

1) Scripture Reading and Notes

Read each passage. Write one clear observation from each.

1. Jeremiah 17:9 (NSV)

----

2. 2 Corinthians 4:4 (NSV)

----

3. James 4:1 (NSV)

----

4. Proverbs 14:12 (NSV)

----

5. Proverbs 4:23 (NSV)

----

6. Galatians 5:16–17 (NSV)

----

7. Philippians 2:13 (NSV)

----

2) Spot the Lie, Speak the Truth

Write one lie that temptation often whispers to you. Keep it short.

The lie: ____

Now write a true statement from what you learned in this chapter.

The truth: ____

Write one sentence you can say in the moment of temptation.

My sentence:

----

3) Map Your Pattern

Think of a recent moment when you felt pulled toward sin. Do not include details you do not want to write down.

1.   What was happening right before the temptation?

----

2.   What did you want in that moment?
     Examples: comfort, control, approval, escape, pleasure.

----

3.   What did you tell yourself to make it feel okay?

----

4.   What was the result in your heart or relationships?

Now write one small change you can make next time.

My change:

----

4) Guard the Springs

Proverbs 4:23 says to guard your heart.

List three inputs that shape your thinking each week.

Examples: music, videos, friends, news, social media, books.

1. ____

2. ____

3. ____

Now answer:

1. Which input helps you love what is good?

    ____

    ____

    ____

2. Which input stirs wrong desires?

    ____

    ____

    ____

3. What boundary will you set this week?

    ____

    ____

    ____

My boundary:

    ____

    ____

    ____

5) Walk by the Spirit Plan

Galatians 5:16 calls you to walk by the Spirit. Write a simple plan you can do.

1. One time each day I will open God's Word:

    ____

    ____

    ____

2. One short prayer I will repeat when tempted:

----

3. One person I can ask for prayer or support:

----

4. One wise step I will take to avoid a common trap:

----

6) Desire Check

Write short answers.

1. A good desire I have is:

----

2. A desire that often tries to rule me is:

----

3. One way that ruling desire has harmed me is:

----

4. One better desire I want God to grow in me is:

Write a prayer for a renewed mind and reordered desires. If you need help, begin here and finish it.

Father, my heart can mislead me.

Shine Your truth on my thoughts.

Help me guard what I take in.

Teach me to walk by Your Spirit when I am tempted.

Change what I want so I want what pleases You.

Amen.

Key Takeaway

Sin bends our thinking and disorders our desires. God gives truth and strength so we can see clearly, choose wisely, and grow in new wants.

CHAPTER 5

HUMAN WORTH AND DIGNITY AFTER THE FALL

After sin entered the world, something stayed true. People are still made by God, and people still matter. The fall damaged the human heart, but it did not erase human worth. This matters because the world often measures value the wrong way. It measures value by strength, beauty, health, money, influence, or usefulness. God does not measure people that way.

Human dignity rests on God's decision to create humans and to set His mark on them. Even in a broken world, God treats human life as weighty. Proverbs 22:2 says, "The rich and the poor meet together; the Lord is the Maker of them all" (NSV). That verse places rich and poor on the same ground. Both are made by God. Both answer to God. Both have worth that money cannot raise or lower.

This truth protects people who are easily pushed aside. It protects the poor, the unborn, the sick, the elderly, the disabled, the refugee, and the forgotten. It also corrects pride in those who feel secure. If you have wealth, health, or status, those gifts do not make you more human than others. If you lack those things, that lack does not make you less human than others.

Human dignity also reshapes how we treat people we dislike. It is easy to respect those who agree with you. It is harder to respect those who offend you or oppose you. But Scripture calls us to treat people with care because they are God's creatures, even when they are wrong, even when they are difficult. This does not mean we excuse sin. It means we refuse to treat people as trash.

The fall did not erase human value, but it did affect how we see ourselves and others. One of the first fruits of sin is shame. Shame makes a person feel dirty, unwanted, or beyond help. Shame whispers, "You are what you did," or "You are what happened to you." But Scripture separates a person's worth from their worst moment. God's Word is honest about sin, yet it still speaks of human dignity.

Psalm 139:14 says, "I praise you, for I am fearfully and wonderfully made" (NSV). This does not mean every person feels wonderful. It means God's workmanship is real. Your life is not random. Your body and your days are known to God. This truth does not remove pain, but it gives a stable base for identity.

Human dignity also shapes how we view justice. In Job 31:15, Job asks, "Did not he who made me in the womb make him?" (NSV). Job uses creation to argue for fair treatment. He is saying, "God made both of us, so I must not crush another person." That is a strong moral line. The worth of a person is not decided by power. It is decided by God.

In Acts 17:26, Scripture says God "made from one man every nation of mankind" (NSV). This truth confronts racial pride and ethnic hatred. It tells us that humans share a common origin. Differences in culture, language, and appearance do not change shared dignity. Racism is not only a social problem. It is a sin against the God who made people.

Human dignity after the fall also changes how we view suffering. Some people assume suffering means God has rejected them. Others assume suffering means they are worthless. Scripture does not teach that. Many faithful people suffered deeply. Suffering can come through living in a fallen world, through the sin of others, through our own sinful choices, or through trials God uses to shape us. But suffering does not cancel dignity. A wounded person is still a person. A struggling person is still valuable.

This also matters for how we speak. Words can cut a person down to size. They can label someone as hopeless. They can reduce a person to a failure, an addiction, or a diagnosis. But God does not speak that way. He speaks truth, yet He also speaks with purpose. He calls sinners to repent, and He also offers mercy to the humble.

Still, we need balance. Saying every person has dignity does not mean every choice is good. The Bible can affirm human worth while also calling sin sin. A person is valuable even when their behavior is evil. If we forget this, we will either become harsh and cruel, or we will become soft and approving. Scripture calls us to a better path: compassion without compromise.

A clear example is how Jesus treated people who were ignored or despised. He did not treat them like props. He listened. He spoke truth. He showed mercy. He also called people to change. Luke 19:10 says the Son of Man came to seek and to save the lost (NSV). That line holds both truths. People are lost, and people are worth seeking.

This is also where Christian hope becomes practical. If God values people, then Christians must value people. That includes protecting life, speaking with care, and refusing to use others for personal gain. It also includes doing good to those who cannot pay you back, and treating the weak as neighbors, not burdens.

Human dignity after the fall also speaks to your view of yourself. Many people swing between pride and despair. Pride says, "I am above others." Despair says, "I am beyond help." Both forget God. A biblical view says, "I am a creature made by God. I am fallen and I need mercy. Yet I have real worth because God made me and God calls me to Himself."

So what do you do with shame and self-hate? You bring them into the light of truth. You name sin where it exists. You do not excuse it. But you also refuse to let sin define your whole identity. In Christ, God forgives and restores. He calls you His own. That does not erase consequences, but it does change your standing before Him.

Human worth also shapes how you handle conflict. If the person in front of you has dignity, you must speak with restraint. You can disagree without contempt. You can correct without cruelty. You can set boundaries without hatred. You can pursue justice without dehumanizing the wrongdoer.

This chapter is meant to steady you. The fall explains why we are broken. But dignity explains why humans are still precious and why love and justice still matter. If you hold both truths together, you can see people clearly. You will not flatter humanity as if sin is small. You also will not crush humanity as if grace is impossible. You will treat people as God's creatures who need truth, mercy, and hope.

1) Scripture Reading and Notes

Read each passage. Write in your journal one observation from each.

1. Proverbs 22:2 (NSV)

____

____

2. Psalm 139:13–16 (NSV)

____

____

3. Job 31:15 (NSV)

____

____

4. Acts 17:26 (NSV)

____

____

5. Luke 19:10 (NSV)

____

____

6. Matthew 25:40 (NSV)

____

____

2) Define Dignity

Write in your journal a simple definition in your own words.

Human dignity means:

____

____

____

____

____

____

Now write one sentence about what dignity does not depend on.

Human dignity does not depend on:

____

____

____

____

3) Identify False Measures of Worth

Circle or copy any that you struggle with. Then answer the questions.

Common false measures: money, success, grades, appearance, strength, health, marriage, children, popularity, productivity.

1. Which false measure pulls you the most?

2. When did you start believing that measure mattered most?

3. What truth from today's passages corrects it?

4) How You Treat Others

Think of one person you tend to dismiss, ignore, or speak about harshly.

1. What makes it hard for you to honor them?

2. What does Matthew 25:40 teach you about how God views "the least"?

----

3. What is one respectful action you will take this week?

----

5) Dignity and Conflict

Write short answers.

1. When you disagree with someone, what words do you often want to use?

----

2. What would it look like to correct without contempt?

----

3. Write one sentence you can use in conflict that shows both truth and respect.

----

6) Shame Check

Answer honestly.

1. What is one shame message you hear in your mind?

----

2. Is that message true, partly true, or false? Explain in one or two sentences.

    ----

3. Replace the shame message with a truth statement from Psalm 139 or Luke 19:10.

    ----

7) Practice Seeing People Clearly

Choose one group that often gets overlooked in your life or community.

Group:

Write one way you can show practical care in the next seven days.

My plan:

Prayer Response

Write a short prayer. If you need help, begin here and finish it.

Father, You are the Maker of every person.

Forgive me for measuring worth by ____________________________ .

Help me treat others with honor, even when it is hard.

Free me from shame that is not from You.

____

____

Teach me to see people as You see them.

____

____

Amen.

Key Takeaway

The fall damaged humanity, but it did not erase human worth. Every person still has dignity because God made them. This truth shapes how you view yourself and how you treat others.

CHAPTER 6

LIVING AS GOD'S IMAGE BEARERS TODAY

The Bible's teaching about humanity is not meant to stay on paper. It is meant to shape daily life. If people are made in God's image, then life has direction. It also has boundaries. Being an image bearer is both a gift and a calling. It means you belong to God. It means your life is meant to reflect Him in the world.

Living as God's image bearer today begins with identity. Many people try to build identity from achievement, approval, comfort, or control. But these things are unstable. They can be taken away. They also can become idols that rule the heart. A stable identity comes from the Creator. You are a creature made by God, not a self-made project. This truth brings humility and peace at the same time.

It also brings responsibility. Image bearers represent God's character in how they live. This does not mean you will reflect God perfectly. Sin still clings. But it does mean you should seek to reflect God truly. Scripture calls believers to grow in holiness and truth because they belong to the Holy God.

One key area is how you use words. Words reveal the heart. Proverbs 18:21 says death and life are in the power of the tongue (NSV). Image-bearing speech is honest, restrained, and aimed at the good of others. It refuses gossip. It refuses cruel humor. It refuses the half-truth meant to protect yourself. It also refuses flattery that hides fear. Instead, it speaks truth with care.

Another key area is how you treat people. Since every person is made by God, you do not have permission to treat anyone as less than human. This includes people you disagree with. It includes people who have harmed you. It includes people who cannot help you. Living as an image bearer means you practice respect, patience, and justice. You do not excuse sin, but you refuse to dehumanize sinners.

This is also where love becomes practical. 1 John 4:20 says if someone claims to love God but hates his brother, he is a liar (NSV). That is strong language. It shows that love for God is tested by how we treat people. Love is not just a warm feeling. It is a pattern of choices that seek another person's good.

Living as God's image bearer today also shapes how you handle your body. Your body is not a toy and not a god. It is a gift. It is also a trust. What you do with your body matters. This includes sexuality, health, rest, and self-control. Many people treat the body as if it belongs to them alone. Scripture teaches you belong to God. That truth leads to wise boundaries and pure living.

Your work also matters. Work is one way image bearers reflect God's order and care. Whether your work is paid or unpaid, it is part of your calling. Honest work is a form of love. It provides. It serves. It builds. It blesses others. It also trains integrity. Even small tasks can be done with faithfulness.

Living as God's image bearer today also means practicing stewardship. God gives resources, then calls you to use them with wisdom. That includes time, money, attention, and energy. Many people waste life by drifting from one distraction to the next. Wisdom says, "My life is not my own. God gave me days, so I will use them well."

This is also how image bearers respond to culture. Some people blend in and let culture shape them. Others fight culture with anger and pride. But Scripture calls believers to be distinct with humility. Living as an image bearer means you test what you hear and see. You do not accept every message. You also do not become bitter and harsh. You stay grounded in truth, and you practice love.

This includes how you use technology. Technology is a tool. It can help you learn, work, connect, and serve. It can also steal attention, feed lust, stir anger, and build envy. An image bearer should not be ruled by a screen. Wisdom sets limits and chooses what builds up.

Living as God's image bearer today also includes responding to sin in your own life. You will fail at times. The question is not whether you will ever sin again. The question is what you do when you sin. Image-bearing life includes confession, repentance, and renewal. You do not hide. You do not blame. You bring your sin to God. You seek forgiveness. You make changes. You pursue accountability. This is how growth happens.

One more key part is hope. Many people look at the world and feel hopeless. They see violence, corruption, and division. But Scripture teaches that God is at work and will complete His plan. Your faithfulness matters even when the world feels dark. A faithful life is not wasted. God sees it. God uses it. God rewards it.

So how do you begin?

Start with one area. Choose your words, your habits, your relationships, your time. Ask God to help you live as His image bearer in daily choices. Big change often begins with small obedience done consistently.

Living as God's image bearer today is not about showing off. It is about reflecting God with a steady life. It is about honoring Him in the ordinary. It is about loving people in real ways. It is about standing in truth with humility. It is about walking in repentance and hope.

This chapter closes Book Two with a simple aim. You were made to reflect God. Sin damaged that reflection. In Christ, God renews His people. As you live with faith and obedience, the reflection grows clearer.

Workbook Section

1) Scripture Reading and Notes

Read each passage. Write in your journal one observation.

1. Proverbs 18:21 (NSV)

   ____

   ____

2. 1 John 4:20 (NSV)

   ____

   ____

3. Micah 6:8 (NSV)

   ____

   ____

4. Colossians 3:12–14 (NSV)

----

5. Romans 12:2 (NSV)

----

6. Ephesians 4:29 (NSV)

----

2) Image Bearer Inventory

Rate yourself from 1 to 5.

1 = weak right now, 5 = strong right now.

Words that build others up:	1	2	3	4	5
Patience with difficult people:	1	2	3	4	5
Honesty and integrity:	1	2	3	4	5
Use of time and attention:	1	2	3	4	5
Self-control in habits:	1	2	3	4	5

Now answer:

1. Which area needs the most attention?

----

2. Which area is a strength you should thank God for?

----

3) Words Practice

Use Ephesians 4:29.

1. Write one kind of speech you need to stop.

    Examples: sarcasm, gossip, harshness, exaggeration.

    ----

2. Write one sentence you can use instead that gives grace.

    ----

3. Who is one person you will encourage this week?

    ----

4) People Practice

Choose one difficult relationship.

1. What is one way you have been tempted to treat this person as less than human?

    ----

2. What does 1 John 4:20 call you to do differently?

    ----

3. What is one respectful action you will take in the next seven days?

    ----

5) Culture and Mind Renewal

Romans 12:2 calls believers not to be shaped by the world.

1. What message from culture most pressures you?

   Examples: "You are what you achieve," "Do what feels right," "Get even."

   ----

2. What truth from Scripture replaces it?

   ----

3. What is one boundary you can set to protect your mind this week?

   ----

6) Stewardship Plan

Write short answers.

1. One time-waster I need to reduce is:

   ----

2. One habit that helps me focus on what matters is:

   ----

3. One act of service I will do this week is:

Write a prayer of daily faithfulness. If you need help, begin here and finish it.

Father, You made me to reflect You.

Forgive me for the ways I have failed in my words and choices.

Help me live as Your image bearer today by_____________________ .

Teach me to love others with truth and patience.

Renew my mind and strengthen my self-control.

Amen.

Key Takeaway

Living as God's image bearer today means reflecting God in ordinary life. It shows up in words, relationships, habits, and choices. God helps His people grow in a clearer reflection through truth, repentance, and daily faithfulness.

BOOK THREE

GRASP HOW SALVATION REALLY WORKS

Salvation is not self-help and it is not something we earn. It is God's rescue for sinners through Jesus Christ. This book will help you see the Bible's full picture of salvation, from God's first move toward us to the new life He produces in us. You will study Christ's saving work, what repentance and faith mean, why justification matters, how growth in holiness happens, and how God gives real assurance. Each chapter includes clear teaching and guided questions so you can understand the gospel more clearly and respond with worship, trust, and obedience.

CHAPTER 1

SALVATION BEGINS WITH GOD'S INITIATIVE

Teaching Section

Many people think salvation begins when a person decides to seek God. The Bible shows a deeper truth. Salvation begins with God seeking the sinner. If God did not move first, no one would come. This is not because people lack the ability to read or learn. It is because sin bends the heart away from God.

Ephesians 2:1 says we were dead in trespasses and sins (NSV). Dead people do not rescue themselves. They do not reach for help. They need life given to them. This verse is meant to humble us, not crush us. It tells the truth about our condition so we will see the greatness of grace.

God's initiative shows up in three clear ways: His choice, His call, and His gift of new life.

First, God chooses. Scripture teaches that God's saving plan is not an emergency fix. It is eternal and intentional. 2 Timothy 1:9 says God saved us and called us, not because of our works, but because of His own purpose and grace, given in Christ before time began (NSV). That means grace is not God reacting to you. Grace is God acting from His own will, according to His own plan.

This does not mean humans are robots. People make real choices. People really believe, really repent, and really follow. But behind that response is God's gracious work. Salvation begins with God, not with human effort.

Second, God calls. John 6:44 says no one can come to Christ unless the Father draws him (NSV). That drawing is not a gentle suggestion that can be ignored without consequence. It is God bringing a person to Himself through truth and the Spirit's work. God uses means like preaching, Scripture reading, a conversation, a warning, or a crisis. The outward moment can look ordinary, but God is doing something deeper.

We see a clear example in Acts 16:14. A woman named Lydia listened to Paul, and the text says the Lord opened her heart to pay attention to what was said (NSV). Lydia heard real words. She used her mind. She responded. Yet Scripture gives the credit to God's work in her heart. That is what divine initiative looks like. God makes the message effective.

Third, God gives new life. Ezekiel 36:26 says God gives a new heart and a new spirit (NSV). He does not simply offer advice or moral improvement. He changes what is inside. He takes a heart of stone and gives a heart of flesh. A stone heart is cold and stubborn. A flesh heart is living and responsive. This new heart is what makes repentance real and faith possible.

If salvation begins with God's initiative, then what is our part?

Our part is to respond to God's call with repentance and faith. God does not save people against their will. He changes the will so the person willingly comes to Christ. The sinner who once loved darkness begins to love the light. The person who once resisted truth begins to receive it. This response is real, personal, and necessary. Yet it is also a gift of grace.

Ephesians 2:8–9 says we are saved by grace through faith, and this is not our own doing (NSV). The whole rescue is God's gift. This removes boasting. No one can say, "I saved myself." It also removes despair. If salvation depended on your strength, you would lose it. If it depends on God's mercy, you can rest in His faithfulness.

God's initiative also shows His character. He is not a reluctant Savior. He is not waiting for sinners to prove they are worth saving. Romans 5:8 says God shows His love in that Christ died for us while we were still sinners (NSV). God loved us at our worst, not after we cleaned ourselves up.

This truth also answers a common fear. Some people think, "I want God, but I do not know if He wants me." Scripture answers that fear with clarity. God invites sinners. He commands repentance. He promises mercy to those who come. Jesus says whoever comes to Him, He will never cast out (John 6:37, NSV). God's initiative does not cancel human responsibility. It gives hope that your coming is not pointless.

God's initiative also changes how we talk about salvation. We do not treat salvation as a product for self-improvement. We do not treat it as a reward for good behavior. We treat it as rescue for helpless sinners. We also treat it as adoption into God's family, not a cold legal transaction alone.

It also changes how we pray for others. If salvation depends on God's work, then prayer is not a last resort. Prayer is a natural response. We ask God to open eyes, soften hearts, and give repentance. We speak the gospel, and we also pray that God will make it fruitful.

God's initiative changes how we view our past, too. Many believers look back and see a trail of sin and regret. They think, "How could God ever want me?" But if salvation starts with God's purpose and grace, then your past does not surprise Him. It does not excuse sin, but it does show the depth of mercy. God is not saving the most impressive people. He is saving sinners.

This truth should produce humility. If God moved first, you cannot look down on others. You cannot treat unbelievers as if you are naturally better. You were dead too. You were blind too. God showed mercy. That mercy should make you patient and compassionate with others.

This truth should also produce confidence. If God began the work, He will not abandon it. He does not start what He cannot finish. When doubts come, you can look away from your performance and look to God's promise.

So here is the main point of this chapter: salvation begins with God's initiative. He plans, He calls, and He gives new life. Our response matters, but it rests on His grace. That truth makes worship deeper, prayer stronger, and hope steadier.

Workbook Section

1) Scripture Reading and Notes

Read each passage. Write one clear truth you learn from it.

1. Ephesians 2:1 (NSV)

----

2. 2 Timothy 1:9 (NSV)

____

____

3. John 6:44 (NSV)

____

____

4. Acts 16:14 (NSV)

____

____

5. Ezekiel 36:26 (NSV)

____

____

6. Ephesians 2:8-9 (NSV)

____

____

7. Romans 5:8 (NSV)

____

____

8. John 6:37 (NSV)

____

____

2) Put It in Your Own Words

Complete these sentences with simple language.

1. Salvation begins with God because:

____

____

____

2. God's call is needed because:

____

____

____

3. A new heart is needed because:

Now write one sentence that explains how this teaching guards you from pride.

My sentence:

Write one sentence that explains how it guards you from despair.

My sentence:

----

3) Trace Your Story

Think back to how you first began to take God seriously. If you do not know Christ yet, answer using what you have seen or heard in your life.

1. What circumstances brought the gospel close to you?

    Examples: a person, a sermon, a Bible reading, a crisis, a quiet season.

    ----

2. What truth began to press on your heart?

    ----

3. What changed in your desires or thinking over time?

    ----

4. Where do you see God's initiative in your story?

----

4) Check Your Assumptions

Choose the statement that sounds most like you, then write a response based on today's passages.

A. "God helps those who help themselves."

B. "I am too far gone for God to want me."

C. "I found God because I was smarter or more serious."

D. "If God is the one who begins salvation, my choices do not matter."

My statement:

Now correct it using one verse from the list above.

Verse and correction:

----

5) Prayer for Someone Who Does Not Believe

Pick one person you care about. Do not write their name if you prefer privacy.

1. What makes you burdened for this person?

----

2. What is one obstacle you see in their life?

----

3. Based on Acts 16:14 and Ezekiel 36:26, what should you ask God to do?

Write a short prayer of intercession:

Father, please work in this person's heart.

Open their mind to Your truth.

Give them a new heart that responds to Christ.

Use Your Word to draw them to Jesus.

Amen.

6) Respond With Gratitude and Obedience

Answer with concrete steps.

1. If salvation is a gift, what is one way you will thank God today?

---

2. What is one habit that helps you stay close to God's Word?

---

3. What is one small act of obedience you will do this week as a response to grace?

Prayer Response

Write a prayer of humility. If you need help, complete these lines.

Lord, I confess that I often want credit for what only You can do.

Thank You for taking the first step toward me.

Thank You for grace that I did not earn.

Help me respond with faith, repentance, and steady obedience.

Amen.

Key Takeaway

Salvation begins with God's initiative. He plans with purpose, calls with power, and gives new life by grace. Our response is real, but it rests on what God has done first.

CHAPTER 2

CHRIST'S WORK SECURES OUR SALVATION

Salvation is not built on what we do. It is built on what Christ has done. If your peace depends on your performance, you will always feel unsure. But if your peace rests on Christ's finished work, you can stand on firm ground.

The Bible teaches that Jesus did not come only to teach. He came to save. He lived a life of perfect obedience, died a real death in our place, and rose from the dead. His work is complete and effective. It does not need to be improved by human effort. It needs to be received by faith.

To understand Christ's work, we need to see why it was necessary.

God is holy. God is just. Sin is not a small problem. It is rebellion against God. Because God is just, sin must be judged. Because God is merciful, He provides a Savior. The cross is where God's justice and mercy meet.

1 Peter 2:24 says, "He himself bore our sins in his body on the tree" (NSV). That sentence is clear. Christ carried our sins. He bore the weight of guilt and judgment. He did not die as a victim of bad politics only. He died as a substitute. He took what we deserved.

This is often called substitution. Substitution means one person stands in the place of another. If Christ did not stand in our place, we would still stand under God's judgment. But Christ took the penalty so that sinners who trust Him can be forgiven.

Isaiah 53:5 says He was pierced for our transgressions and crushed for our iniquities (NSV). That passage shows the same truth. Christ suffered for sins that were not His. He was not paying for His own guilt. He was paying for ours.

Christ's work also includes His obedient life. Jesus did not only die. He lived in perfect faithfulness. He obeyed the Father in every thought, word, and action. Where Adam failed, Christ obeyed. Romans 5:19 says, "By the one man's obedience the many will be made righteous" (NSV). Christ's obedience counts for those who belong to Him. This is part of what it means to be saved by grace.

Christ's work is also a sacrifice. Ephesians 5:2 says Christ loved us and gave Himself up for us, a fragrant offering to God (NSV). In the Old Testament, sacrifices pointed forward. They showed that sin requires death and that God provides a way for guilt to be covered. Those sacrifices were limited. They were repeated. They could not change the heart. But Christ's sacrifice is final and sufficient.

Hebrews 10:12 says Christ offered one sacrifice for sins forever, then sat down at the right hand of God (NSV). Sitting down shows completion. Priests stood daily because their work was never finished. Christ sat down because His saving work was done.

Christ's work also includes redemption. Redemption means being bought back. Sin enslaves. It binds people through guilt and corrupt desires. Christ paid the price to free His people. Mark 10:45 says the Son of Man came to give His life as a ransom for many (NSV). A ransom is a payment that sets someone free. Christ's blood is that payment.

Christ's work also includes reconciliation. Sin breaks fellowship with God. It creates distance and hostility. But Christ brings peace. Colossians 1:20 says God made peace by the blood of His cross (NSV). Peace with God does not come from trying harder. It comes through Christ removing the barrier of guilt.

Then there is the resurrection. If Jesus stayed dead, we would have no hope. The resurrection is God's public declaration that Christ's sacrifice was accepted. It shows Christ has conquered death. It also guarantees that believers will be raised. 1 Corinthians 15:20 says Christ has been raised as the firstfruits of those who have fallen asleep (NSV). Firstfruits means the first part of a harvest that promises the rest will follow. Christ's resurrection is the promise of our resurrection.

The resurrection also proves Christ is Lord. Romans 1:4 says He was declared to be the Son of God in power by His resurrection (NSV). That does not mean He became God then. It means His identity was shown with power and clarity.

So how does Christ's work secure salvation?

It secures salvation because it deals with the real problem. The real problem is guilt before a holy God. The cross deals with guilt. The real problem is death and separation. The resurrection deals with death. The real problem is bondage to sin. Christ's ransom frees. The real problem is hostility with God. Christ reconciles.

This also means salvation is not fragile. If Christ's work is complete, then the foundation does not shift with your feelings. You can have weak faith and still have a strong Savior. Your faith is not the power. Christ is the power. Faith is the hand that receives Him.

Still, this teaching must be held with care. Some people hear "Christ did it all" and think obedience does not matter. But the Bible never uses grace to excuse sin. It uses grace to change sinners. 1 Peter 2:24 says Christ bore our sins so that we might die to sin and live to righteousness (NSV). Salvation produces a new direction.

Christ's work also leads to worship. When you see the cost of your redemption, pride dies. Gratitude grows. When you see the mercy of God, fear of earning fades. Love and obedience rise.

This chapter is meant to steady your heart. When you feel accused, look to the cross. When you feel hopeless, look to the empty tomb. When you feel trapped, look to the ransom Christ paid. Salvation is secure because Christ's work is secure.

Workbook Section

1) Scripture Reading and Notes

Read each passage. Write one clear truth about Christ's work.

1. 1 Peter 2:24 (NSV)

    ____

    ____

2. Isaiah 53:5 (NSV)

    ____

    ____

3. Romans 5:19 (NSV)

    ____

    ____

4. Ephesians 5:2 (NSV)

5. Hebrews 10:12 (NSV)

6. Mark 10:45 (NSV)

7. Colossians 1:20 (NSV)

8. 1 Corinthians 15:20 (NSV)

2) Put the Gospel in One Paragraph

Write 4 to 6 sentences that explain what Christ did to save sinners. Keep it simple.

My paragraph:

3) Substitution and the Cross

Answer with your own words.

1. What does it mean that Christ "bore our sins"?

2. Why is substitution necessary if God is just?

----

3. What happens if you remove substitution from the gospel?

----

4) Finished Work Check

Hebrews 10:12 says Christ sat down after offering one sacrifice.

1. What does "finished" mean in this context?

----

2. Where are you tempted to add your own efforts to Christ's work?

   Examples: trying to earn forgiveness, trying to deserve love, fear-based performance.

----

3. What truth from today's passages corrects that fear?

----

5) The Resurrection and Hope

Answer with short, clear sentences.

1. Why does the resurrection matter for forgiveness?

----

2. What does "firstfruits" tell you about your future?

----

3. How should resurrection hope shape the way you face suffering?

----

6) Application: From Gratitude to Obedience

Use 1 Peter 2:24.

1. What is one sin pattern you need to "die to"?

----

2. What is one righteous habit you want to practice instead?

----

3. What is one small step you will take in the next 48 hours?

Prayer Response

Write a prayer of thanks. If you need help, complete these lines.

Lord Jesus, thank You for bearing my sins.

Thank You for Your obedience and Your sacrifice.

Thank You that Your work is complete and enough.

Help me die to sin and live to righteousness as a response to Your mercy.

Amen.

Christ's obedient life, atoning death, and resurrection secure salvation. His work is complete, and it gives real peace to sinners who trust Him.

CHAPTER 3

FAITH AND REPENTANCE ARE BOTH REQUIRED

The Bible teaches that salvation is a gift of grace, received through faith. It also teaches that a saved person turns from sin. These two responses belong together. Faith and repentance are not competing ideas. They are two sides of one response to the gospel.

Jesus began His public preaching with a clear call: "Repent and believe in the gospel" (Mark 1:15, NSV). Notice the order and the pairing. Repent and believe. Not repent without believing. Not believe without repenting. The gospel calls you to trust Christ and to turn from sin.

Faith means trusting Jesus Christ as Savior and Lord. Faith is not mere agreement with facts. It is personal reliance. It is resting your hope on Christ, not on yourself. Romans 10:9 says if you confess with your mouth that Jesus is Lord and believe in your heart that God raised Him from the dead, you will be saved (NSV). Faith involves the heart and the life. It includes believing and confessing.

Faith also means you stop trying to earn God's acceptance. You stop presenting your record as if it could save you. You come empty-handed. You receive Christ as your only hope. Faith is not a work that earns salvation. Faith is the open hand that receives a gift.

Repentance means turning away from sin and turning to God. It includes a change of mind, a change of direction, and a change in what you love. In Acts 2, Peter preached Christ. The people were cut to the heart and asked what they should do. Peter answered, "Repent and be baptized" (Acts 2:38, NSV). He did not offer them a way to fix themselves. He called them to turn from sin and to come to Christ.

Repentance is often misunderstood. Some people think repentance means paying for sin through shame. Others think repentance means promising God you will never fail again. Scripture presents a better picture. Repentance is honest turning. It is agreeing with God about sin and turning away from it because you trust God's mercy.

2 Corinthians 7:10 says godly grief produces repentance that leads to salvation without regret, while worldly grief produces death (NSV). That verse helps us see the difference between true repentance and mere regret.

Worldly grief is sadness because of consequences. It says, "I got caught," or "I ruined my life," or "I look bad." It may feel intense, but it often stays self-focused. It can lead to despair, bitterness, or more sin.

Godly grief is sorrow that begins with God. It says, "I have sinned against the Lord." It takes responsibility. It does not blame others. It does not excuse. It does not hide behind weak apologies. It turns toward God, trusting His mercy, and it produces change over time.

Repentance also does not mean you clean yourself up before coming to Christ. You repent by coming. You do not fix your heart first, then come. You come with your sin, confess it, and ask God to change you. Repentance is not a price you pay. It is the posture of a person who knows they need grace.

Some people worry that repentance adds works to the gospel. It does not. Repentance does not earn forgiveness. Christ earns forgiveness. Repentance is the right response to forgiveness offered. If someone says they trust Christ but refuses to turn from known sin, their claim is empty. A person cannot cling to rebellion and claim loyalty to Jesus at the same time.

This is why faith and repentance must stay together. Faith without repentance becomes empty words. Repentance without faith becomes self-salvation. Faith says, "Christ is my hope." Repentance says, "Sin is not my master." Both are part of turning to God.

True faith always leads to a changed direction, even if growth is slow. When the heart truly trusts Christ, it begins to hate what God hates and love what God loves. That does not mean instant perfection. It means a new path.

Repentance also continues throughout the Christian life. It is not only the first step. Believers still fight sin. Believers still need confession. Believers still need to turn from wrong desires and wrong habits. The difference is that repentance now happens within a relationship of grace. You do not repent to become God's child. You repent because you are God's child.

Here is a simple way to remember it:

- Faith looks to Christ.

- Repentance turns from sin.

- Both responses happen as you come to God.

This chapter also helps with assurance. Some people look for assurance only in feelings. Feelings rise and fall. Scripture points you to Christ's work and to the fruit of a changed life. If you trust Christ and your life shows a growing pattern of turning from sin, that is evidence of real faith. If you claim faith but love sin without resistance, that should warn you.

At the same time, repentance should not become self-hate. Some people confess sin with no hope. They stay stuck in shame. Godly repentance leads to life. It leads to honesty, humility, and change. It also leads to deeper joy because it brings you back into the light.

A steady gospel response is not complicated. You turn from sin and you trust Christ. You do not save yourself. You come to the One who saves. You do not bargain. You do not pretend. You come with honest confession and true reliance.

So the main point is this: faith and repentance are both required because the gospel is a call to receive Christ and to leave sin. Christ does not only forgive. He also leads. When you come to Him, you come to a Savior and a Lord.

Workbook Section

1) Scripture Reading and Notes

Read each passage. Write one clear truth from each.

1. Mark 1:15 (NSV)

   ----

2. Romans 10:9 (NSV)

   ----

3. Acts 2:37–38 (NSV)

----

4. 2 Corinthians 7:10 (NSV)

----

5. Luke 13:3 (NSV)

----

6. Acts 20:21 (NSV)

----

2) Define the Terms

Write simple definitions in your own words.

Faith is:

Repentance is:

Now write one sentence that explains why they belong together.

They belong together because:

----

3) Worldly Grief or Godly Grief

Use 2 Corinthians 7:10. Think of a time you felt sorry about a wrong choice.

1. What were you most upset about at first?

----

2. Did you focus more on consequences or on sin against God?

    ____

    ____

    ____

3. What did your sorrow produce?

    Examples: excuses, hiding, anger, confession, change, seeking help.

    ____

    ____

    ____

4. What would godly grief look like in a similar situation next time?

    ____

    ____

    ____

4) Faith Check

Romans 10:9 connects belief and confession.

1. Write one sentence that states who Jesus is to you.

    ____

    ____

    ____

2. Write one sentence that states what you are trusting Him for.

    ____

    ____

    ____

3. Write one sentence that shows what you are no longer trusting for acceptance with God.

    Examples: good works, church attendance, being "better than others."

    ____

    ____

    ____

5) Repentance in Real Life

Choose one area where you need to turn from sin. Keep it specific.

1. The sin pattern is:

   ----

2. The common trigger is:

   ----

3. The lie I tend to believe is:

   ----

4. The truth from today's passages that corrects the lie is:

   ----

5. One change I will make this week is:

   ----

6) Two-Part Response Plan

Write a short plan that includes both faith and repentance.

Faith step: One way I will look to Christ daily this week is:

Repentance step: One way I will turn from sin daily this week is:

Add one support step.

Support step: One person I can ask to pray for me or check in with me is:

----

7) Confession Practice

Write a short confession that is clear and direct. Avoid vague words like "mistakes."

I have sinned by:

I was wrong because:

____

____

I ask God to forgive me through Christ because:

____

____

I will take this step of change:

____

____

Prayer Response

Write a short prayer. If you need help, use these lines and complete them.

Lord Jesus, I turn from my sin and I turn to You.

____

____

I trust You as my Savior and my Lord.

____

____

Forgive me for ____ .

Give me strength to walk in a new direction, starting with ________ .

____

Thank You for mercy that is real and free.

____

____

Amen.

Key Takeaway

Faith receives Christ. Repentance turns from sin. Both belong together as the gospel response, because Christ saves sinners and leads them into a new way of life.

CHAPTER 4

JUSTIFIED BY FAITH ALONE

Teaching Section

Many people think salvation means God helps good people become better. The Bible teaches something more shocking and more hopeful. God justifies sinners. To justify means God declares a person righteous in His court. It is a legal verdict. It is not God pretending you never sinned. It is God counting you as righteous because of Jesus Christ.

Romans 3:24 says people are "justified by his grace as a gift, through the redemption that is in Christ Jesus" (NSV). Notice the words grace and gift. Justification is not payment for good behavior. It is God's free act toward those who do not deserve it.

This raises a question. How can a just God declare guilty people righteous? Romans 3:26 answers it by showing what Christ did. God is "just and the justifier of the one who has faith in Jesus" (NSV). God remains just because sin is truly judged. God can justify because Jesus took the penalty and provided perfect righteousness.

Justification is connected to Christ in two ways.

First, Christ's death removes guilt. Romans 4:25 says Jesus was delivered up for our trespasses and raised for our justification (NSV). His death deals with the charge against us. His resurrection confirms the verdict.

Second, Christ's obedience provides righteousness. God does not justify by lowering His standard. His standard is perfect righteousness. The good news is that Christ met that standard. When you trust Him, God counts Christ's righteousness to you. This is why justification brings peace. It does not rest on your best day. It rests on Christ.

Galatians 2:16 says a person is not justified by works of the law but through faith in Jesus Christ (NSV). This verse is direct. Works cannot justify. Law-keeping cannot justify. Even religious effort cannot justify. Faith is the means God uses, because faith looks away from self and toward Christ.

Faith is not a good deed that earns a reward. Faith is reliance. It is resting your hope on Christ alone. Romans 4:5 says God justifies "the one who does not work but believes" (NSV). That verse does not praise laziness. It attacks pride. It says you cannot earn your verdict. You must receive it.

This is why the phrase "faith alone" matters. It does not mean faith is alone in the Christian life. True faith produces obedience over time. But faith alone is the only instrument of justification. Your works are not part of the basis for God's verdict. If they were, you would never have peace.

Justification also differs from sanctification. Justification is God's once-for-all verdict. It does not increase over time. You are either justified or not. Sanctification is the lifelong process of growth in holiness. It does increase over time. Many people confuse these two. When they sin, they think God's verdict has changed. But if you are justified, the verdict is settled.

This does not make sin harmless. Sin still grieves God and damages fellowship and joy. But sin does not overturn justification. A judge does not reverse a lawful verdict every time the adopted child stumbles. In Christ, the verdict stands. That truth helps you repent with hope instead of panic.

Justification also answers the question of boasting. If salvation is partly earned, people will compare themselves. They will feel proud or crushed. Romans 3:27 says boasting is excluded (NSV). Faith shuts the mouth of pride. It leaves room only for gratitude.

Justification also brings peace with God. Romans 5:1 says, "Since we have been justified by faith, we have peace with God through our Lord Jesus Christ" (NSV). Peace is not just a calm feeling. It is a real change in relationship. God is no longer against you as judge. He is for you as Father.

This truth changes how you face accusation. You may be accused by your own conscience. You may be accused by other people. You may even feel spiritual accusation. The answer is not to list your good deeds. The answer is to point to Christ. Your hope is not, "I did better." Your hope is, "Christ is enough."

This truth also changes how you treat others. If you were justified by grace, you cannot treat people with cold pride. You cannot look down on those who struggle. You can speak truth, but with patience. You can correct, but without contempt. You can forgive, because you were forgiven at great cost.

It also changes how you serve. You do not obey to earn God's love. You obey because you already have it in Christ. You serve out of gratitude, not fear. This makes service steadier. It also makes it more joyful.

Philippians 3:9 shows Paul's heart. He wanted to be found in Christ, not having a righteousness of his own, but the righteousness that comes through faith (NSV). That is the goal of every believer. Not self-righteousness, but Christ-righteousness. Not a shaky record, but a solid Savior.

So here is the main point. Justification is God's gracious verdict, given to sinners through faith in Jesus Christ. It is not earned by works. It is not improved by works. It produces peace, humility, and a life of grateful obedience.

Workbook Section

1) Scripture Reading and Notes

Read each passage. Write one clear truth about justification.

1. Romans 3:24 (NSV)

   ____

   ____

2. Romans 3:26 (NSV)

   ____

   ____

3. Galatians 2:16 (NSV)

   ____

   ____

4. Romans 4:5 (NSV)

   ____

   ____

5. Romans 4:25 (NSV)

6. Romans 5:1 (NSV)

7. Philippians 3:9 (NSV)

2) Define the Word

Write a simple definition.

Justification means:

Now write one sentence that explains what justification is not.

Justification is not:

3) Two Common Confusions

Answer in short sentences.

1. How is justification different from "God making me a better person"?

2. How is justification different from sanctification?

3. Why does mixing these up steal peace?

----

4) Replace Self-Talk With Truth

Write one sentence you say to yourself when you feel guilty or afraid.

My guilt sentence:

Now replace it with a truth statement based on Romans 5:1 or Romans 3:24.

My truth statement:

Write one sentence you can say out loud when you feel accused.

My spoken sentence:

----

5) Works and the Heart

Galatians 2:16 says works cannot justify.

1. Where are you tempted to "prove" yourself to God?
    Examples: being perfect, never failing, doing more, being noticed.

----

2. What fear is under that impulse?

----

3. What truth from today's passages answers that fear?

____

____

____

6) Peace With God Practice

Romans 5:1 speaks of peace with God.

1. What do you think God feels toward you on your worst day?

____

____

____

2. What does Romans 5:1 say is true if you are justified by faith?

____

____

____

3. How should that truth change the way you pray this week?

____

____

____

7) Gratitude Response

Write three short lines of gratitude that flow from being justified.

1. Thank You, Lord, for:

____

____

2. Thank You, Lord, for:

____

____

3. Thank You, Lord, for:

____

____

Now write one act of obedience you will do this week as a response to grace.

My act of obedience:

Write a prayer of trust. If you need help, complete these lines.

Father, thank You for justifying sinners by grace.

I stop trying to earn what Christ has already secured.

When I feel accused, help me rest in Your verdict.

Teach me to obey You out of gratitude, not fear.

Amen.

Key Takeaway

Justification is God's once-for-all verdict that a sinner is righteous in Christ. It is received by faith, not earned by works, and it brings real peace with God.

CHAPTER 5

SANCTIFIED FOR A NEW WAY OF LIFE

Teaching Section

God does not save people only to forgive them. He saves people to change them. This change is called sanctification. Sanctification is the process by which God makes His people more like Christ in real life. It is not instant perfection. It is steady growth. It is learning to put sin to death and to practice obedience from the heart.

1 Thessalonians 4:3 says, "This is the will of God, your sanctification" (NSV). That verse is simple. God's will for His people is not a mystery. He wants you to grow in holiness. Holiness means being set apart for God, living in a way that fits His character.

Sanctification is different from justification. Justification is God's verdict. It happens once. Sanctification is God's work of growth. It continues throughout your life. Justification changes your status. Sanctification changes your conduct. Both are gifts of grace, but they are not the same.

Sanctification begins with union with Christ. If you belong to Christ, you are joined to Him. That union is real. Romans 6:11 tells believers to consider themselves dead to sin and alive to God in Christ Jesus (NSV). That means your relationship to sin has changed. Sin is no longer your master. You still feel temptation. You still can fall. But you do not belong to sin anymore.

Sanctification also involves a real fight. Galatians 5:17 says the flesh desires what is against the Spirit, and the Spirit desires what is against the flesh (NSV). That conflict is part of the Christian life. Some believers feel discouraged by the fight. They think, "If I were really saved, I would not struggle." Scripture says the opposite. The struggle often shows that the Spirit is at work. A heart that is dead in sin does not fight sin. A living heart does.

God sanctifies His people through truth. John 17:17 says, "Sanctify them in the truth; your word is truth" (NSV). God uses Scripture to shape thinking, expose sin, and guide obedience. If you neglect God's Word, you will not grow well. You might still have religious activity, but your inner life will stay weak.

Sanctification also happens through daily choices. Romans 12:2 says believers are transformed by the renewal of the mind (NSV). The mind is renewed when you replace lies with truth, and when you practice thinking God's thoughts. This affects desires and habits over time.

Sanctification includes putting off sin and putting on righteousness. Ephesians 4:22-24 teaches this pattern. Put off the old self, be renewed, and put on the new self (NSV). This helps you think clearly about change. You do not only stop bad habits. You replace them with good habits. If you stop lying, you practice truth. If you stop bitterness, you practice forgiveness. If you stop lust, you pursue purity and wise boundaries. This is a practical pathway for growth.

Sanctification also includes discipline. Discipline is training, not punishment. Hebrews 12:10 says God disciplines us for our good, that we may share His holiness (NSV). God's discipline can include conviction, correction through Scripture, and hard lessons that expose idols. Discipline is proof of God's fatherly care. A loving father trains his children.

This is where many believers need balance. Some people treat sanctification as if it depends mainly on willpower. They try harder, fail, and then feel crushed. Others treat sanctification as if effort does not matter. They say, "God will change me if He wants," and they stay passive. Scripture calls you to active dependence. God works, and you work. Philippians 2:12-13 says work out your salvation with fear and trembling, for God is the one who works in you (NSV). That passage holds both truths. You do not grow without God. You also do not grow without effort.

Sanctification is also shaped by the church. God does not grow His people in isolation. He uses preaching, fellowship, correction, encouragement, and shared worship. Hebrews 10:24-25 calls believers to stir one another up to love and good works and not neglect meeting together (NSV). If you try to live the Christian life alone, you will be more vulnerable to sin and discouragement.

Sanctification also includes suffering. God uses trials to refine faith. James 1:2–4 says trials produce steadfastness, and steadfastness leads toward maturity (NSV). That does not mean suffering is pleasant. It means suffering is not wasted in God's hands. God can use hardship to expose pride, deepen prayer, and strengthen obedience.

Over time, sanctification produces fruit. You may not notice change day to day, but you can often see it over months and years. Growth may look like slower anger, quicker confession, more self-control, more patience, more love for Scripture, and more desire to serve others. Growth also includes learning to hate sin, not only because it has consequences, but because it dishonors God.

Sanctification does not mean you never fail. When you fail, you return to Christ. You confess sin. You ask for help. You make changes. You keep going. Proverbs 24:16 says the righteous falls seven times and rises again (NSV). That verse does not excuse sin. It describes persistence. God's people get up because God gives grace.

Sanctification also protects assurance. Not because your growth earns salvation, but because growth is evidence of life. If a tree is alive, it bears fruit in time. If a believer is alive in Christ, change will show. That change may be slow. It may be uneven. But it will be real.

So here is the main point. Sanctification is God's work of making His people holy in real life. It is a process that includes truth, effort, church life, discipline, and grace. You are not saved by your growth, but you are saved for growth. A new Savior leads to a new way of life.

Workbook Section

1) Scripture Reading and Notes

Read each passage. Write one clear truth about sanctification.

1. 1 Thessalonians 4:3 (NSV)

____

____

2. John 17:17 (NSV)

____

____

3. Romans 6:11 (NSV)

----

4. Philippians 2:12–13 (NSV)

----

5. Hebrews 12:10 (NSV)

----

6. Hebrews 10:24–25 (NSV)

----

7. James 1:2–4 (NSV)

----

2) Clarify the Difference

Write short answers.

1. Justification is:

----

2. Sanctification is:

----

3. Why does confusing them hurt your faith?

----

3) Identify One Growth Area

Choose one area where you want to grow. Keep it specific.

My growth area is:

Now answer:

1. What usually triggers this sin or weakness?

    ----

2. What lie do you tend to believe in that moment?

    ----

3. What truth from Scripture corrects that lie?

    ----

4) Put Off and Put On Plan

Use the pattern from Ephesians 4:22–24.

Put off: What must I stop or resist?

Put on: What must I practice instead?

Renew: What truth will I repeat to my mind?

Now write one action step you will take in the next 48 hours.

My action step: ____

----

5) Active Dependence

Philippians 2:12–13 shows you work because God works.

1. What does it look like for you to "work out" obedience in your growth area?

   ----

2. What does it look like for you to depend on God while you work?

   ----

3. Who can support you through prayer or accountability?

   ----

6) Church and Growth

Answer honestly.

1. How connected are you to a local church right now?

   ----

2. What is one way you can pursue stronger Christian community this month?

   ----

3. What is one fear that keeps you from being known by others?

   ----

7) Respond to Failure

Think of a time you failed recently.

1. What was your first response?

    Examples: hiding, excuses, anger, despair, confession.

    ----

2. What would a better response look like next time?

    ----

3. What is one step you can take to reduce the chance of repeat failure?

Prayer Response

Write a prayer for growth. If you need help, complete these lines.

Father, Your will is my sanctification.

Thank You that sin is not my master in Christ.

Use Your Word to change my mind and desires.

Help me put off sin and put on obedience in ____________________ .

Give me strength to persevere when growth feels slow.

Amen.

Sanctification is God's lifelong work of shaping His people into a new way of life. It is real growth in holiness that happens through truth, effort, community, and grace.

CHAPTER 6

ASSURANCE AND ENDURANCE IN SALVATION

Many believers struggle with fear. They wonder if God will keep them. They wonder if their faith is real. They look at their failures and feel unsure. The Bible speaks to these fears with both comfort and clarity. God gives assurance to His people, and God calls His people to endure.

Assurance means confidence that you belong to Christ. It is not arrogance. It is not pretending you never doubt. It is steady trust based on God's promises and God's work in you. Endurance means continuing in faith. It means staying with Christ over time, through temptation, suffering, and seasons of weakness.

Assurance begins with God's character. God does not lie. God keeps His word. Titus 1:2 says God never lies (NSV). If God promises salvation to those who trust His Son, that promise is sure. Your assurance is not first built on your strength. It is built on God's faithfulness.

Assurance also rests on what Christ has done. Hebrews 7:25 says Jesus is able to save completely those who draw near to God through Him, since He always lives to intercede for them (NSV). This is strong comfort. Christ does not save halfway. He saves completely. He also prays for His people. Your salvation is not guarded by your grip on Christ alone. It is guarded by Christ's grip on you.

John 10:28–29 teaches that Christ gives eternal life and that no one can snatch His sheep from His hand (NSV). The Father is greater than all. This does not mean believers never struggle. It means the final outcome is secure because God is strong.

Still, many believers have shaky assurance. Why?

Sometimes assurance is weak because a person has never understood the gospel clearly. They think salvation is based on Christ plus their performance. That will always lead to fear. Scripture teaches salvation is by grace through faith. Works follow as fruit, not as the foundation.

Sometimes assurance is weak because of ongoing, unconfessed sin. Sin clouds the heart. It steals joy. It makes prayer feel heavy. It also dulls the conscience. A believer can still be saved and yet feel far from God because they are resisting Him. Confession restores fellowship and strengthens assurance.

Sometimes assurance is weak because of suffering or depression. A person may feel numb. They may feel abandoned. But feelings are not the final judge of truth. Psalm 42 shows a believer speaking to his own soul, calling himself to hope in God. The Bible makes room for real sadness, yet it calls believers to hold to God's promises.

Sometimes assurance is weak because of a tender conscience. Some believers are quick to see sin and slow to accept grace. They look inward too much. They measure salvation by their emotions. They need to look outward to Christ's work and to God's promises.

So how does Scripture say we can grow in assurance?

First, by trusting God's promises. 1 John 5:13 says these things are written so believers may know they have eternal life (NSV). God wants His people to know. Assurance is not a rare luxury. It is a normal gift God intends for believers.

Second, by looking for the fruit of new life. 1 John often points to signs of real faith, like obedience, love for other believers, and a pattern of turning away from sin. These signs do not earn salvation. They show it. Fruit is evidence, not the root.

Third, by using the means God provides. God strengthens assurance through Scripture, prayer, fellowship, the preaching of the Word, and the Lord's Supper. When believers neglect these, assurance often fades. When believers practice these with sincerity, assurance often grows.

Now we must also talk about endurance.

Scripture calls believers to continue. Colossians 1:23 speaks of continuing in the faith, stable and steadfast (NSV). Hebrews gives repeated warnings not to harden the heart. These warnings are real. They are part of how God keeps His people. God uses warnings to wake believers up and pull them back from danger.

Some people get confused here. They hear about security and endurance and think the Bible is contradicting itself. It is not. Scripture teaches both: God keeps His people, and God's people keep following. Endurance is not proof that you saved yourself. Endurance is proof that God is sustaining you.

Philippians 1:6 says God will bring to completion the good work He began (NSV). That is God's promise. Jude 24 says God is able to keep you from stumbling and present you blameless (NSV). That is God's power. At the same time, Hebrews 12:1 calls believers to run with endurance (NSV). That is your calling.

Endurance looks ordinary most of the time. It looks like praying when you feel tired. It looks like resisting sin when nobody is watching. It looks like keeping your promises. It looks like staying in the Word. It looks like staying in the church. It looks like returning to Christ after failure, not giving up.

Endurance also grows through testing. James 1 teaches that trials test faith and produce steadfastness (NSV). Again, this does not mean suffering is pleasant. It means God uses it. A tested faith becomes sturdier than an untested faith.

What if someone falls away?

Scripture teaches that some people appear to believe for a time, then leave. They may have religious activity, but their heart was never truly renewed. 1 John 2:19 says some went out because they were not truly of us (NSV). That verse is not meant to make believers paranoid. It is meant to urge honesty. It calls people to examine whether they truly trust Christ and whether their life shows a new direction.

At the same time, believers can stumble badly and still be restored. Peter denied Christ, yet Christ restored him. Failure is not the same as final apostasy. The difference is repentance. A true believer may fall, but will not stay content in sin. God brings His people back.

So how do you pursue assurance and endurance in a healthy way?

Start with Christ. Keep returning to what He has done. Then examine your life with honesty, not with panic. Confess sin quickly. Seek help when you are weak. Stay connected to a faithful church. Use God's Word daily. Pray for perseverance. Encourage other believers and receive encouragement.

Assurance and endurance are not meant to make you self-focused. They are meant to make you Christ-focused. The more you look to Christ, the more peace grows. The more you walk with Him, the more steady your faith becomes.

The goal is not a life without struggle. The goal is a life that keeps coming back to Jesus. God keeps His people, and His people endure. That is hope you can live on.

Workbook Section

1) Scripture Reading and Notes

Read each passage. Write one truth about assurance or endurance.

1. Titus 1:2 (NSV)

   ____

   ____

2. Hebrews 7:25 (NSV)

   ____

   ____

3. John 10:28–29 (NSV)

   ____

   ____

4. 1 John 5:13 (NSV)

   ____

   ____

5. Philippians 1:6 (NSV)

   ____

   ____

6. Hebrews 12:1 (NSV)

   ____

   ____

7. Jude 24 (NSV)

   ____

   ____

8. Colossians 1:23 (NSV)

\-

\-

2) What You Base Assurance On

Answer honestly.

1. When you feel unsure, what do you usually look at first?

    Examples: your feelings, your recent behavior, your past, God's promises.

    \-

    \-

    \-

2. What is dangerous about basing assurance only on feelings?

    \-

    \-

    \-

3. What is one promise from the passages above you can return to?

    \-

    \-

    \-

3) Signs of Life Check

These are not ways to earn salvation. They are possible evidences of new life.

Rate each from 1 to 5.

1 = weak right now, 5 = strong right now.

Desire to obey Christ:	1	2	3	4	5
Conviction when I sin:	1	2	3	4	5
Love for believers:	1	2	3	4	5
Desire for God's Word:	1	2	3	4	5
Willingness to repent:	1	2	3	4	5

Now write:

1. One area where you see God's grace at work.

    ----

2. One area where you need growth.

    ----

4) Confession and Renewal

If unconfessed sin is weighing on you, write it here in general terms.
The sin I need to confess is:

Write one step of repentance you will take.

My step:

Write one person you can ask to pray for you, if needed.

My support:

----

5) Endurance Plan

Hebrews 12:1 calls believers to run with endurance.

1. What is one "weight" that slows you down?

    Examples: distraction, bitterness, unhealthy habits, fear of
    people.

    ----

2. What is one "sin" that trips you often?

____

____

3. What is one practical change you will make this week?

____

____

4. What is one habit that helps you keep going?

____

____

6) When You Feel Weak

Write answers you can return to later.

1. When I feel weak, I will open: (choose one)
    A Bible passage:

____

____

A psalm:

____

____

A gospel account:

____

____

2. When I feel weak, I will pray this short prayer:
    Write a one-sentence prayer:

____

____

3. When I feel weak, I will reach out to:
    Write one person or group:

____

____

Prayer Response

Write a prayer for assurance and perseverance. If you need help, begin here and finish it.

Father, thank You that You do not lie and You keep Your promises.

Lord Jesus, thank You that You save completely and intercede for Your people.

Help me rest in Your Word when I feel unsure.

Help me confess sin quickly and keep following You with endurance.

Keep me faithful until the end.

Amen.

Key Takeaway

Assurance rests on God's promises and Christ's finished work. Endurance is the ongoing path of faith. God keeps His people, and His people keep coming back to Him.

BOOK FOUR
LIVE BY THE SPIRIT GOD HAS GIVEN

God does not leave His people to live the Christian life by effort alone. He gives the Holy Spirit. The Spirit is not a mood, a force, or a vague feeling. He is God, and He works in real ways. This book will help you learn what Scripture teaches about the Spirit's person and power. You will study how He gives life, unites believers to Christ, grows fruit in daily character, and strengthens the church. Each chapter includes clear teaching and guided questions so you can depend on the Spirit with faith, wisdom, and steady obedience.

CHAPTER 1

THE SPIRIT IS GOD - NOT AN INFLUENCE

Teaching Section

Many people speak about the Holy Spirit as if He is a feeling. They may say, "I felt the Spirit," meaning they felt moved. Feelings can happen during worship, prayer, or repentance. But the Holy Spirit is not a feeling. He is not an "it." He is not an invisible energy. Scripture teaches the Spirit is a person, and the Spirit is God.

This matters because your view of the Spirit shapes your Christian life. If you think the Spirit is only a boost of emotion, you will chase moods. You will think God is near only when you feel warm inside. But if you know the Spirit is God, you will trust Him even when feelings are quiet. You will learn to depend on His truth and His presence in every season.

The Bible shows the Spirit is a person because He acts like a person.

First, the Spirit speaks and directs. In Acts 13:2, the Holy Spirit said to set apart Barnabas and Saul for the work God called them to (NSV). Speaking is personal action. Directing people is personal action. The Spirit is not a passive force.

Second, the Spirit has a will. 1 Corinthians 12:11 says the Spirit distributes gifts to each one as He wills (NSV). A will is not a cloud. A will belongs to a person who chooses and acts.

Third, the Spirit can be grieved. Ephesians 4:30 warns believers not to grieve the Holy Spirit of God (NSV). You cannot grieve electricity. You can grieve a person. The Spirit is personal, and He is holy.

Fourth, the Spirit teaches. 1 Corinthians 2:10 says the Spirit searches everything, even the depths of God (NSV). That same section explains that the Spirit knows God's thoughts. Knowing and teaching are personal actions.

The Bible also shows the Spirit is God.

In Acts 5:3–4, Peter confronts Ananias. He says Ananias lied to the Holy Spirit, then says he lied to God (NSV). Peter treats the Spirit as God, not as a created messenger.

2 Corinthians 3:17 says, "The Lord is the Spirit" (NSV). This does not erase the Father and the Son. It teaches the Spirit shares the divine nature. He is not less than God. He is the Lord.

The Spirit also has divine attributes. He is everywhere. Psalm 139:7 says there is no place you can flee from God's Spirit (NSV). Only God is present everywhere. The Spirit's presence is not limited by space.

The Spirit also does divine work. He is involved in creation. Genesis 1:2 says the Spirit of God was hovering over the waters (NSV). Creation is God's work. The Spirit is present and active in it.

The Spirit also gives life, which is God's work. Job 33:4 says the Spirit of God made the speaker, and the breath of the Almighty gives life (NSV). Giving life is not something a mere influence can do.

So why do people reduce the Spirit to an influence?

One reason is that people confuse the Spirit's work with emotions. The Spirit can bring conviction, joy, comfort, and awe. But feelings are not the Spirit Himself. Feelings rise and fall. The Spirit remains.

Another reason is that people fear being misled. Some have seen claims of "Spirit-led" behavior that ignored Scripture and harmed others. That is real harm. But the answer is not to shrink the Spirit into an idea. The answer is to honor the Spirit the way Scripture does. The Spirit never contradicts God's Word. He works through truth. He also produces holiness, not chaos.

Knowing the Spirit is God also protects you from a common mistake. Some people treat the Spirit as optional, as if serious Christianity is only about Jesus, and the Spirit is an extra. Scripture does not allow that. The Spirit is central to Christian life. No one comes to Christ without the Spirit's work. No believer grows without the Spirit's help.

Knowing the Spirit is a person also changes how you relate to Him. You do not use Him. You do not command Him. You do not treat Him like a tool. You honor Him. You listen. You ask for help with humility. You seek to please God, not to control spiritual experiences.

This also shapes your worship. Worship is not about getting a certain feeling. Worship is responding to God in truth. The Spirit helps you worship with sincerity. He opens your eyes to Christ. He presses God's truth into your heart. He strengthens faith when you feel weak.

It also shapes your obedience. When you are tempted, you do not need a rush of emotion to obey. You need truth, prayer, and strength. The Spirit supplies strength that is steady, not flashy. He helps you say no to sin and yes to righteousness. He helps you endure when life is hard.

So the main point is clear. The Holy Spirit is God, and He is a person. He is not an influence. He speaks, wills, teaches, and can be grieved. He is present everywhere. He gives life. When you know who the Spirit is, you can depend on Him with reverence and confidence.

Workbook Section

1) Scripture Reading and Notes

Read each passage. Write one clear observation from each.

1. Acts 13:2 (NSV)

    ----

2. 1 Corinthians 12:11 (NSV)

    ----

3. Ephesians 4:30 (NSV)

    ----

4. Acts 5:3–4 (NSV)

    ----

5. 2 Corinthians 3:17 (NSV)

    ----

6. Psalm 139:7 (NSV)

____

____

7. Genesis 1:2 (NSV)

____

____

8. Job 33:4 (NSV)

____

____

2) Person or Influence

Write "person" or "influence" next to each statement.

1. The Spirit teaches and guides.

____

____

2. The Spirit is a power I can control.

____

____

3. The Spirit can be grieved by sin.

____

____

4. The Spirit is just a worship feeling.

____

____

5. The Spirit chooses how gifts are given.

____

____

6. The Spirit is fully God.

____

____

Now write one sentence explaining why it matters that the Spirit is a person.

My sentence:

----

3) Correct a Wrong Idea

Choose one wrong idea you have heard or believed.

Common wrong ideas:

- "The Spirit is a force."
- "The Spirit is only for certain Christians."
- "The Spirit always shows up as strong emotion."
- "The Spirit leads people away from Scripture."

The wrong idea I want to reject is:

Now correct it using one verse from today's list.

Verse and correction:

----

4) Reverence Check

Ephesians 4:30 says the Spirit can be grieved.

1. What kinds of sin tend to dull your spiritual sensitivity?

   Examples: harsh speech, secret compromise, bitterness, dishonesty.

   ----

2. What is one step of repentance you will take this week?

____

____

____

3. What is one habit that helps you walk in holiness?

____

____

____

5) Dependence Practice

Write short answers you can use in prayer.

1. One area where I need the Spirit's help today is:

____

____

2. One truth I will rely on is:

____

____

3. One choice of obedience I will make is:

____

____

4. One way I will seek God's Word today is:

____

____

6) Worship and Feelings

Answer honestly.

1. When you do not feel much in worship, what do you assume?

____

____

2. What is a better truth to hold based on Psalm 139:7?

____

____

____

3. Write one sentence you will remind yourself of next time feelings are low.

Write a short prayer of honor and dependence. If you need help, complete these lines.

Holy Spirit, You are God, not an influence.

Forgive me for treating You lightly or ignoring You.

Teach me to listen to Your Word and obey with a willing heart.

Help me worship in truth, even when my feelings change.

Lead me in holiness today.

Amen.

Key Takeaway

The Holy Spirit is a real person and fully God. He speaks, wills, teaches, and can be grieved. Knowing who He is leads to reverent trust and steady dependence.

CHAPTER 2

THE SPIRIT BRINGS LIFE

The Christian life does not begin with a better attitude. It begins with new life. The Bible teaches that the Holy Spirit brings that life. Without the Spirit, a person can hear Bible words and still stay spiritually dead. A person can join a church, learn religious habits, and still lack true life with God. The Spirit changes that. He makes the gospel real to the heart.

Jesus explained this clearly when He spoke with Nicodemus. He said, "Unless one is born of water and the Spirit, he cannot enter the kingdom of God" (John 3:5, NSV). New birth is not a self-made upgrade. It is a work of God. The Spirit gives a kind of life that did not exist before. This is why Christianity is not first a set of rules. It is a rescue that includes a new heart.

Jesus also said, "That which is born of the flesh is flesh, and that which is born of the Spirit is spirit" (John 3:6, NSV). Flesh here points to human nature on its own. Humans can produce human efforts, but they cannot produce spiritual life. Only the Spirit gives spiritual life. The Spirit does not improve your old nature. He gives new life that begins a new direction.

This new birth is mysterious in its inner workings, but clear in its results. Jesus compared the Spirit's work to the wind. You cannot see the wind itself, but you can see its effects (John 3:8, NSV). In the same way, you may not be able to explain the exact moment your heart changed, but you can see the fruit. New life shows up in new desires. A person begins to care about truth. A person begins to feel conviction over sin. A person begins to hunger for God's Word. A person begins to love Christ and want to obey Him.

Titus 3:5 calls this work "the washing of regeneration and renewal of the Holy Spirit" (NSV). Regeneration means new birth. Renewal means a new direction of mind and heart. The Spirit cleans, not by scrubbing the outside only, but by changing what is inside. This is why salvation is not earned by good deeds. If the Spirit must bring life, then no one can boast.

The Spirit also brings life by giving spiritual sight. Without the Spirit, the gospel can seem dull or foolish. But when the Spirit opens a person's heart, Christ becomes precious. Sin becomes serious. Grace becomes amazing. That does not mean every believer feels strong emotion all the time. It means the Spirit changes what you value. He teaches you to see reality the way God sees it.

The Spirit's life-giving work is also seen in conversion. 1 Corinthians 6:11 speaks to people who once lived in many sins. Then it says, "But you were washed, you were sanctified, you were justified in the name of the Lord Jesus Christ and by the Spirit of our God" (NSV). That verse shows the Spirit's power to change real people with real pasts. The Spirit does not only forgive. He also sets apart. He also makes a new path possible.

The Spirit brings life in another important way. He strengthens believers to keep going. Romans 8:11 says the Spirit who raised Jesus from the dead dwells in believers, and He gives life to their mortal bodies (NSV). This points to present help and future hope. In the present, the Spirit strengthens you for obedience. In the future, the Spirit's presence guarantees resurrection life.

This matters because many believers try to live the Christian life with the wrong fuel. They try to change through shame, fear, or pure willpower. Shame might produce short bursts of effort, but it cannot produce lasting life. Fear can produce outward behavior, but it cannot produce a willing heart. Willpower can help with certain habits, but it cannot cleanse the conscience or remake the heart. The Spirit does what human effort cannot do.

This does not mean effort is useless. Believers are called to pursue holiness. But the order matters. The Spirit gives life first. Then effort becomes a response, not an attempt to earn God's favor. When the Spirit is the source, obedience can be steady. When self is the source, obedience becomes fragile.

So how do you know if the Spirit has brought life?

Do you trust Christ as your Savior and Lord? Do you have a growing awareness of sin and a desire to turn from it? Do you desire God's Word, even if your discipline is weak? Do you love God's people, even if you still struggle with selfishness? Do you keep coming back to Christ when you fail? These are signs of life. They are not reasons to brag. They are reasons to thank God.

What if you feel spiritually dry?

Dryness can happen for many reasons. Sometimes it comes from neglect of Scripture and prayer. Sometimes it comes from unconfessed sin. Sometimes it comes from suffering, grief, or depression. Dryness does not always mean you are lost. But it is a call to return to the means God uses. Open the Word. Pray simply. Seek help from mature believers. Confess known sin. Ask God for renewed strength.

The Spirit brings life, and that life is meant to grow. A newborn baby is alive, but still needs food, care, and time. In the same way, new spiritual life needs feeding. The Spirit uses Scripture to nourish faith. He uses prayer to grow dependence. He uses fellowship to strengthen endurance.

The main point is clear. The Holy Spirit brings life. He causes new birth. He renews the heart. He opens spiritual eyes. He strengthens believers to obey and to persevere. If you belong to Christ, you are not trying to create life from nothing. You are learning to live from the life the Spirit has already given.

Workbook Section

1) Scripture Reading and Notes

Read each passage. Then write one clear truth you learn about the Spirit bringing life.

1. John 3:5 (NSV)

   ----

2. John 3:6 (NSV)

   ----

3. John 3:8 (NSV)

----

4. Titus 3:5 (NSV)

----

5. 1 Corinthians 6:11 (NSV)

----

6. Romans 8:11 (NSV)

----

2) New Life in Your Own Words

Write a simple description.

New spiritual life means:

Now write one sentence that explains what new life is not.

New spiritual life is not:

----

3) Signs of Life Check

These are not a scorecard. They help you observe fruit.

Rate each from 1 to 5.

1 = weak right now, 5 = strong right now.

Desire to trust Christ:	1	2	3	4	5
Conviction when I sin:	1	2	3	4	5
Desire for Scripture:	1	2	3	4	5
Desire to pray:	1	2	3	4	5
Love for believers:	1	2	3	4	5
Willingness to repent:	1	2	3	4	5

Now write:

1. One area where you see evidence of life:

    ----

2. One area where you want growth:

    ----

4) Wind and Evidence

John 3:8 compares the Spirit's work to the wind.

1. What is one effect of the Spirit's work you can see in your life
    today?

    ----

2. What is one effect you want to see more clearly in the next
    month?

    ----

3. What is one habit that could support that growth?

    ----

5) From Dry to Fed

If you feel spiritually dry, answer these with honesty.

1. One possible cause of dryness for me is:

    Examples: distraction, fear, unconfessed sin, exhaustion, grief.

    ----

2. One step I will take this week to seek renewed strength is:

    ----

3. One person I can ask for prayer or counsel is:

    ----

6) Washed and Renewed

Titus 3:5 speaks of washing and renewal.

1. What is one old pattern you want God to wash away?

____

____

____

____

____

2. What is one new pattern you want God to grow in you?

____

____

____

____

3. Write one sentence of hope that you can say when you feel stuck.

____

____

____

7) Prayer Response

Write a prayer asking God for life and renewal. If you need help, begin here and finish it.

Holy Spirit, thank You for bringing life where I could not.

____

____

Give me fresh desire for God's Word.

____

____

Expose what needs to change in my heart.

____

____

Strengthen me to repent and obey.

Help me live from the new life You have given.

Amen.

Key Takeaway

The Holy Spirit brings life through new birth and renewal. He changes the heart, opens spiritual sight, and strengthens believers to keep following Christ.

CHAPTER 3

THE SPIRIT UNITES BELIEVERS TO CHRIST

Teaching Section

When a person is saved, God does more than forgive. He joins that person to Jesus Christ. This union is real. It is not a picture only. It is not a warm idea. It is a true spiritual connection created by the Holy Spirit. The Spirit unites believers to Christ so that what belongs to Christ becomes ours by grace.

This matters because many believers live as if Christianity is only trying harder. They think of Jesus as a helper on the outside. But Scripture describes something deeper. Christ lives in His people, and His people live in Him. That is union. The Spirit is the one who makes this union real and active.

1 Corinthians 6:17 says, "He who is joined to the Lord becomes one spirit with him" (NSV). This does not mean believers become divine. It means believers share a real spiritual bond with Christ. Through this bond, Christ's life becomes the source of the believer's life.

Romans 8:9 says, "Anyone who does not have the Spirit of Christ does not belong to him" (NSV). The Spirit is not optional. The Spirit is the mark of belonging. If you have the Spirit, you belong to Christ. If you belong to Christ, you have the Spirit. This union is not earned. It is given.

The Spirit unites believers to Christ in several key ways.

First, the Spirit joins us to Christ's death and resurrection. Romans 6:4 says believers were buried with Christ by baptism into death so that, just as Christ was raised, we too might walk in newness of life (NSV). This verse is about more than water. It is about what water points to. The Spirit joins you to Christ so that His death counts as your death to sin, and His resurrection becomes your new life.

This changes how you view sin. Sin is not your master anymore. You may still feel its pull, but you are not its property. You belong to Christ. Union means a change of ownership. You were under sin. Now you are under Christ.

Second, the Spirit makes Christ's benefits real in you. These benefits include forgiveness, peace with God, adoption, and hope. Ephesians 1:13 says believers were sealed with the promised Holy Spirit when they heard the word of truth and believed (NSV). A seal shows ownership and protection. The Spirit's presence is God's mark that you are His.

This sealing also serves as a guarantee. Ephesians 1:14 says the Spirit is the guarantee of our inheritance (NSV). That means your future with God is not a guess. The Spirit is like God's down payment, showing that He will finish what He started. You may feel weak, but God's promise is strong.

Third, the Spirit creates fellowship with Christ that changes daily life. Galatians 2:20 says, "It is no longer I who live, but Christ who lives in me" (NSV). Paul is not saying he disappeared. He is saying his old identity as self-ruler died. Christ now rules his life. This is a lived reality. Union changes what you want, how you decide, and what you pursue.

Fourth, the Spirit unites believers to Christ and also to each other. 1 Corinthians 12:13 says believers were all baptized by one Spirit into one body (NSV). The Spirit does not only create personal faith. He creates a people. He forms the church as Christ's body. This means union with Christ always has a community shape. If you belong to Jesus, you belong to His people.

This also challenges pride and isolation. Pride says, "I do not need others." Isolation says, "I will keep faith private." But the Spirit joins believers together. This does not mean church is always easy. It means church is part of God's design. The Spirit works through mutual care, correction, and encouragement.

Union with Christ also changes how you handle guilt. Many believers live with ongoing shame even after confession. They keep replaying failure. But union means you are not standing before God on your own. You stand in Christ. When God looks at you, He sees you in His Son. This does not excuse sin, but it does answer condemnation. Romans 8:1 says there is now no condemnation for those who are in Christ Jesus

(NSV). "In Christ" is union language. The Spirit places you there.

Union also changes how you face suffering. If you belong to Christ, your suffering is not meaningless. You are not abandoned. God is present. Christ is with you. The Spirit comforts and strengthens. Romans 8:17 says believers are heirs with Christ, provided they suffer with Him in order that they may also be glorified with Him (NSV). This does not mean suffering earns glory. It means suffering is part of the path God uses, and union guarantees the end.

Union changes how you pursue holiness too. Growth is not about trying to become someone else. It is about living out what is already true. You are united to Christ, so you learn to live like you belong to Him. You fight sin because you are alive, not to become alive. You obey because you are accepted, not to become accepted.

So how do you live in light of union with Christ?

You remember who you belong to. You stop treating sin like a safe friend. You seek the help of the Spirit in prayer. You stay near God's Word because it tells you what is true. You stay connected to the church because the Spirit uses the body of Christ to strengthen you. You also learn to preach the gospel to yourself. When shame speaks, you answer with truth: you are in Christ, and the Spirit is the seal of that reality.

The main point is simple. The Holy Spirit unites believers to Christ. Through this union, Christ's death and resurrection shape your life. His benefits become yours. Your identity becomes steadier. Your hope becomes stronger. You are not trying to live the Christian life alone. You are living from your union with Jesus.

Workbook Section

1) Scripture Reading and Notes

Read each passage. Write one clear truth about union with Christ and the Spirit's role.

   1. 1 Corinthians 6:17 (NSV)

----

2. Romans 8:9 (NSV)

____

____

3. Romans 6:4 (NSV)

____

____

4. Ephesians 1:13 (NSV)

____

____

5. Ephesians 1:14 (NSV)

____

____

6. Galatians 2:20 (NSV)

____

____

7. 1 Corinthians 12:13 (NSV)

____

____

8. Romans 8:1 (NSV)

____

____

2) Define Union in Plain Words

Finish the sentence.

Union with Christ means:

____

____

____

Now write one sentence that explains how the Spirit makes this union real.

The Spirit makes union real by:

----

3) Identity Check

Answer honestly.

1. When you fail, what do you tend to say about yourself?

    ----

2. How does Romans 8:1 correct your self-talk?

    ----

3. Write one truth statement you will repeat when guilt rises.

    ----

4) Ownership Change

Union means you belong to Christ.

1. What sin do you still treat like it belongs in your life?

    ----

2. What does Romans 6:4 call you to do instead?

    ----

3. What is one boundary you can set this week that matches your
    new ownership?

    ----

5) Sealed and Secure

Ephesians 1:13–14 speaks about being sealed.

1. What fears make you doubt God will keep you?

   ____

   ____

2. What does it mean that the Spirit is God's seal on you?

   ____

   ____

3. Write one sentence of assurance based on Ephesians 1:14.

   ____

   ____

6) Union and the Church

1 Corinthians 12:13 says the Spirit forms one body.

1. How connected are you to a local church right now?

   ____

   ____

2. What is one way you can pursue stronger connection in the next two weeks?

   ____

   ____

3. What is one barrier that keeps you from fellowship?

   ____

   ____

4. What is one step you will take to move past that barrier?

   ____

   ____

7) Daily Practice: Live From What Is True

Write a simple daily plan for the next seven days.

1. One short passage I will read each day is:

   ____

   ____

2. One prayer I will pray each day is:

----

3. One act of obedience that fits my union with Christ is:

----

4. One person I will encourage or reach out to is:

Prayer Response

Write a prayer of gratitude and dependence. If you need help, begin here and finish it.

Father, thank You for uniting me to Christ by Your Spirit.

Thank You that I belong to Jesus and He lives in me.

Help me walk in newness of life and resist sin as a true response to grace.

Strengthen my faith when I feel weak.

Keep me close to Christ and close to His people.

Amen.

The Holy Spirit unites believers to Christ. This union changes identity, breaks sin's ownership, secures hope, and connects believers to the body of Christ.

CHAPTER 4

THE SPIRIT PRODUCES FRUIT, NOT JUST GIFTS

Many Christians talk about spiritual gifts. Gifts matter. God gives them for the good of the church. But Scripture puts strong focus on something else too: fruit. Fruit is the Spirit's work in your character. Gifts can be seen quickly. Fruit is seen over time. Gifts can draw attention. Fruit shows maturity.

A person can have visible gifts and still have a harsh spirit. A person can speak well and still lack self-control. A person can serve in public and still be proud in private. That is why the Bible points us to fruit. The Spirit does not only give ability. He forms a kind of person.

Galatians 5:22–23 lists the fruit of the Spirit: love, joy, peace, patience, kindness, goodness, faithfulness, gentleness, and self-control (NSV). This list is not a set of personality traits some people are born with. It is the Spirit's work in believers. It describes what the Spirit grows in a life that is learning to follow Christ.

Fruit is also connected to staying close to Christ. Jesus said, "Whoever abides in me and I in him, he it is that bears much fruit" (John 15:5, NSV). Fruit does not come from trying harder in your own strength. It comes from abiding. Abiding means staying close, staying dependent, staying connected. A branch does not strain to produce grapes. It stays connected to the vine, and life flows into it.

This helps us think about growth in a healthy way. Some believers try to change through fear and pressure. Others give up and assume they will never change. The Spirit offers a better path. You depend on Christ. You obey in small steps. You repent when you fail. Over time, the Spirit grows fruit that is real.

Now consider the difference between gifts and fruit.

Gifts are abilities given by God for service. Fruit is character shaped by God for holiness. Gifts are distributed in different ways. Not everyone has the same gift. Fruit is for every believer. No Christian is called to pursue "some" fruit and ignore the rest. The Spirit's fruit is meant to shape the whole person.

Gifts can also be present in immature believers. This may surprise some people, but it is true. A person can have a gift and still need deep growth. Fruit is a clearer sign of maturity. Fruit shows what rules the heart when nobody is watching.

Fruit also protects the church. A church can be impressed by talent and energy. But talent without fruit can lead to harm. Leaders and teachers must be marked by character. The Spirit's fruit helps keep the church safe and healthy.

Let's walk through the fruit of the Spirit in a practical way.

Love is active good for others. It is not only affection. It is seeking another person's good, even when it costs you. Love is patient in conflict. Love refuses bitterness. Love tells the truth with care.

Joy is not constant cheerfulness. Joy is deep gladness rooted in God. It can exist in sorrow. It does not depend on a perfect week. Joy grows when you remember God's mercy and trust His promises.

Peace is not the absence of problems. Peace is a settled heart that trusts God. Peace also shows up in how you handle conflict. A peaceful person is not always quiet, but they are not ruled by chaos.

Patience is long-suffering. It is staying steady under delay, weakness, or irritation. Patience does not explode quickly. It can endure frustration without cruelty.

Kindness is practical care. Kindness notices needs. Kindness uses words that heal instead of wound. Kindness is not weakness. It is strength used for another person's good.

Goodness is moral integrity. It is choosing what is right, even when it costs you. Goodness refuses hidden compromise. Goodness is sincere.

Faithfulness is reliability. It is keeping your word. It is being steady over time. Faithfulness shows up in marriage vows, work habits, church commitments, and private obedience.

Gentleness is controlled strength. Gentleness does not mean you never confront sin. It means you confront with humility, not harshness. Gentleness is careful with people who are weak.

Self-control is restraint. It is the ability to say no to wrong desires and yes to obedience. Self-control matters in speech, food, spending, sexuality, time, and anger. It is not grit alone. It is Spirit-enabled discipline.

Fruit grows through repeated choices. A tree does not produce fruit by trying once. It grows through seasons. In the same way, the Spirit grows fruit as you practice obedience again and again.

2 Peter 1:5–8 speaks about growth like this. It calls believers to make every effort to add virtue, knowledge, self-control, steadfastness, godliness, brotherly affection, and love (NSV). This does not contradict grace. It shows the shape of a responsive life. God gives life, and believers respond with effort that depends on God. Growth is not passive.

Philippians 1:9–11 also connects fruit to the Spirit's work. Paul prays that believers will abound in love with knowledge and discernment, so they approve what is excellent, and be filled with the fruit of righteousness that comes through Jesus Christ (NSV). That passage shows fruit has roots. Love grows with truth. Discernment grows with practice. Righteous fruit grows through Christ.

This is why the Spirit's fruit is so important for discernment. Many people try to measure spiritual life by dramatic moments. But fruit shows what is steady. A life that keeps producing love, patience, and self-control is showing the Spirit's work.

Fruit also helps you evaluate your use of gifts. Gifts should serve love. Gifts should build up others. If a gift makes you proud, it is being misused. If a gift becomes your identity, it becomes an idol. Fruit keeps gifts in their proper place.

Fruit also grows best in the soil of repentance. When the Spirit convicts you, do not hide. Confess sin. Turn from it. Ask God to reshape your desires. Repentance is not shame-driven self-punishment. It is returning to God with trust.

Fruit also grows in community. You cannot practice patience with nobody. You cannot practice gentleness in isolation. The church is one place God uses to grow fruit, because it puts you near real people with real needs. That is where love becomes practical.

So what should you aim for?

Aim for a life that looks like Christ. Ask God for fruit more than attention. Ask Him for love more than applause. Ask Him for self-control more than comfort. Ask Him for gentleness more than the last word. Over time, the Spirit forms a steady Christian who can serve with gifts and also live with integrity.

The main point of this chapter is simple. The Spirit produces fruit that reflects Christ. Gifts matter, but fruit matters more. Fruit shows who you are becoming.

Workbook Section

1) Scripture Reading and Notes

Read each passage. Write one clear observation from each.

1. Galatians 5:22–23 (NSV)

    ----

2. John 15:5 (NSV)

    ----

3. 2 Peter 1:5–8 (NSV)

    ----

4. Philippians 1:9–11 (NSV)

    ----

5. Titus 2:11–12 (NSV)

    ----

2) Fruit Inventory

Rate each fruit from 1 to 5.

1 = weak right now, 5 = strong right now.

Love:	1	2	3	4	5
Joy:	1	2	3	4	5
Peace:	1	2	3	4	5
Patience:	1	2	3	4	5
Kindness:	1	2	3	4	5
Goodness:	1	2	3	4	5
Faithfulness:	1	2	3	4	5
Gentleness:	1	2	3	4	5
Self-control:	1	2	3	4	5

Now write:

1. Two fruits I thank God for today:

   ----

2. Two fruits I want to grow in the next month:

   ----

3) Abiding Practice

John 15:5 connects fruit to abiding.

Write a simple plan for the next seven days.

1. Time of day I will read Scripture:

   ----

2. Place where I will pray:

   ----

3. One distraction I will limit during that time:

   ----

4. One short prayer I will pray before reading:

----

4) Fruit in Conflict

Choose one recent conflict. Keep details general.

1. What fruit was hardest to show in that moment?

----

2. What did you do instead?

----

3. What would love plus truth look like next time?

----

4. Write one sentence you could say next time that shows gentleness.

----

5) Fruit in Private

Fruit is tested in private choices.

Choose one area where you need more self-control.

Examples: speech, spending, screen time, food, lust, anger, laziness.

My area:

Now write:

1. The usual trigger is:

----

2. The lie I tend to believe is:

----

3. A true statement from Scripture that corrects the lie is:

----

4. One boundary I will set this week is:

----

5. One replacement habit I will practice is:

----

6) Gifts and Fruit Together

Write short answers.

1. One gift or strength God has given me is:

----

2. One way I can use it to serve others is:

----

3. One fruit I need so this gift does not become pride is:

----

4. One step of humility I will take is:

----

7) Growth Plan With 2 Peter 1

Pick one quality named in 2 Peter 1:5–8 and set a plan.

The quality I will pursue is:

Two practical steps I will take this week:

1. ____

____

____

2. ____

____

____

One person I will ask to pray for me:

Write a short prayer. If you need help, complete these lines.

Holy Spirit, thank You for growing fruit in Your people.

____

____

Help me abide in Christ and depend on Him.

____

____

Grow love and self-control in me where I am weak.

____

____

Make my character steady so my service is safe and helpful.

____

____

Amen.

The Spirit does more than give gifts. He grows fruit. Fruit is Christlike character formed over time through abiding, repentance, truth, and steady obedience.

CHAPTER 5

THE SPIRIT BUILDS AND GUIDES THE CHURCH

Teaching Section

God does not save people and then leave them alone. He gathers them. He forms a church. The church is not a club for like-minded people. It is the people of God, called out of sin and brought together in Christ. The Holy Spirit is the one who builds and guides this church.

Many believers think of the Spirit mainly in personal terms, like comfort, conviction, or strength for obedience. Those are real. But Scripture also shows the Spirit working in a public way through the church. The Spirit forms a people who worship, learn, serve, and grow together.

The Spirit builds the church in at least four clear ways: He gives unity, He gives gifts, He guides leadership, and He guards truth.

First, the Spirit gives unity.

Ephesians 4:3 calls believers to be "eager to maintain the unity of the Spirit in the bond of peace" (NSV). Unity is not something Christians create from scratch. The Spirit creates it by joining believers to Christ and to one another. Our job is to maintain it. That means we must protect unity from pride, gossip, and stubbornness.

Unity does not mean everyone thinks the same about every topic. It means believers share one Lord, one faith, one baptism, and one hope. It means we refuse to treat secondary issues as if they are more important than the gospel.

Unity also requires humility. Philippians 2:3–4 calls believers to do nothing from selfish ambition, but to count others more significant than themselves (NSV). Pride is one of the fastest ways to fracture a church. The Spirit builds unity through humble people who are willing to listen, repent, and forgive.

Second, the Spirit gives gifts for service.

1 Corinthians 12:4-7 says there are different gifts, but the same Spirit, and gifts are given for the common good (NSV). This means gifts are not badges for status. They are tools for love. God gives gifts so the church will be built up, cared for, taught, and strengthened.

Some gifts are more visible, like teaching. Others are less visible, like service, helps, or giving. Scripture teaches that every part of the body matters. A church becomes unhealthy when it praises certain gifts and ignores others. The Spirit gives a variety of gifts so that no one person becomes the center.

The Spirit also teaches believers to use gifts with love. 1 Corinthians 13 shows that gifts without love are empty. A person can speak well, but if they are harsh, their words do not build. A person can lead, but if they are proud, they harm. The Spirit's gifts must be guided by the Spirit's fruit.

Third, the Spirit guides the church through the Word and through qualified leaders.

The Spirit does not guide churches by sudden impressions that ignore Scripture. He guides through truth. Acts 20:28 says the Holy Spirit made overseers to care for the church of God (NSV). This shows the Spirit's role in appointing leaders. It also shows leaders have a sacred responsibility. They must shepherd God's people with care, not control.

The Spirit also equips leaders to teach sound doctrine and correct error. Titus 1:9 says a leader must hold firm to the trustworthy word, so he can give instruction and rebuke those who contradict it (NSV). The Spirit's guidance never pulls away from Scripture. The Spirit is the author of Scripture. He does not fight Himself.

Fourth, the Spirit guards the church by protecting truth and exposing error.

In Acts 15, the church faced a major doctrinal conflict. The leaders met, searched the Scriptures, and made a decision. Acts 15:28 says, "It has seemed good to the Holy Spirit and to us" (NSV). That line shows that the Spirit guided the church as they sought truth together. The Spirit did not give a secret revelation that replaced Scripture. He guided through the Word, prayer, and wise counsel.

The Spirit also guides the church in mission.

Acts 1:8 says believers will receive power when the Holy Spirit comes, and they will be witnesses (NSV). The Spirit strengthens believers to speak the gospel with courage and clarity. He also opens doors for ministry. He brings conviction to hearers. He draws people to Christ.

This does not mean every Christian is called to preach publicly. It means every Christian is part of a Spirit-empowered witness. The Spirit gives boldness, wisdom, and love for people who need Christ.

The Spirit also shapes the church's worship. Believers sing, pray, and hear Scripture. The Spirit works through these ordinary means. Sometimes worship feels powerful. Sometimes it feels quiet. Either way, the Spirit is present when God's people gather in truth.

So how should you respond to this teaching?

First, commit to the local church. If the Spirit builds the church, then the church matters. You cannot treat church as optional and still follow Scripture well. Online sermons can help, but they cannot replace real relationships, accountability, and shared life.

Second, serve with your gifts. Ask, "How can I build others up?" Do not wait for perfect conditions. Start small. Help where there is need. Use your time and skills for the good of the body.

Third, protect unity. Refuse gossip. Refuse unnecessary fights. Speak directly when needed. Be quick to forgive. Be slow to assume the worst.

Fourth, stay anchored in truth. Test teachings. Read Scripture. Learn sound doctrine. The Spirit uses truth to keep the church healthy.

Fifth, pray for leaders. Church leaders carry heavy responsibility. Pray they would be humble, wise, and faithful to Scripture. Pray they would not fear people. Pray they would not abuse power. Pray they would care for the weak and protect the church from error.

The main point is this: the Spirit builds and guides the church. He creates unity, gives gifts, appoints and equips leaders, guards truth, and strengthens mission. When you honor the Spirit's work in the church, you will grow and the church will be strengthened.

1) Scripture Reading and Notes

Read each passage. Write one clear observation from each.

1. Ephesians 4:3 (NSV)

   ----

2. 1 Corinthians 12:4–7 (NSV)

   ----

3. Acts 20:28 (NSV)

   ----

4. Acts 15:28 (NSV)

   ----

5. Acts 1:8 (NSV)

   ----

6. Philippians 2:3–4 (NSV)

   ----

7. Titus 1:9 (NSV)

   ----

2) Church Commitment Check

Answer honestly.

1. What has helped you stay connected to a local church?

   ----

2. What has made church connection hard for you?

----

3. What is one step you can take in the next two weeks to strengthen your involvement?

----

3) Unity and Peace

Ephesians 4:3 calls believers to maintain unity.

1. What usually threatens unity in your church setting?

    Examples: gossip, pride, unresolved conflict, factions, politics.

    ----

2. What role do you tend to play when conflict rises?

    Examples: avoider, fixer, fighter, silent critic, peacemaker.

    ----

3. What is one change you will make to protect unity?

    ----

4) Gifts for the Common Good

1 Corinthians 12 says gifts are for others.

1. One strength or gift I can use to serve is:

    ----

2. One need I see in my church or group is:

----

3. One way I can meet that need this month is:

----

4. What might keep you from serving?

----

5) Leaders and Care

Acts 20:28 speaks about leaders caring for the church.

1. What is one quality you should look for in church leadership?

----

2. What is one way you can support leaders in a healthy way?

----

3. Write a short prayer for your leaders.

----

6) Truth and Discernment

Titus 1:9 ties leadership to holding fast to the Word.

1. What is one false idea you have heard that sounds "Christian" but does not fit Scripture?

----

2. What is one practice that helps you stay grounded in truth?

----

3. What is one Bible habit you want to strengthen?

---

7) Mission and Witness

Acts 1:8 connects Spirit power to witness.

1. Who is one person you want to speak to about Christ?

---

2. What fear holds you back?

---

3. What is one step you can take this week?

    Examples: pray, invite, share a short testimony, offer to read Scripture together.

Prayer Response

Write a prayer for the church. If you need help, complete these lines.

Holy Spirit, thank You for building Christ's church.

Protect our unity and guard us from pride and division.

Help us use our gifts for the good of others.

Give our leaders wisdom and faithfulness to Your Word.

Make us bold witnesses with love and truth.

Amen.

Key Takeaway

The Spirit builds and guides the church by creating unity, giving gifts for service, equipping leaders, guarding truth, and empowering witness.

CHAPTER 6

WALKING BY THE SPIRIT DAILY

Many believers want to follow Christ, but they feel stuck. They know what is right, yet they struggle to do it. They start strong, then lose consistency. The Bible does not tell Christians to rely on willpower alone. It calls them to walk by the Spirit.

Galatians 5:16 says, "Walk by the Spirit, and you will not gratify the desires of the flesh" (NSV). This verse is both a command and a promise. It does not say believers will never feel temptation. It says believers do not have to obey temptation. The Spirit gives a new power and a new direction.

Walking by the Spirit is not a special experience for a few Christians. It is normal Christian life. It is not mystical. It is daily dependence on God, guided by Scripture, expressed through obedience.

To walk by the Spirit, you must understand what the "flesh" is. In Galatians 5, the flesh refers to the sinful nature that still pulls at the believer. It is the old pattern of life that wants to rule again. The flesh says, "Do what feels good now." The Spirit says, "Trust God and obey." The conflict is real. Galatians 5:17 explains that these desires are opposed (NSV). This is why you may feel torn inside. The answer is not to pretend the conflict is not there. The answer is to learn how to walk.

Walking is a picture of steady movement. It is not a leap. It is not a sprint. It is repeated steps in one direction. Walking by the Spirit means choosing the Spirit's path again and again.

Here are several practical parts of walking by the Spirit.

First, walking by the Spirit starts with believing what is true.

Romans 8:14 says those who are led by the Spirit of God are sons of God (NSV). If you belong to Christ, you are not trying to earn adoption.

You are living from it. When you forget who you are, you will live like the old self. When you remember you belong to God, you can resist sin with hope.

Second, walking by the Spirit means staying close to God's Word.

The Spirit never contradicts Scripture. He works through it. Colossians 3:16 says, "Let the word of Christ dwell in you richly" (NSV). A Spirit-led life is a Word-filled life. If Scripture is absent, you will rely on mood, impulse, or the opinions of others. Scripture gives a steady path when feelings shift.

This does not mean you must read huge amounts to be faithful. It means you must be consistent. A few verses each day, read with attention and prayer, will shape you more than occasional long sessions followed by neglect.

Third, walking by the Spirit means prayerful dependence.

Ephesians 6:18 calls believers to pray at all times in the Spirit (NSV). This does not mean non-stop talking. It means a posture of dependence. It means you ask for help before you are in trouble, not only after. It means you speak to God honestly when you feel weak. It means you bring temptation into the light through prayer.

Prayer can be short. It can be as simple as, "Lord, help me obey right now." The key is not fancy words. The key is real dependence.

Fourth, walking by the Spirit includes active obedience.

The Spirit helps you obey, but He does not obey for you. You still choose. You still turn from sin. You still take steps of wisdom. You still set boundaries. The Spirit empowers, guides, and strengthens, but you must walk.

This is why the Bible speaks about putting sin to death. Romans 8:13 says if by the Spirit you put to death the deeds of the body, you will live (NSV). Notice both parts. You put sin to death, and you do it by the Spirit. This is active dependence again. You fight, and God supplies power.

Fifth, walking by the Spirit means learning your patterns.

Many sins repeat because people ignore their triggers. Some are tempted when tired. Some are tempted when lonely. Some are tempted when angry. Some are tempted when bored. Wisdom pays attention. It does not excuse sin, but it prepares for battle. If you know your weak moments, you can plan for them. You can avoid certain settings. You can set limits on screens. You can call a friend. You can go to bed earlier. You can step away from conflict for a moment. These are not unspiritual choices. They are wise choices that support obedience.

Sixth, walking by the Spirit means staying in Christian community.

The Spirit builds the church for a reason. We need encouragement. We need correction. We need prayer. Hebrews 3:13 says believers should exhort one another daily so none are hardened by the deceitfulness of sin (NSV). Sin is deceitful. It tells lies that sound reasonable. Other believers can help you see what you cannot see.

Seventh, walking by the Spirit includes quick repentance.

When you sin, do not hide. Do not delay confession. Confession keeps your heart soft. Delay hardens the heart. A Spirit-led person is not sinless, but they are responsive. They do not make peace with sin. They return to God, ask for forgiveness, and take steps of change.

Walking by the Spirit also helps with decision-making.

Some believers want the Spirit to guide them by secret signs. Scripture points us to wisdom. Wisdom is Spirit-shaped thinking. It uses Scripture, prayer, counsel, and careful judgment. The Spirit often guides by shaping your desires toward what is good and by giving clarity through God's Word. When a choice involves sin, Scripture already answers. When a choice is morally neutral, wisdom helps you choose what is best.

Walking by the Spirit also guards you from pride.

A Spirit-led life does not produce boasting. It produces gratitude. When you obey, you thank God for help. When you fail, you return to Christ. The focus stays on God's grace, not on your record.

So what should you expect as you walk by the Spirit?

Expect a real fight. Expect slow growth in some areas. Expect stronger fruit over time. Expect that obedience becomes more natural as habits change and desires are trained. Also expect that God will use ordinary means, not only dramatic moments. A steady Christian life is often built through small choices made over years.

This chapter closes Book Four with a simple call. The Spirit is not only for the start of faith. He is for every day. Walking by the Spirit is daily dependence that shows up in truth, prayer, boundaries, repentance, and love. God does not ask you to live for Christ alone. He gives you the Spirit so you can follow with strength that is not your own.

Workbook Section

1) Scripture Reading and Notes

Read each passage. Write one clear truth about walking by the Spirit.

1. Galatians 5:16 (NSV)

   ----

2. Galatians 5:17 (NSV)

   ----

3. Romans 8:13–14 (NSV)

   ----

4. Colossians 3:16 (NSV)

   ----

5. Ephesians 6:18 (NSV)

   ----

6. Hebrews 3:13 (NSV)

   ----

2) What "Walking" Looks Like

Answer in simple words.

Walking by the Spirit means I will:

Now write one sentence that describes what walking by the Spirit is not.

It is not:

----

3) Daily Plan for the Next 7 Days

Write a plan you can keep.

1. Bible time:

    When: ____

    Where: ____

    How long: ____

2. Prayer plan:

    One short prayer I will use in temptation:

    ----

3. One obedience focus:

    The habit I want to practice this week:

    ----

4) Trigger and Boundary

Choose one sin you often struggle with. Keep it specific.

The sin pattern:

Now answer:

1. My common trigger is:

    ----

2. The lie I tend to believe is:

----

3. A truth from Scripture that corrects it is:

----

4. One boundary I will set this week is:

----

5. One replacement habit I will practice is:

----

5) Put Sin to Death by the Spirit

Romans 8:13 says you do this "by the Spirit."

1. What does active dependence look like for you in your struggle?

----

2. What is one step you can take today, not later?

----

3. Who can support you with prayer or accountability?

----

6) Community Step

Hebrews 3:13 calls believers to exhort one another.

1. One person I can reach out to this week is:

----

2. One way I can encourage them is:

----

3. One way they can help me stay honest is:

----

7) Quick Repentance Practice

If you have sinned recently, write a short confession in plain words.

I sinned by:

I was wrong because:

I ask God to forgive me through Christ because:

I will take this step of change:

Prayer Response

Write a short prayer of dependence. If you need help, complete these lines.

Holy Spirit, I need Your help today.

Lead me through Your Word and strengthen me to obey.

Help me resist the desires of the flesh in _________________________ .

Teach me to repent quickly and walk in a new direction.

Make my life steady and faithful, one step at a time.

____

____

Amen.

Walking by the Spirit is daily dependence that shows up in truth, prayer, obedience, wise boundaries, community, and quick repentance. The Spirit gives strength to resist sin and live a new way of life.

BOOK FIVE

HOLD FAST TO THE FUTURE GOD HAS PROMISED

God's promises about the future are not meant to satisfy curiosity. They are meant to strengthen faith and steady daily obedience. This book will help you learn what Scripture teaches about Christ's return, the resurrection, final judgment, and the life to come. It will also help you see how future hope shapes present choices, especially in suffering, temptation, and fear. Each chapter includes clear teaching and guided questions so you can hold fast to God's promises, live with watchful faith, and keep your hope anchored in what God will surely do.

CHAPTER 1

JESUS WILL RETURN IN POWER

Teaching Section

Christians do not only look back to the cross and resurrection. They also look forward. Jesus will return. This is not a vague hope. It is a clear promise. The return of Christ is central to Christian faith because it completes God's plan in history. It brings justice, rescue, and renewal.

Acts 1:11 records an angel speaking to the disciples after Jesus ascended. The angel said Jesus will come in the same way they saw Him go into heaven (NSV). That promise ties Christ's return to real history. Jesus left in a real body. He will return in a real way. His return will not be an idea. It will be an event.

Jesus also taught that His return will be visible and powerful. Matthew 24:30 speaks of the Son of Man coming on the clouds of heaven with power and great glory (NSV). The point is not to map every detail. The point is certainty and majesty. Christ's return will not be hidden. It will not be small. It will reveal His authority over all.

The New Testament also teaches that Christ's return will be sudden. 1 Thessalonians 5:2 says the day of the Lord will come like a thief in the night (NSV). This does not mean Jesus is sneaky. It means His return will be unexpected to those who are not ready. People will be living ordinary life, making plans, assuming time will continue as usual. Then Christ will come.

Because the timing is unknown, Scripture calls believers to watchfulness. Jesus said, "You do not know on what day your Lord is coming" (Matthew 24:42, NSV). This is why the Bible does not encourage date-setting. It encourages readiness. The right question is not, "When will it happen?" The right question is, "Am I living faithfully today?"

Christ's return will also bring judgment. 2 Thessalonians 1:7–8 says the Lord Jesus will be revealed from heaven with mighty angels, in flaming fire, inflicting vengeance on those who do not know God and do not obey the gospel (NSV). This is serious. It shows that history has accountability. Evil will not go unaddressed forever. Christ's return will bring justice.

At the same time, Christ's return is comfort for believers. The same passage says Christ comes to be glorified in His saints (NSV). For those who belong to Christ, His return is not terror. It is rescue. It is the end of sin's presence. It is the end of death's threat. It is the end of the long struggle.

Titus 2:13 calls Christ's return "our blessed hope" (NSV). Hope in the Bible is not wishful thinking. It is confident expectation based on God's promise. The return of Christ is called blessed because it completes redemption. It means believers will see their Savior. It means faith will become sight.

Still, many believers do not think about Christ's return much. Some avoid it because it feels confusing. Some avoid it because it feels scary. Some avoid it because they are busy with life. But the Bible teaches that remembering Christ's return helps you live with clarity.

Here are three ways Christ's return shapes daily life.

First, it calls you to holiness. 1 John 3:3 says everyone who hopes in Christ purifies himself as Christ is pure (NSV). Hope has moral power. When you know you will stand before Christ, you take sin more seriously. You do not make peace with what Christ died to defeat.

Second, it steadies you in suffering. If life is painful, you may feel like evil is winning. But Christ's return guarantees that evil will not rule forever. God will set things right. This gives strength to endure without bitterness.

Third, it motivates faithful work. The Bible does not teach believers to stop living and wait passively. It teaches believers to live responsibly and serve with diligence, because Christ will return. Faithfulness now matters.

Christ's return will also expose what is hidden. Many injustices are never corrected in this world. Many lies are never admitted. Many faithful acts are never noticed. But Christ sees all. His return will reveal the truth. That should comfort the oppressed and warn the proud.

Christ's return will also gather God's people. 1 Thessalonians 4:16–17 speaks of the Lord descending, the dead in Christ rising, and believers being gathered to be with the Lord forever (NSV). That passage is meant to comfort grieving believers. It teaches that separation is not final for those in Christ.

So how should you respond?

Do not treat Christ's return as a topic for speculation. Treat it as a call to faithfulness. Live with clean hands and a steady heart. Keep short accounts with God. Confess sin quickly. Love your neighbor. Serve your church. Pray for endurance. Share the gospel with compassion. When Christ returns, you want to be found trusting Him and obeying Him.

The main point is clear. Jesus will return in power. His return will be visible, certain, and final. For those who reject Him, it brings judgment. For those who trust Him, it brings rescue and joy. Holding this hope shapes how you live today.

Workbook Section

1) Scripture Reading and Notes

Read each passage. Write one clear truth about Christ's return.

1. Acts 1:11 (NSV)

    ____

    ____

2. Matthew 24:30 (NSV)

    ____

    ____

3. Matthew 24:42 (NSV)

    ____

    ____

4. 1 Thessalonians 5:2 (NSV)

    ____

    ____

5. 2 Thessalonians 1:7–8 (NSV)

----

6. Titus 2:13 (NSV)

----

7. 1 John 3:3 (NSV)

----

8. 1 Thessalonians 4:16–17 (NSV)

----

2) Expectation and Readiness

Answer in short, honest sentences.

1. When you think about Jesus returning, what do you feel first?

----

2. Why do you think you feel that way?

----

3. What truth from today's passages steadies you most?

----

3) Watchfulness Check

Matthew 24:42 calls believers to watch.

1. What distractions most pull your heart away from readiness?
   Examples: busyness, entertainment, fear, money, anger, comfort.

----

2. What is one change you can make this week to live more watchfully?

---

4) Holiness and Hope

1 John 3:3 links hope to purity.

1. What sin are you tempted to treat as "normal"?

---

2. What would repentance look like in one concrete step?

---

3. Who can support you in this change?

---

5) Comfort in Suffering

If you are in a hard season, answer these.

1. What is the hardest part right now?

---

2. How does the promise of Christ's return help you endure?

---

3. Write one sentence of hope you can say when you feel overwhelmed.

---

6) Faithful Work Until He Comes

Write short answers.

1. One responsibility God has placed in my hands right now is:

   ----

2. One way I can be more faithful in it this week is:

   ----

3. One person I can encourage with this hope is:

Prayer Response

Write a prayer of readiness and hope. If you need help, complete these lines.

Lord Jesus, thank You that You will return in power and glory.

Help me live ready, not careless.

Strengthen me to turn from sin and pursue holiness.

Comfort me and others with the promise that You will set all things right.

Keep me faithful until the day You come.

Amen.

Jesus will return in power. His return is certain, visible, and final. This hope calls believers to watchfulness, holiness, endurance, and faithful living.

CHAPTER 2

THE DEAD WILL BE RAISED

The Bible teaches that death is real, but it is not the end. God will raise the dead. This is not poetry only. It is a promise rooted in the resurrection of Jesus Christ. Christians do not hope in a vague afterlife. They hope in resurrection.

Resurrection means the body will live again. It is not the idea of a soul floating forever. It is not becoming an angel. It is not being absorbed into some higher spirit. Scripture teaches that God will raise people, and they will live in a real, renewed way.

The clearest teaching on resurrection is found in 1 Corinthians 15. Paul begins by reminding the church of the gospel. Christ died for our sins, was buried, and was raised (NSV). Then Paul draws a straight line from Christ's resurrection to ours. If Christ is raised, believers will be raised. If Christ is not raised, faith is empty and we are still in our sins.

1 Corinthians 15:20 says, "Christ has been raised from the dead, the firstfruits of those who have fallen asleep" (NSV). Firstfruits means the first part of a harvest that guarantees the rest. Christ's resurrection is the beginning of the harvest. The rest of the harvest is the resurrection of His people. This gives strong assurance. Your future is tied to Christ's victory.

Jesus also taught resurrection clearly. In John 5:28–29, He said that an hour is coming when all who are in the tombs will hear His voice and come out (NSV). That is an authority statement. Jesus has power over death. He will call the dead, and they will rise. The verse also says there will be a resurrection to life and a resurrection to judgment. Resurrection is not only for believers. All will be raised. The difference is what follows.

This truth is both comforting and sobering.

It is comforting because death does not win. Many believers have buried loved ones. Many have faced death themselves. Resurrection means separation is not final for those who are in Christ. It also means the body is not worthless. God made the body. Sin and death harmed it. God will redeem it. That is part of salvation.

It is sobering because resurrection includes accountability. People will not disappear. They will stand before God. Life is not a closed system. History has an ending, and every person will face the truth.

So what will resurrection be like?

1 Corinthians 15 explains that the resurrection body will be changed. Paul uses the picture of a seed. A seed is planted, and what grows is connected, yet transformed. He says the body is sown in weakness and raised in power (NSV). He also says it is sown perishable and raised imperishable (NSV). That means the resurrection body will not decay. It will not break down. It will not be headed toward death again.

Paul also calls the resurrection body "spiritual" (NSV). That word can be misunderstood. It does not mean non-physical. It means a body fully animated and directed by the Spirit, free from sin's corruption. Jesus' own resurrection helps us understand this. After His resurrection, Jesus could be seen, touched, and recognized. He ate food. He spoke. He was not a ghost. He was bodily alive. Yet His body was also transformed, no longer subject to death.

Resurrection also connects to creation. Romans 8:23 says believers groan as they wait for adoption as sons, the redemption of our bodies (NSV). Notice the phrase redemption of our bodies. Redemption is not escape from the body. Redemption is the body being made new and free from decay.

This helps correct two common errors.

One error is to treat the body as everything. Some people live as if the body is the highest good, so comfort and pleasure become the goal. That leads to idolatry.

The other error is to treat the body as nothing. Some people act as if the body is a shell and what you do in the body does not matter. That leads to sin and dishonor.

The Bible teaches a balanced truth. The body matters, and it will be raised. What you do with your body matters, because it belongs to God. Resurrection hope encourages holiness. You do not treat the body as a toy. You treat it as a gift and a trust.

Resurrection hope also strengthens endurance. 1 Thessalonians 4:13–14 says believers should not grieve as those without hope, because God will bring with Jesus those who have fallen asleep in Him (NSV). This does not cancel grief. Grief is real. But grief is not hopeless. Christians grieve with expectation.

Resurrection hope also helps you face suffering. Pain can make people feel trapped. Disease can make people fear the future. Aging can make people feel loss. Resurrection says, "This is not the final form." The present body is fragile. The future body will be raised and made whole. That hope does not remove sorrow, but it gives strength.

Resurrection also helps you live with courage. If death is not the end, you do not have to live in fear. You can do hard things. You can obey God when it costs you. You can serve others even when it is inconvenient. You can speak truth even when it brings opposition. Resurrection hope frees you from slavery to self-protection.

So how should you hold this truth?

Hold it with gratitude. Christ's resurrection is your guarantee. Hold it with humility. Resurrection is God's act, not human achievement. Hold it with holiness. If God will raise your body, honor Him with your body now. Hold it with comfort. Your loved ones in Christ are not lost. They are waiting. Hold it with urgency. All will be raised, and all will face God.

The main point of this chapter is clear. The dead will be raised. Christ's resurrection guarantees it. Believers will be raised to life, with bodies transformed and made whole. This hope strengthens faith, steadies grief, and shapes how we live today.

1) Scripture Reading and Notes

Read each passage. Write one clear truth about resurrection.

1. 1 Corinthians 15:20 (NSV)

----

2. John 5:28–29 (NSV)

----

3. 1 Corinthians 15:42–44 (NSV)

----

4. Romans 8:23 (NSV)

----

5. 1 Thessalonians 4:13–14 (NSV)

----

6. Philippians 3:20–21 (NSV)

----

2) Define Resurrection

Write a simple definition.

Resurrection means:

Now write one sentence that says what resurrection is not.

Resurrection is not:

----

3) Firstfruits and Assurance

1 Corinthians 15:20 calls Christ "firstfruits."

1. What does firstfruits mean in your own words?

    ----

2. How does this give confidence about your future?

    ----

3. Write one sentence you can say when fear of death rises.

    ----

4) Grief With Hope

If you have lost someone, you may answer these. If not, answer as preparation.

1. What do you most fear about death or loss?

    ----

2. How does 1 Thessalonians 4:13–14 correct that fear?

    ----

3. What is one way you can comfort someone else with this hope?

    ----

5) Body Honor Check

Romans 8:23 speaks of the redemption of our bodies.

1. Do you tend to treat your body as everything, or as nothing, or as a gift?

    ----

2. What is one way you can honor God with your body this week?

____

____

____

3. Examples: purity, rest, self-control, caring for health, refusing harmful habits.

____

____

____

4. What is one habit that dishonors God with your body?

____

____

____

5. What is one boundary you will set to fight that habit?

____

____

____

6) Live With Courage

Answer with concrete steps.

1. What is one obedience step you have delayed because of fear?

____

____

____

2. How does resurrection hope give you courage to do it?

____

____

____

3. What is one step you will take in the next 48 hours?

____

____

Write a prayer of hope. If you need help, complete these lines.

Father, thank You that death is not the end.

Thank You that Christ's resurrection guarantees the resurrection of His people.

Comfort those who grieve and strengthen those who fear.

Help me honor You with my body and live with courage and hope.

Keep my eyes on the life to come.

Amen.

Key Takeaway

The dead will be raised. Christ's resurrection is the guarantee. This hope comforts grief, strengthens courage, and shapes a holy life in the present.

CHAPTER 3

HEAVEN AND HELL ARE REAL AND FINAL

The Bible teaches that every human life has an end, and every human life also has an eternal outcome. Heaven and hell are real. They are not symbols. They are not myths meant to scare people into behaving. They are part of God's final judgment and final mercy. Scripture speaks about them with clarity and seriousness because eternity is not a small topic.

Many people prefer to avoid this subject. Some think it is too heavy. Some think it is unkind. Some think it is embarrassing. But the Bible does not treat it that way. Jesus spoke about final judgment more than many people realize. He did not do it to entertain curiosity. He did it to warn, to call for repentance, and to offer real hope.

Heaven is the final home of those who belong to Christ. Hell is the final judgment for those who reject God. Both are final. There is no second death for believers, and there is no later escape for those judged. This truth makes the gospel urgent and precious.

Let's begin with heaven.

Heaven is described as being with the Lord. Revelation 21:3 says God's dwelling will be with His people, and He will be their God (NSV). That is the heart of heaven. It is not mainly about comfort. It is about communion. The greatest gift is God Himself.

Heaven is also described as a place without sin and without death. Revelation 21:4 says God will wipe away every tear, and death will be no more, and mourning and pain will be gone (NSV). This is not temporary relief. It is final healing. Sin will not threaten peace again. Death will not return. Loss will not repeat.

Heaven is also described as joyful worship. Revelation 7:9–10 shows a great multitude from every nation praising God and the Lamb (NSV).

This shows heaven is not dull. It is full of life. Worship there is not forced. It is the natural response of redeemed people who finally see God's glory without the fog of sin.

Heaven is also described as inheritance. 1 Peter 1:4 says believers have an inheritance that is imperishable, undefiled, and unfading, kept in heaven (NSV). That means it cannot be stolen. It cannot rot. It cannot be lost. This gives security. What God promises is safe.

Now we must speak about hell.

Hell is real, and it is final. Scripture describes it as judgment, separation from God's favorable presence, and conscious punishment. 2 Thessalonians 1:9 says those who do not obey the gospel will suffer the punishment of eternal destruction, away from the presence of the Lord and from the glory of His might (NSV). That verse stresses both punishment and separation.

Jesus also spoke of final judgment in Matthew 25:46. He said some will go away into eternal punishment, but the righteous into eternal life (NSV). Notice the parallel. The same word eternal describes both outcomes. Jesus presents two final destinations with lasting results. This is why the church has always taken hell seriously.

Some people ask, "How can a good God allow hell?" Scripture gives several truths that help us think rightly.

First, God is just. Justice means God does what is right. If God never judged evil, He would not be morally good. Many people demand justice when they are harmed. They want wrongs to be answered. Hell shows that evil matters and God's court is not asleep.

Second, sin is serious. Sin is not only harming others. It is rebellion against God. It is refusing God's rightful rule. The weight of sin is measured by the One sinned against. God is holy and infinite in worth. Sin against Him is not trivial.

Third, hell is not God losing control. It is God judging in truth. Judgment is not an emotional outburst. It is a settled verdict from the righteous Judge.

Fourth, God offers mercy. The Bible does not present hell without also presenting the gospel. God warns so people will flee to Christ. Ezekiel 33:11 says God takes no pleasure in the death of the wicked, but that the wicked turn from his way and live (NSV). God's warning is a form of mercy.

Fifth, people are responsible. Scripture presents unbelief as willful. People love darkness rather than light. They refuse to come to Christ. Hell is not a trap God hides. It is the end of chosen rebellion.

Another question people ask is, "Will everyone finally be saved?" Some hope so, but Scripture does not teach it. Jesus speaks of a narrow gate and a hard way that leads to life, and a wide way that leads to destruction (Matthew 7:13–14, NSV). This is not meant to make believers proud. It is meant to call people to repentance.

Another question is, "Do Christians go to heaven when they die, or do they wait for the resurrection?" Scripture points to both present comfort and future fullness. Believers who die are with the Lord in a real sense. Yet the final state includes resurrection and the new creation. Heaven is not only a disembodied existence. The Bible's final picture includes a renewed world where God dwells with His people.

So how does this teaching shape life now?

It shapes your priorities. If heaven is real, you do not live for temporary approval alone. Colossians 3:2 says to set your mind on things above (NSV). That does not mean you neglect responsibilities. It means you keep eternal values in view.

It shapes your comfort. If you are suffering, Revelation 21:4 gives true hope. Pain is not forever for those in Christ. Tears will end. Death will end. God will heal.

It shapes your urgency. If hell is real and final, people need the gospel. Love does not stay silent when the danger is real. This does not mean you preach with harshness. It means you speak with humility and compassion, remembering you are saved by grace.

It shapes your worship. If you understand what you have been saved from and what you have been saved to, gratitude grows. Worship becomes more sincere.

It also shapes your view of justice. When you see evil that seems unpunished, you do not need to take vengeance into your own hands. God will judge. That frees you to pursue justice in lawful ways, but not with bitterness.

The main point is this. Heaven and hell are real and final. Heaven is the home of God's people, marked by God's presence, joy, and the end of death. Hell is God's just judgment on sin, marked by separation and lasting punishment. This truth calls you to repentance, faith, humility, and compassionate witness.

Workbook Section

1) Scripture Reading and Notes

Read each passage. Write one clear truth about heaven or hell.

1. Revelation 21:3–4 (NSV)

    ----

2. 1 Peter 1:4 (NSV)

    ----

3. Revelation 7:9–10 (NSV)

    ----

4. Matthew 25:46 (NSV)

    ----

5. 2 Thessalonians 1:9 (NSV)

    ----

6. Ezekiel 33:11 (NSV)

    ----

7. Matthew 7:13–14 (NSV)

    ----

8. Colossians 3:2 (NSV)

    ----

2) Two Real Destinations

Write two short statements.

Heaven is real because:

Hell is real because:

Now write one sentence that explains why both matter for the gospel.

They matter because:

----

3) What You Expect From Heaven

Answer in clear sentences.

1. What do you most look forward to about being with the Lord?

    ----

2. Which promise in Revelation 21:3–4 comforts you most?

    ----

3. How should this hope shape your choices this week?

    ----

4) Respond to the Warning

Matthew 25:46 speaks of eternal outcomes.

1. What does this passage teach you about the seriousness of sin?

    ----

2. What does it teach you about God's justice?

____

____

3. What does it teach you about the need for the gospel?

____

____

5) Compassionate Witness

Think of one person who does not know Christ.

1. What makes it hard to speak to them about spiritual things?

____

____

2. What fear holds you back?

____

____

3. What is one kind and clear step you can take in the next seven days?

Examples: pray with them, ask a question, share a short testimony, offer to read Scripture.

____

____

4. Write one sentence you could say that is truthful and gentle.

6) Set Your Mind Above

Colossians 3:2 calls you to set your mind on things above.

1. What earthly thing most steals your focus?

____

____

2. What is one habit that would help you reset your focus daily?

____

____

____

3. What is one practical way you can store up eternal value this week?

Examples: serving, giving, forgiving, sharing the gospel.

____

____

____

7) Prayer Response

Write a prayer that holds both hope and seriousness. If you need help, complete these lines.

Father, thank You for the sure hope of being with You forever.

____

____

Thank You that You will wipe away tears and end death.

____

____

Help me take Your warnings seriously and turn from sin.

____

____

Give me compassion for those who do not know Christ.

____

____

Help me speak truth with humility and love.

____

____

Amen.

Key Takeaway

Heaven and hell are real and final. Heaven is life with God, with sin and death removed. Hell is God's just judgment on sin. This truth shapes worship, priorities, and compassionate witness.

CHAPTER 4

GOD WILL MAKE ALL THINGS NEW

The Bible's final hope is not escape from the world. It is renewal. God will make all things new. This is not a small touch-up. It is a complete restoration of what sin has damaged. God will remove evil, heal what is broken, and bring His people into a renewed creation where righteousness dwells.

Revelation 21:5 says, "Behold, I am making all things new" (NSV). That sentence is spoken from the throne. It is God's promise. It does not say, "I am making some things better." It says all things new. This points to God's power and God's plan.

This truth matters because many believers feel tired. They see death, sickness, injustice, and conflict. They wonder if anything will ever truly change. Scripture says yes. Change is coming, and it will be God's work. The future is not a human project. It is God's final act.

To understand renewal, we need to see what sin did.

Sin brought disorder. It broke fellowship with God. It corrupted human hearts. It brought decay into the created world. Romans 8:20–21 says creation was subjected to futility and is in bondage to corruption, but it will be set free (NSV). This is important. Creation itself is waiting for liberation. God's plan includes the created order, not just human souls.

Renewal also includes the end of the curse. Revelation 22:3 says, "No longer will there be anything accursed" (NSV). That means what sin brought into the world will be removed. The world will no longer be marked by frustration, decay, and death. Work will no longer be painful in the same way. Relationships will no longer be poisoned by selfishness. The curse will be gone.

Renewal also includes the visible presence of God among His people. Revelation 22:4 says God's servants will see His face (NSV). This is stunning. In the present age, we walk by faith. We see God's goodness through His Word and His works. In the new creation, there will be direct fellowship without the barrier of sin. God will not feel distant. His presence will be clear and constant.

This renewed future is tied to Christ's victory. Colossians 1:19–20 says God was pleased to reconcile all things to Himself, making peace by the blood of Christ's cross (NSV). "All things" includes people and creation. The cross is not only the answer to personal guilt. It is the foundation of cosmic restoration. Christ's work is wide enough to heal what sin shattered.

This also means the future is physical and real. The Bible speaks of a new heaven and a new earth. It speaks of life with God in a renewed world. Some believers have been taught to think heaven means floating in the clouds forever. Scripture gives a fuller picture. God's people will live in God's renewed world, with resurrected bodies, in a life marked by holiness and joy.

2 Peter 3:13 says, "According to his promise we are waiting for new heavens and a new earth in which righteousness dwells" (NSV). Righteousness dwelling means it is at home there. Sin will not be tolerated. Evil will not return. The new creation will be the right world, ordered under God, filled with peace.

This future also answers a deep longing in the human heart. People long for justice, beauty, safety, and lasting love. Those desires often get twisted, but the longing itself points to something real. We were made for God's world as it was meant to be. The new creation is that world, restored and purified.

But how does God make all things new?

Scripture shows two key parts.

First, God removes evil. He judges sin. He defeats the final enemies. Death is called the last enemy to be destroyed (1 Corinthians 15:26, NSV). God does not coexist with evil forever. He brings it to an end.

Second, God restores what is good. He heals. He renews. He brings His people into a life where worship and work are pure and joyful. In the new creation, serving God is not a burden. It is a delight.

This truth also protects you from despair. You may work for justice now and still see limited results. You may fight sin and still feel weakness. You may lose people you love. You may see brokenness that cannot be fixed in this life. Renewal means your labor is not wasted. God will finish what you cannot.

It also protects you from idolatry. Some people place all hope in progress, politics, or technology. Others place all hope in personal comfort. Scripture says do good now, but do not place ultimate hope in this age. Only God can bring final renewal.

Renewal also shapes how you view suffering. Suffering is not the final word. Romans 8:18 says present sufferings are not worth comparing with the glory to be revealed (NSV). That does not minimize pain. It places pain in a larger story. The coming renewal is so great that it will put present sorrow in its place.

Renewal also shapes how you treat creation. If God plans to renew creation, then creation matters. Christians should not treat the world as disposable. We should act as good stewards. We cannot save the world by our effort, but we can honor God by caring for what He made. Stewardship is part of love for God and neighbor.

Renewal also shapes the church's mission. We do not preach only "escape." We preach reconciliation with God through Christ. We invite people into a future with God. We also show signs of that future now through acts of mercy, truth, justice, and love. These acts do not create the new creation, but they point toward it.

So how do you live with this promise?

You hold it in your mind when the world feels heavy. You remind yourself that God is not finished. You choose faithfulness in small tasks. You repent of sin because it will not fit the coming world. You serve others because love belongs to God's future. You keep worship steady because God will dwell with His people.

The main point is clear. God will make all things new. The curse will end. Creation will be set free. God will dwell with His people in a renewed world where righteousness is at home. This promise gives endurance, steadies sorrow, and shapes faithful living today.

1) Scripture Reading and Notes

Read each passage. Write one clear truth about God's renewal.

1. Revelation 21:5 (NSV)

    ----

2. Romans 8:20–21 (NSV)

    ----

3. Revelation 22:3–4 (NSV)

    ----

4. 2 Peter 3:13 (NSV)

    ----

5. Colossians 1:19–20 (NSV)

    ----

6. 1 Corinthians 15:26 (NSV)

    ----

7. Romans 8:18 (NSV)

    ----

2) Define "All Things New"

Write a simple definition.

God making all things new means:

Now write one sentence that explains what this promise does not mean.

It does not mean:

----

3) Hope for a Tired Heart

Answer honestly.

1. What part of the world's brokenness weighs on you most?

   ----

2. Which promise from today's passages speaks to that weight most clearly?

   ----

3. Write one sentence of hope you can repeat when you feel discouraged.

   ----

4) Renewal and Repentance

If God will bring a world where righteousness dwells, sin does not fit.

1. What sin do you need to stop treating as "small"?

   ----

2. What is one step of repentance you will take this week?

   ----

3. What is one replacement habit you will practice instead?

   ----

5) Stewardship in the Present

Romans 8 says creation will be set free.

1. What is one way you can care for what God has made this week?

    Examples: reduce waste, act responsibly at work, care for your home, avoid careless harm.

    ----

2. What is one way you can show love for your neighbor through practical care?

    ----

6) Signs of the Coming World

Write two ways your life can point to God's coming renewal.

1. One act of mercy I will do this week is:

    ----

2. One act of truth and integrity I will do this week is:

Prayer Response

Write a prayer of hope and faithfulness. If you need help, complete these lines.

Father, thank You that You will make all things new.

When I feel tired, remind me that You are not finished.

Help me repent of sin that does not fit Your coming world.

Teach me to serve and steward with hope, not despair.

Keep my eyes on the day when righteousness will dwell and the curse will end.

Amen.

God will make all things new. He will end the curse, free creation from corruption, and dwell with His people in a renewed world where righteousness is at home.

CHAPTER 5

LIVE TODAY IN LIGHT OF THE END

Teaching Section

God's promises about the end are not given so we can argue over timelines. They are given so we can live wisely now. The future shapes the present. If you believe Jesus will return, the dead will be raised, and God will judge and renew all things, then your daily choices matter. You are not drifting. You are moving toward a real meeting with God.

The Bible often connects end-time truth to daily faithfulness. One clear example is 2 Peter 3:11. After speaking about the day of the Lord, Peter asks, "What sort of people ought you to be in lives of holiness and godliness?" (NSV). He does not say, "What charts should you draw?" He says, "What kind of life should you live?" The end should make you serious about holiness and steady obedience.

Living in light of the end begins with watchfulness. Jesus said, "Be ready, for the Son of Man is coming at an hour you do not expect" (Matthew 24:44, NSV). Readiness is not panic. It is steady faithfulness. It means keeping your heart soft, your conscience clean, and your priorities aligned with God's will.

Watchfulness also means you do not fall asleep spiritually. Many people live as if life will always stay the same. They assume they will have endless time to change, to repent, to reconcile, or to obey. Scripture calls that foolishness. James 4:14 says you do not know what tomorrow will bring, and life is like a mist (NSV). That is not meant to make you afraid. It is meant to make you wise.

Living in light of the end also means living with holiness. Holiness is not being strange. Holiness is being set apart for God. It is living in a way that matches His character. 1 Peter 1:15–16 says, "As he who called you is holy, you also be holy in all your conduct" (NSV). The end-time hope that God will remove sin should make you want to remove sin now, not make peace with it.

Holiness includes private choices. It includes what you do when nobody is watching. It includes what you click, what you say, what you imagine, and what you hide. Living in light of the end means you stop treating hidden sin as safe. God sees it. The end will expose what is hidden. Wisdom confesses now.

This future hope also shapes relationships. If you know you will stand before God, you will take love and forgiveness seriously. Romans 12:18 says, "If possible, so far as it depends on you, live peaceably with all" (NSV). You cannot control others, but you can pursue peace with humility and truth. You can refuse revenge. You can seek reconciliation where possible. You can speak honestly without cruelty.

Living in light of the end also changes how you use time and money. Temporary things are real, but they are not ultimate. Jesus taught people to store up treasure in heaven, where it cannot be destroyed or stolen (Matthew 6:19–20, NSV). He does not forbid possessions. He forbids worshiping them. He calls you to invest in what lasts.

This affects daily spending. It affects generosity. It affects how you use free time. It affects what you chase. It calls you to ask, "Will this matter in eternity?" Not every activity must feel spiritual. Rest and enjoyment are gifts. But the end calls you to avoid wasting your life on what cannot satisfy.

Living in light of the end also shapes your work. Colossians 3:24 says you serve the Lord Christ (NSV). That means your job is not only for income. It is an assignment from God. Even small tasks can be done in faith. The end reminds you that God sees hidden labor. Faithful work done with integrity is not wasted.

This future hope also shapes your witness. If heaven and hell are real and final, then people need the gospel. Love speaks. Paul says in 2 Corinthians 5:10–11 that we must all appear before the judgment seat of Christ, and therefore we persuade others (NSV). Persuading does not mean manipulating. It means speaking with clarity and care because the stakes are real.

The end also shapes how you handle suffering. When pain comes, it can tempt you to bitterness or despair. But the end reminds you that pain is not forever. God will make all things new. That hope helps you endure with patience. It also helps you keep doing good even when life is hard.

Living in light of the end also protects you from two common errors.

The first error is obsession. Some people become consumed with end-time details. They chase predictions and arguments. They become anxious or proud. Scripture calls for readiness, not obsession. The end should lead to obedience, not endless speculation.

The second error is neglect. Some people ignore the future entirely. They live as if Jesus will not return. They drift into comfort and distraction. Scripture calls that spiritual sleep. The end is meant to wake you up.

So what does a faithful life look like in light of the end?

It looks like daily repentance. It looks like prayer and Scripture. It looks like faithful church life. It looks like honest work. It looks like love for neighbor. It looks like generosity. It looks like resisting sin and practicing holiness. It looks like hope in suffering. It looks like speaking the gospel with gentleness and respect.

You do not need to do all of this perfectly. You need to keep turning toward Christ. The end is not meant to crush you. It is meant to clarify what matters. It is meant to pull you out of trivial living. It is meant to strengthen you for steady faithfulness.

The main point is simple. The end is certain, so live faithfully now. Christ will return. Judgment will come. Renewal will arrive. Let that future shape your habits, your relationships, your priorities, and your witness today.

1) Scripture Reading and Notes

Read each passage. Write one clear truth about living in light of the end.

1. 2 Peter 3:11 (NSV)

2. Matthew 24:44 (NSV)

3. James 4:14 (NSV)

4. 1 Peter 1:15–16 (NSV)

5. Romans 12:18 (NSV)

6. Matthew 6:19–20 (NSV)

7. Colossians 3:24 (NSV)

8. 2 Corinthians 5:10–11 (NSV)

2) Life Audit: What Matters Most

Write short answers.

1. What do you spend most of your time thinking about?

   ----

2. What do you spend most of your money on?

   ----

3. What do these patterns say about your priorities?

   ----

4. What is one priority you want to change in the next 30 days?

   ----

3) Watchfulness Plan

Matthew 24:44 calls you to be ready.

1. One habit that makes me spiritually sleepy is:

   ----

2. One habit that helps me stay ready is:

   ----

3. One change I will make this week is:

   ----

4) Holiness Step

1 Peter 1:15–16 calls believers to holiness.

1. One hidden sin I need to bring into the light is:

   ----

2. One step of repentance I will take in the next 48 hours is:

----

3. One boundary I will set is:

----

4. One replacement habit I will practice is:

----

5) Relationship Repair

Romans 12:18 calls you to pursue peace.

1. Is there a relationship you need to address?

----

2. What is one humble step you can take this week?

----

3. Examples: apologize, ask for a conversation, stop gossip, forgive.

----

4. Write one sentence you can say that is truthful and peaceful.

----

6) Treasure That Lasts

Matthew 6:19–20 speaks of treasure in heaven.

1. One way I will practice generosity this month is:

----

2. One way I will invest time in what lasts is:

----

3. One distraction I will reduce is:

----

7) Witness Step

2 Corinthians 5:10–11 speaks of persuasion in light of judgment.

1. One person I want to pray for is:

----

2. One way I can show love and open a door for conversation is:

----

3. One simple gospel sentence I can share is:

Prayer Response

Write a prayer for faithfulness. If you need help, complete these lines.
Father, teach me to live in light of the end.

Help me stay ready for Christ's return.

Strengthen me to pursue holiness and peace with others.

Help me use my time and money for what lasts.

Give me courage and love to speak the gospel with care.

Keep me faithful until the day You complete Your work.

Amen.

Key Takeaway

The end is certain, so daily faithfulness matters. Watchfulness, holiness, wise priorities, peacemaking, and humble witness are the right response to God's promised future.

CHAPTER 6

HOPE THAT NEVER FADES

Teaching Section

Life changes fast. Health can turn overnight. Jobs can disappear. Relationships can break. Even good seasons do not last. That is why God gives a hope that does not fade. Christian hope is not wishful thinking. It is confident expectation based on God's promise and God's character.

1 Peter 1:3 says God has caused believers to be born again to a living hope through the resurrection of Jesus Christ from the dead (NSV). That verse tells us where hope comes from. It comes from new birth, and it is anchored in Christ's resurrection. Because Jesus rose, the believer's future is secure. Hope is living because Christ is living.

This hope does not depend on circumstances. It does not rise when life feels easy and collapse when life feels hard. It rests on what God has promised to do. God's promises are steady even when feelings are not.

Scripture also says this hope will not fade because it is protected by God. 1 Peter 1:5 says believers are guarded by God's power through faith for a salvation ready to be revealed (NSV). Your hope is not protected by your mood. It is protected by God's power. Faith may feel weak at times, but the One who guards you is not weak.

Hope that never fades also has content. It is not vague. It is not simply "things will work out." God tells us what we are hoping for.

We hope for the return of Christ. We hope for resurrection. We hope for the end of sin and death. We hope for God to make all things new. We hope for life with God in righteousness and joy. These hopes are not separate. They are one future held together by God's promise.

This hope is meant to shape how you live today, especially in suffering.

Romans 15:13 calls God "the God of hope" and prays that He would fill believers with joy and peace in believing, so they abound in hope by the power of the Holy Spirit (NSV). That verse teaches two important things. First, hope is connected to believing. When faith is fed, hope grows. Second, hope is strengthened by the Spirit. You are not left to create hope from nothing. God supplies it.

Hope also helps you endure hardship with patience. Romans 8:25 says if we hope for what we do not see, we wait for it with patience (NSV). Hope and patience work together. Without hope, waiting feels pointless. With hope, waiting becomes meaningful.

Hope also keeps you from giving up when you fail. Many believers fall into despair because they see their sin and weakness. They think, "I will never change." Hope answers that lie. If you belong to Christ, God will finish His work. He will complete what He began. Your growth may be slow, but your future is certain.

Hope also helps you resist sin. Sin offers short comfort with long damage. Hope offers long joy rooted in God. When you hold hope firmly, the bait of sin looks smaller. You can say no because you know what you are living for.

Hope also shapes grief. Grief is real. The Bible does not tell believers to pretend loss does not hurt. But Christian grief is different because it is not final. You can weep and still hope. You can miss a loved one and still trust God's promise. Hope does not erase tears. It keeps tears from turning into despair.

Hope that never fades also shapes how you see yourself.

Many people build identity from what they can control. When control is lost, identity collapses. But hope anchors identity in Christ. You belong to God. You are being kept. Your future is secure. That creates stability in a changing world.

Hope that never fades also protects you from cynicism.

Cynicism is the belief that nothing will change and nothing matters. Cynicism often comes from repeated disappointment. People get hurt and they stop expecting good. But Christian hope refuses to surrender to cynicism because it rests on God, not on people. People fail. God does not fail. The world breaks promises. God keeps promises.

Hope that never fades also protects you from shallow optimism.

Optimism says, "Everything will be fine." Hope says, "God will be faithful." Optimism often ignores evil. Hope looks at evil honestly and still trusts God's final victory. Hope can stand in a hospital room, at a funeral, or in persecution and still say, "God is still true, and His promises stand."

So how do you keep hope strong?

First, feed hope with Scripture. Hope grows when you remember what God has promised. When Scripture is neglected, hope often shrinks. Your mind fills with fear and noise. God's Word cuts through that.

Second, pray for hope. Romans 15:13 connects hope to prayer and to the Spirit's power. Ask God to strengthen your hope. Ask Him to help you believe. Ask Him to keep your eyes on what is coming.

Third, practice gratitude. Gratitude does not replace hope, but it supports it. When you thank God for present mercy, your heart is reminded that God is good and active even now.

Fourth, stay close to God's people. Isolation feeds despair. Fellowship strengthens hope. Other believers can remind you of truth when your own mind feels foggy.

Fifth, keep obedience connected to hope. Do not treat hope as a theory. Use hope as fuel. When you choose purity, you are choosing the future over the moment. When you forgive, you are living like the coming kingdom is real. When you serve, you are storing up treasure that lasts.

Hope that never fades is also meant to produce courage.

Hebrews 6:19 says hope is "a sure and steadfast anchor of the soul" (NSV). An anchor does not remove storms. It keeps you from drifting. When fear and pressure rise, hope holds you steady.

So what should you do when you feel hope fading?

Start by returning to Christ's resurrection. 1 Peter 1:3 roots hope there. Then name what is draining hope. Is it unconfessed sin? Is it constant fear? Is it exhaustion? Is it isolation? Bring it to God with honesty. Ask for help. Take one small step of obedience. Open Scripture. Speak with a trusted believer. Do not wait for a perfect feeling before you move. Often hope grows as you return to the means God uses.

The main point is clear. Christian hope never fades because it rests on the living Christ, the guarding power of God, and the promised future God will bring. This hope steadies suffering, strengthens patience, and fuels faithful living until the day faith becomes sight.

Workbook Section

1) Scripture Reading and Notes

Read each passage. Write one clear truth about hope.

1. 1 Peter 1:3 (NSV)

    ____

    ____

2. 1 Peter 1:5 (NSV)

    ____

    ____

3. Romans 15:13 (NSV)

    ____

    ____

4. Romans 8:25 (NSV)

    ____

    ____

5. Hebrews 6:19 (NSV)

    ____

    ____

6. Lamentations 3:21–23 (NSV)

    ____

    ____

2) Define Hope

Write a simple definition.

Christian hope means:

____

____

Now write one sentence that explains how hope is different from optimism.

Hope is different because:

----

3) Hope Drainers and Hope Feeders

Write short answers.

1. One thing that drains my hope is:

    ----

2. Another hope drainer is:

    ----

3. One thing that feeds my hope is:

    ----

4. Another hope feeder is:

Now write one change you will make this week to reduce a hope drainer.

My change:

----

4) Anchor Practice

Hebrews 6:19 calls hope an anchor.

1. What storm are you facing right now?

    ----

2. What promise from today's passages can anchor you in that storm?

____

____

3. Write one sentence you will repeat when fear rises.

____

____

5) Waiting With Patience

Romans 8:25 links hope and patience.

1. What are you waiting for right now?

____

____

2. What makes waiting hard for you?

____

____

3. What is one faithful step you can take while you wait?

____

____

6) Obedience Fueled by Hope

Choose one area where you need to obey God in a hard way.

1. The obedience step is:

____

____

2. What fear or excuse holds you back?

____

____

3. How does hope in God's future help you obey today?

____

____

4. What is one step you will take in the next 48 hours?

____

____

Write a prayer for steady hope. If you need help, complete these lines.

Father, thank You for a living hope through the resurrection of Jesus.

When my hope feels weak, remind me that You are faithful and Your promises stand.

Guard my heart from despair and cynicism.

Fill me with joy and peace in believing by the power of Your Spirit.

Help me live faithfully while I wait for what You have promised.

Amen.

Key Takeaway

Hope that never fades is anchored in the living Christ and guarded by God's power. It steadies the soul in storms, strengthens patience in waiting, and fuels obedience until God's promises are fully seen.

CONCLUSION

HOLD THE WHOLE COUNSEL OF GOD CLOSE

You just finished a full workbook set on the big truths of the Bible: God, humanity, salvation, the Holy Spirit, and the future. These are not small topics. Yet God did not give them to confuse you. He gave them to steady you. He gave them so you can know Him, trust Him, obey Him, and endure with hope.

Systematic theology can sound like a school word. But the goal is simple. It means learning Bible truth in an ordered way, so your faith is not built on guesses. When your view of God is clear, your life becomes clearer. When your view of sin is honest, grace becomes sweeter. When your view of salvation is firm, fear loses its grip. When your view of the Spirit is biblical, you stop trying to live the Christian life alone. When your view of the future is sure, you can suffer without despair and serve without quitting.

This workbook set was written to be used, not just read. If you only read the teaching sections, you gained knowledge. But the workbook sections are where truth becomes practice. They help you slow down, name what is real, and respond to God with faith and obedience. The exercises were meant to help you build habits that last. Habits matter because you will not always feel strong. You will not always feel focused. But habits can carry you when your feelings are weak.

What you can take with you from each book

Book One helped you start where the Bible starts: with God.

You looked at God's self-revelation, His triune life, His rule over all things, His goodness, His relationship with time, and worship that is shaped by truth. This matters because every other doctrine depends on God. If you get God wrong, everything else bends. If you think God is small, you will live with small faith. If you think God is harsh, you will hide. If you think God is distant, you will stop praying. But if you know God as He has revealed Himself, you can live with reverence and peace at the same time.

A steady takeaway from Book One is this: God invites you. He is not confused, rushed, or threatened. He is worthy of trust. When life feels out of control, God is not. When you do not know what to do next, God does. Your job is not to carry the world. Your job is to obey the God who carries it.

Book Two helped you face the truth about humanity.

You saw the dignity of being made in God's image. You also faced the damage of the fall and how sin bends thinking and desire. You learned that human worth remains even after sin, and you ended with what it means to live as an image bearer today.

This matters because people often swing between pride and shame. Pride says, "I am above others." Shame says, "I am beyond hope." Both are lies. The Bible gives a better view. You are made by God, and you matter. You are also fallen, and you need mercy. That balance protects you from self-worship and self-hate at the same time.

A steady takeaway from Book Two is this: you cannot understand your life if you refuse to face sin. But you also cannot live wisely if you deny dignity. God calls you to truth and love together. That means you treat people as people, even when they sin. It also means you treat your own sin as serious, without treating yourself as worthless.

Book Three helped you grasp salvation as God's rescue.

You learned that salvation begins with God's initiative. You saw Christ's saving work. You faced the call to faith and repentance. You studied justification by faith alone. You learned what sanctification is and how it grows. You ended with assurance and endurance.

This matters because many Christians live with constant fear. They think God's love rises and falls with their performance. That creates either pride or despair. But the gospel gives a firmer foundation. Christ is enough. Your standing with God is secured by Christ, not by your mood. That does not remove the call to obedience. It places obedience in the right place. You obey because you are saved, not to earn saving.

A steady takeaway from Book Three is this: if you are in Christ, you can repent without panic. You can face sin without hiding. You can work hard at growth without trying to buy God's love. You can also rest, because your hope is not built on your record.

Book Four helped you live by the Spirit God has given.

You learned the Spirit is God, not a force. You learned the Spirit brings life, unites believers to Christ, grows fruit, builds and guides the church, and helps you walk daily.

This matters because many believers try to live the Christian life by sheer effort. Some burn out. Some pretend. Some give up. The Spirit is not an optional extra. He is God's gift for the whole Christian life. He opens eyes, strengthens obedience, grows character, and keeps the church healthy through truth and love.

A steady takeaway from Book Four is this: you do not need to chase feelings to follow God. You need truth, prayer, repentance, wise boundaries, and steady dependence. The Spirit works through ordinary faithfulness more often than sudden moments.

Book Five helped you hold fast to the future God has promised.

You learned Christ will return, the dead will be raised, heaven and hell are real and final, God will make all things new, you must live in light of the end, and hope does not fade.

This matters because many people live like this life is all there is. That produces panic, greed, and despair. But Christian hope is anchored in God's promise. The future is not fog. It is not fantasy. God will finish His work. Evil will be judged. Death will end. God will dwell with His people. This hope does not make you passive. It makes you faithful.

A steady takeaway from Book Five is this: the future makes the present meaningful. Your choices are not random. Your pain is not pointless. Your labor in the Lord is not wasted. Hope does not erase tears. It keeps tears from becoming the end of the story.

What to do now that you finished the set

It is easy to finish a workbook and move on. But the best fruit comes when you return to it. Think of this set like a tool kit. You will need it again in different seasons.

Here are practical ways to use what you learned.

1) Pick one "anchor truth" for each book

An anchor truth is a short sentence you can remember. Keep it plain. Keep it usable.

Examples you can adapt:

- **God:** "God is worthy of trust, even when I do not understand."
- **Humanity:** "People bear God's image, and sin is real."
- **Salvation:** "Christ is enough, and grace changes me."
- **Spirit:** "The Spirit helps me obey in ordinary life."
- **Future:** "God will finish what He promised, so I will be faithful today."

Write your own anchors on paper. Put them where you will see them.

2) Build a weekly rhythm that protects your faith

Many people fail because they rely on motivation. Motivation comes and goes. Rhythm is steadier.

A simple rhythm can include:

- A set time to read Scripture most days.
- One longer time each week to reflect and write.
- One time each week to gather with God's people.
- One person you can speak to with honesty.
- A plan for confession and repentance when you fall.

You do not need an impressive plan. You need a plan you will actually keep.

3) Use the workbook questions when life gets hard

Hard seasons often bring the same questions.

- "Where is God?"
- "Why do I feel numb?"
- "Why is my sin still here?"
- "Will God keep me?"
- "What is the point of staying faithful?"

When those questions rise, open this book set again. Use the questions to slow down and tell the truth. Pray in plain words. Ask for help. Take one step of obedience, not ten.

4) Study with others when possible

Some truths become clearer when you say them out loud. A small group, a spouse, a friend, or a mentor can help. You do not need a big group. Two or three can be enough.

If you study with others, keep it simple:

- Read the teaching section.
- Answer a few workbook questions.
- Share one "I learned" and one "I will do".
- Pray for each other with short prayers.

5) Keep doctrine connected to love

It is possible to learn theology and become cold. That is not the goal. Truth should grow worship, humility, and love. If learning makes you harsh, slow down and check your heart. Ask God to give you tenderness and courage together.

Truth without love becomes pride. Love without truth becomes confusion. God calls you to both.

A final reminder about growth

God does not measure growth the way people do. People notice big moments. God often grows people through small faithfulness.

Growth can look like:

- You confess sin sooner than you used to.
- You forgive faster than you used to.
- You choose restraint in speech more often.
- You pray even when you feel weak.
- You keep going after a hard week.
- You serve without needing praise.
- You stop making excuses and start taking steps.

Do not despise small growth. A tree grows quietly most days. But over time, it changes.

Also remember this: some seasons feel slow because God is doing deep work. Roots grow before fruit shows. Keep showing up. Keep repenting. Keep trusting. Keep obeying.

Copy this section. Keep it in your Bible, notebook, or on your wall. Use it daily, weekly, and monthly. If you miss a day, do not quit. Start again.

Daily Checklist: 10 minutes that steady your soul

- I read a portion of Scripture today.
- I asked God for help in plain words.
- I named one temptation I faced and brought it into the light.
- I took one small step of obedience.
- I thanked God for one clear mercy today.
- I spoke words that build, not words that tear down.
- I chose one boundary that protects my mind or body.
- I asked, "How can I love someone today?" and I acted on it.

Daily Heart Check: quick questions

- Did I treat God as real today, or as distant?
- Did I trust my feelings more than God's truth today?
- Did I hide sin, or confess it?
- Did I use people, or serve people?
- Did I spend time on what lasts, or mostly on what fades?

Weekly Checklist: set your direction again

- I gathered with a local church or a faithful group of believers.
- I reviewed one chapter's workbook pages from any book in this set.
- I wrote one confession and one request for help.
- I encouraged one believer with a message, call, or visit.
- I served in a practical way, even if it felt small.
- I gave time or money to support God's work as I am able.
- I rested in a wise way, without guilt and without laziness.
- I made peace where I could, by speaking or forgiving.

Weekly Doctrine Check: keep the foundations firm

- God is holy, good, and worthy of trust.
- People bear God's image and have real dignity.

- Sin is real and it damages the heart.
- Salvation is by grace through faith in Christ.
- I am justified by faith, not by works.
- The Spirit is God and He helps me obey.
- Christ will return, and God will judge and renew all things.
- My hope is anchored in God's promise, not my mood.

Monthly Checklist: deeper review and repair

- I chose one sin pattern to confront with a clear plan.
- I set or renewed one wise boundary (time, media, spending, speech).
- I had one honest talk with a mature believer about my walk with God.
- I reviewed my use of time and adjusted one habit that wastes it.
- I checked my relationships and took one step toward peace or repair.
- I served someone who cannot repay me.
- I re-read one full book introduction and one chapter that I need most.
- I prayed for someone who does not know Christ.

Crisis Checklist: when you feel weak, numb, or afraid

- I stopped and admitted what I feel without pretending.
- I asked, "What is true about God right now?" and wrote one sentence.
- I confessed any known sin, without excuses.
- I reached out to one trusted believer for prayer or help.
- I took one small step of obedience today, not ten.
- I rested if I am exhausted.
- I remembered the promised future and refused despair.

One-Page Commitment: sign and date

Write this in your own words, then sign it.

- I will seek God in Scripture and prayer with steady habits.
- I will take sin seriously and repent quickly.

- I will trust Christ's finished work when guilt rises.
- I will depend on the Holy Spirit for daily obedience.
- I will stay connected to the church and serve with humility.
- I will live in light of Christ's return with hope and faithfulness.

Signature: ____________________

Date: ______________________

Final encouragement

If you are trusting Christ, you are not alone. God is with you. He has spoken. He has saved. He has given His Spirit. He has promised a future that will not fail. The goal now is not to become impressive. The goal is to be faithful.

Keep returning to God's Word. Keep praying in plain speech. Keep repenting when you sin. Keep loving your neighbor. Keep serving the church. Keep your hope anchored in what God has promised.

And when you feel tired, remember this: the God who began His work in you does not quit halfway. He will finish what He has started.

APPENDIX
BIBLE STUDY PLANS AND MEMORY WORK

This appendix turns the whole 5-in-1 workbook into a simple program you can repeat. It is built for real life. It uses short readings, clear prompts, and small next steps.

Important note: **This appendix lists Scripture references only.** It does not print any Bible verses.

Part 1: How to Study the Bible in Four Steps

Use these four steps every time you read.

Step 1: Observe

Ask: **What does it say?**

- o   Who is speaking?
- o   Who is listening?
- o   What happens?
- o   What words repeat?
- o   What command is given?
- o   What promise is given?

Write 2–3 facts you can point to in the passage.

Step 2: Understand

Ask: **What does it mean?**

- o   What is the main point?
- o   What does this teach about God?
- o   What does this teach about people?
- o   What does this show about sin or grace?

Write one short sentence: "This passage means ..."

Step 3: Apply

Ask: **What should I do?**

- o What sin should I confess?
- o What truth should I believe?
- o What habit should I start?
- o What habit should I stop?
- o Who should I love or serve?

Write one action step you can do in 24–48 hours.

Step 4: Pray

Ask: **What should I ask God for?**

Pray in simple words:

- o Praise: "God, You are..."
- o Confess: "I have..."
- o Ask: "Please help me..."
- o Thanks: "Thank You for..."

Part 2: 10-Week Bible Reading Plan (50 Readings)

Plan: 5 days per week (Monday–Friday).

Weekend: review your notes and answer the weekly questions.

Each day includes:

- Read (NSV reference)
- Notice (2 questions)
- Do (1 action)
- Pray (1 prompt)
- One-sentence summary

Week 1: Know God as He Has Revealed Himself

Day 1 (Mon) Read: Exodus 34:6–7

Notice: What does God say about Himself? What do you learn about mercy and justice?

Do: Write one reason you can trust God today.

____

____

Pray: Ask God to help you believe His name is good.

____

____

Summary: God tells the truth about who He is.

____

____

Day 2 (Tue) Read: Deuteronomy 6:4–5

Notice: What does God command? What does love look like here?

____

____

Do: Choose one time today to speak love for God out loud.

____

____

Pray: Ask God to unite your heart to love Him.

Summary: God calls for whole-heart love.

Day 3 (Wed) Read: Isaiah 55:8–9

Notice: How are God's ways different from ours? What does this correct in you?

Do: Write one area where you will stop demanding your own way.

Pray: Ask for humility to accept God's wisdom.

Summary: God is higher than our plans.

Day 4 (Thu) Read: Psalm 145:8–9

Notice: What words describe God's heart? Who receives His care?

Do: Show patience to one person today.

Pray: Thank God for His steady compassion.

Summary: God's kindness reaches far.

Day 5 (Fri) Read: John 17:3

Notice: What is eternal life in this verse? What does it say about knowing God?

Do: Write one sentence that defines eternal life in plain words.

Pray: Ask God to help you know Him truly.

Summary: Life is found in knowing God.

Weekend Review (No new reading)

- What truth about God was most clear this week?

- What did you learn about trusting Him?

- What is one habit you want to keep next week?

Day 6 (Mon) Read: Matthew 3:16–17

Notice: Who is present in this scene? What does the Father say?

Do: Write three short lines: Father, Son, Spirit. What does each do here?

Pray: Praise God for His unity and love.

Summary: God is one, and God is three persons.

Day 7 (Tue) Read: Matthew 28:18–20

Notice: What authority does Jesus claim? What name are disciples baptized into?

Do: Write one step to obey Jesus this week.

Pray: Ask for courage to follow Christ's command.

Summary: The triune name stands over the church.

Day 8 (Wed) Read: John 14:16–17

Notice: What does Jesus promise? What does this teach about the Spirit?

Do: Write one area where you need help and comfort.

Pray: Ask God to strengthen you by His Spirit.

Summary: The Spirit is given to help and stay.

Day 9 (Thu) Read: 2 Corinthians 13:14

Notice: What gift is named from each person of the Trinity?

Do: Write one sentence of thanks for grace, love, and fellowship.

Pray: Thank God for His care in three persons.

Summary: God's blessings flow from Father, Son, and Spirit.

Day 10 (Fri) Read: Ephesians 1:3–5

Notice: What does the Father plan? What does this show about His love?

Do: Write one fear you will answer with God's adoption love.

Pray: Thank the Father for choosing to bless His people.

Summary: The Father's plan is loving and sure.

Weekend Review (No new reading)

- What part of the Trinity teaching was new to you?

- How does it change prayer?

- What is one way to honor God with your worship?

Week 3: Recognize God's Sovereignty in All Things

Day 11 (Mon) Read: Daniel 4:34–35

Notice: Who rules? What does this say about human power?

Do: Hand one worry to God in writing.

Pray: Tell God you trust His rule.

Summary: God's rule cannot be stopped.

Day 12 (Tue) Read: Proverbs 19:21

Notice: What do people plan? What finally stands?

Do: List your plans for the week, then write "God is Lord" below them.

Pray: Ask for peace with God's will.

Summary: God's purpose holds.

Day 13 (Wed) Read: Psalm 115:3

Notice: Where is God? What does He do?

Do: Say one sentence today: "God can do what He pleases."

Pray: Ask God to shape your desires to match His.

Summary: God is free and able.

Day 14 (Thu) Read: Isaiah 46:9–10

Notice: What does God declare? What does He promise to do?

Do: Write one promise from this passage in your own words.

Pray: Praise God for His sure plan.

Summary: God's plan stands from start to end.

Day 15 (Fri) Read: Romans 11:36

Notice: Where do all things come from? What is the right response?

Do: Write one sentence of worship that gives God glory.

Pray: Praise God for His greatness.

Summary: All things are from God and for God.

Weekend Review (No new reading)

- Where did you see God's rule in your week?

- What did you learn about control?

- What will you do next week when plans change?

Week 4: Trust God's Moral Goodness

Day 16 (Mon) Read: Psalm 34:8

Notice: What is the invitation? What is the result of trusting?

Do: Write one way you will "taste" God's goodness today (obedience choice).

Pray: Ask God to help you trust His goodness.

Summary: God invites trust, not fear.

Day 17 (Tue) Read: Nahum 1:7

Notice: What is God like? Who does He know?

Do: Write your name next to "those who take refuge."

Pray: Ask God to be your safe place today.

Summary: God is a safe refuge.

Day 18 (Wed) Read: James 1:17

Notice: What comes from God? What does this say about His character?

Do: List three good gifts you received this week.

Pray: Thank God for steady goodness.

Summary: God gives what is good.

Day 19 (Thu) Read: Psalm 86:5

Notice: What does God give? Who can call on Him?

Do: Make one honest request to God today.

Pray: Ask God to help you come without shame.

Summary: God is ready to forgive.

Day 20 (Fri) Read: Romans 8:32

Notice: What did God give? What does that prove?

Do: Write one fear, then write "God did not spare His Son" beside it.

Pray: Thank God for love shown in Christ.

Summary: The cross proves God's goodness.

Weekend Review (No new reading)

- Where do you doubt God's goodness most?

- What truth helped you this week?

- What will you do when you feel bitterness rise?

Week 5: Understand God's Relationship with Time

Day 21 (Mon) Read: Psalm 90:1–2

Notice: How long has God been God? What does that mean for you?

Do: Write one worry you will place under God's eternal care.

Pray: Praise God for being everlasting.

Summary: God is before all time.

Day 22 (Tue) Read: 2 Peter 3:8–9

Notice: How does God view time? What does this show about patience?

Do: Write one place where you need patience today.

Pray: Thank God for His patience with sinners.

Summary: God is patient and purposeful.

Day 23 (Wed) Read: Ecclesiastes 3:1

Notice: What does this say about seasons? How does that comfort you?

Do: Name your current season in one word.

Pray: Ask God for wisdom in your season.

Summary: God orders seasons.

Day 24 (Thu) Read: Isaiah 40:28

Notice: What does God never do? What does that mean for your weak days?

Do: Write one sentence: "God does not grow tired."

Pray: Ask God to give strength today.

Summary: God is never worn out.

Day 25 (Fri) Read: Revelation 1:8

Notice: What titles does God claim? What does that say about His control?

Do: Write "He is" at the top of a page, then list what God is.

Pray: Praise God as the beginning and the end.

Summary: God holds all time.

Weekend Review (No new reading)

- What changed in your view of time?

- What does patience look like for you?

- What is one habit that helps you live wisely in your days?

Week 6: Worship God in Truth

Day 26 (Mon) Read: John 4:23–24

Notice: What kind of worshipers does God seek? What must worship include?

Do: Write one way you will worship today in truth (not just feeling).

Pray: Ask God to help you worship with a true heart.

Summary: Worship must be true and Spirit-shaped.

Day 27 (Tue) Read: Psalm 96:9

Notice: What does it mean to worship in holy splendor?

Do: Remove one distraction for your next prayer time.

Pray: Ask God for reverence.

Summary: Worship calls for reverence.

Day 28 (Wed) Read: Hebrews 12:28–29

Notice: What kind of worship is fitting? What does it say about God?

Do: Write one sentence of gratitude for God's kingdom.

Pray: Ask for a thankful, careful heart.

Summary: God is holy and worthy.

Day 29 (Thu) Read: Colossians 3:17

Notice: What does "in the name of the Lord Jesus" cover?

Do: Pick one task today and do it as worship.

Pray: Ask God to shape your daily life as worship.

Summary: All of life can honor Christ.

Day 30 (Fri) Read: Psalm 100:4–5

Notice: What actions are commanded? What reason is given?

Do: Write a short list of thanks (5 items).

Pray: Thank God for His steadfast love.

Summary: Gratitude is part of worship.

Weekend Review (No new reading)

- What makes your worship shallow?

- What makes your worship steadier?

- What is one change you will keep?

Day 31 (Mon) Read: Genesis 1:27

Notice: What does this say about God's image? What does it say about male and female?

Do: Write one way you will honor human dignity today.

Pray: Ask God to help you treat people with honor.

Summary: Humans bear God's image.

Day 32 (Tue) Read: Genesis 3:6–7

Notice: What choice is made? What is the first result?

Do: Write one lie you are tempted to believe.

Pray: Ask God to help you trust His word.

Summary: Sin brings shame and hiding.

Day 33 (Wed) Read: Romans 3:23

Notice: Who has sinned? What do we lack?

Do: Write one area you need God's mercy.

Pray: Confess sin plainly.

Summary: All need grace.

Day 34 (Thu) Read: Jeremiah 17:9–10

Notice: What is the heart like? What does God do?

Do: Ask God to search one motive in you.

Pray: Ask for a clean heart.

Summary: God sees deeper than we do.

Day 35 (Fri) Read: Psalm 51:10

Notice: What does David ask for? What does that show about change?

Do: Write one request for inner change, not just outer change.

Pray: Ask God for renewal.

Summary: God can renew the heart.

Weekend Review (No new reading)

- What did you learn about dignity and sin?

- What is one habit that helps you fight hiding?

- What is one way to show honor to others?

Week 8: Grasp Salvation in Christ

Day 36 (Mon) Read: Ephesians 2:4–5

Notice: What moves God to act? What does He give?

Do: Write one sentence: "God made me alive by grace."

Pray: Thank God for mercy.

Summary: Salvation comes from God's mercy.

Day 37 (Tue) Read: Romans 5:1

Notice: What do we have through faith? Who gives it?

Do: Write one fear that peace with God answers.

Pray: Thank God for peace through Christ.

Summary: Faith brings peace with God.

Day 38 (Wed) Read: Acts 4:12

Notice: Where is salvation found? What is excluded?

Do: Write the name "Jesus" and circle it.

Pray: Thank God for a sure Savior.

Summary: Salvation is in Christ alone.

Day 39 (Thu) Read: 2 Corinthians 5:17

Notice: What changes in Christ? What becomes new?

Do: Write one "old" pattern you want to leave behind.

Pray: Ask God to grow new life in you.

Summary: In Christ, new life begins.

Day 40 (Fri) Read: Romans 8:1

Notice: What is removed? Who is this for?

Do: Write one sentence to answer guilt today.

Pray: Thank God for no condemnation in Christ.

Summary: Condemnation is removed for those in Christ.

Weekend Review (No new reading)

- What part of salvation teaching helped most?

- What part is still hard to believe?

- What will you do when guilt rises?

Week 9: Live by the Spirit God Has Given

Day 41 (Mon) Read: Acts 5:3–4

Notice: Who is the Spirit called? What does that teach?

Do: Write one sentence that honors the Spirit as God.

Pray: Ask for a reverent heart.

Summary: The Spirit is God.

Day 42 (Tue) Read: Titus 3:5–6

Notice: Who renews? What does God pour out?

Do: Write one area where you need renewal.

Pray: Ask God for renewal by the Spirit.

Summary: The Spirit brings new life.

Day 43 (Wed) Read: Romans 8:9

Notice: What marks belonging to Christ?

Do: Write one reason to be grateful if you belong to Christ.

Pray: Thank God for His presence in you.

Summary: The Spirit marks God's people.

Day 44 (Thu) Read: Galatians 5:22–23

Notice: What fruit is named? Which fruit do you need most now?

Do: Choose one fruit to practice today.

Pray: Ask the Spirit to grow it in you.

Summary: The Spirit grows Christlike character.

Day 45 (Fri) Read: 1 Corinthians 12:7

Notice: Why are gifts given? Who benefits?

Do: Plan one act of service this week.

Pray: Ask God to help you build up others.

Summary: Gifts are for the common good.

Weekend Review (No new reading)

- Where do you depend on self instead of the Spirit?

- What fruit do you want to grow next week?

- How can you serve the church in a small way?

Week 10: Hold Fast to the Future God Has Promised

Day 46 (Mon) Read: Acts 1:11

Notice: What promise is given? What does it say about Jesus returning?

Do: Write one sentence of readiness: "I will live ready."

Pray: Ask God to keep you watchful.

Summary: Jesus will return.

Day 47 (Tue) Read: 1 Corinthians 15:52

Notice: What happens at the last trumpet? What changes?

Do: Write one fear of death, then write "God will raise the dead."

Pray: Ask God for courage.

Summary: Resurrection is real.

Day 48 (Wed) Read: Matthew 25:46

Notice: What two outcomes are named? What does "eternal" teach?

Do: Pray for one person who needs Christ.

Pray: Ask God to give mercy and repentance.

Summary: Eternity is final.

Day 49 (Thu) Read: Revelation 21:5

Notice: Who speaks? What promise is made?

Do: Write one broken thing you long to see made new.

Pray: Ask God to keep your hope steady.

Summary: God will make all things new.

Day 50 (Fri) Read: Hebrews 6:19

Notice: What is hope compared to? What does an anchor do?

Do: Write one promise you will cling to this week.

Pray: Ask God to anchor your soul.

Summary: Hope holds you steady.

Final Weekend Review (No new reading)

- What truth from the whole plan mattered most to you?

- What changed in your habits?

- What do you want to repeat in the next 10 weeks?

Part 3: Scripture Memory Path

How to use this

- Write the verse reference on a card.

- Write the first letter of each word (or write the verse in your own notebook).

- Say it out loud once a day for 5 days.

- Review older verses every week.

Week 1	Week 2
1. Psalm 23:1	6. John 1:14
2. Isaiah 26:3	7. Hebrews 1:3
3. Proverbs 3:5–6	8. Colossians 1:15–16
4. Psalm 46:10	9. John 14:6
5. Deuteronomy 31:8	10. Philippians 2:10–11

Week 3

11. Psalm 103:8
12. Lamentations 3:22–23
13. Numbers 23:19
14. 1 Samuel 2:2
15. Psalm 118:24

Week 5

21. John 3:16
22. Romans 6:23
23. 1 Timothy 1:15
24. Isaiah 1:18
25. Acts 3:19

Week 7

31. James 1:22
32. Micah 6:8
33. Colossians 3:12
34. 1 Peter 2:9
35. Matthew 5:16

Week 9

41. Matthew 6:33
42. Luke 9:23
43. 1 Thessalonians 5:16–18
44. Proverbs 15:1
45. Hebrews 10:24

Week 4

16. Genesis 2:7
17. Psalm 8:4–5
18. Job 33:4
19. Ecclesiastes 7:20
20. Proverbs 4:23

Week 6

26. Romans 10:13
27. John 6:37
28. Ephesians 1:7
29. 2 Corinthians 5:21
30. Hebrews 9:27–28

Week 8

36. Galatians 2:20
37. Romans 8:14
38. Zechariah 4:6
39. 2 Timothy 1:7
40. 1 Corinthians 6:19–20

Week 10

46. John 14:3
47. 1 Thessalonians 4:16
48. Revelation 22:12
49. 2 Peter 3:13
50. Romans 15:13

Part 4: Troubleshooting Pages
(When You Feel Stuck)

These pages are short on purpose. Use them when you feel stuck. Read the references, then answer the prompts.

A) If You Feel Spiritually Dry

Read (NSV): Psalm 63:1–2; Isaiah 41:10; John 7:37–39

- What do you want from God right now?

  ____

  ____

- What is one thing you are avoiding: prayer, Scripture, confession, church?

  ____

  ____

- What is one small step you can take today, not later?

  ____

  ____

- Who can pray with you this week?

  ____

  ____

- Prayer prompt: Ask God for fresh desire and steady faith.

  ____

  ____

B) If You Feel Crushed by Guilt

Read (NSV): Psalm 32:1–2; 1 John 1:9; Hebrews 4:16

- What sin do you need to confess plainly?

  ____

  ____

- What makes you want to hide?

  ____

  ____

- What does it mean to come to God with confidence?

- What is one repair step you need to take with another person?

- Prayer prompt: Confess, then thank God for forgiveness in Christ.

C) If You Feel Stuck in Temptation

Read (NSV): 1 Corinthians 10:13; Matthew 26:41; Psalm 119:9

- What is your most common trigger?

- What lie does temptation tell you?

- What "way of escape" can you take right now?

- What boundary will you set for the next 7 days?

- Prayer prompt: Ask God for a clear mind and strength to obey.

Read (NSV): Psalm 13:1–2; Job 1:21; Romans 11:33

- What loss or pain is under your anger?

- What do you wish God would change?

- What is one truth you can hold even while you hurt?

- Who can listen and pray with you without judging you?

- Prayer prompt: Tell God the truth, then ask Him to help you trust Him.

E) If You Feel Anxious About the Future

Read (NSV): Matthew 6:34; Philippians 4:6–7; Psalm 121:1–2

- What is your biggest fear right now?

- What is one thing you can do today that is wise and simple?

- What is one thing you need to release because you cannot control it?

- What is one promise you can repeat this week?

- Prayer prompt: Ask God for peace and a steady mind.

10-Week Progress Tracker

Check one box each day you complete.

Week 1		Week 2	
Mon	[ ]	Mon	[ ]
Tue	[ ]	Tue	[ ]
Wed	[ ]	Wed	[ ]
Thu	[ ]	Thu	[ ]
Fri	[ ]	Fri	[ ]
Weekend Review	[ ]	Weekend Review	[ ]

Week 3		Week 4	
Mon	[ ]	Mon	[ ]
Tue	[ ]	Tue	[ ]
Wed	[ ]	Wed	[ ]
Thu	[ ]	Thu	[ ]
Fri	[ ]	Fri	[ ]
Weekend Review	[ ]	Weekend Review	[ ]

Week 5		Week 6	
Mon	[ ]	Mon	[ ]
Tue	[ ]	Tue	[ ]
Wed	[ ]	Wed	[ ]
Thu	[ ]	Thu	[ ]
Fri	[ ]	Fri	[ ]
Weekend Review	[ ]	Weekend Review	[ ]

<table>
<tr><td colspan="2">Week 7</td><td colspan="2">Week 8</td></tr>
<tr><td>Mon</td><td>[ ]</td><td>Mon</td><td>[ ]</td></tr>
<tr><td>Tue</td><td>[ ]</td><td>Tue</td><td>[ ]</td></tr>
<tr><td>Wed</td><td>[ ]</td><td>Wed</td><td>[ ]</td></tr>
<tr><td>Thu</td><td>[ ]</td><td>Thu</td><td>[ ]</td></tr>
<tr><td>Fri</td><td>[ ]</td><td>Fri</td><td>[ ]</td></tr>
<tr><td>Weekend Review</td><td>[ ]</td><td>Weekend Review</td><td>[ ]</td></tr>
<tr><td colspan="2">Week 9</td><td colspan="2">Week 10</td></tr>
<tr><td>Mon</td><td>[ ]</td><td>Mon</td><td>[ ]</td></tr>
<tr><td>Tue</td><td>[ ]</td><td>Tue</td><td>[ ]</td></tr>
<tr><td>Wed</td><td>[ ]</td><td>Wed</td><td>[ ]</td></tr>
<tr><td>Thu</td><td>[ ]</td><td>Thu</td><td>[ ]</td></tr>
<tr><td>Fri</td><td>[ ]</td><td>Fri</td><td>[ ]</td></tr>
<tr><td>Weekend Review</td><td>[ ]</td><td>Weekend Review</td><td>[ ]</td></tr>
</table>

Check each one when you can say it from memory.

1. .... [ ]	26. .... [ ]
2. .... [ ]	27. .... [ ]
3. .... [ ]	28. .... [ ]
4. .... [ ]	29. .... [ ]
5. .... [ ]	30. .... [ ]
6. .... [ ]	31. .... [ ]
7. .... [ ]	32. .... [ ]
8. .... [ ]	33. .... [ ]
9. .... [ ]	34. .... [ ]
10. .... [ ]	35. .... [ ]
11. .... [ ]	36. .... [ ]
12. .... [ ]	37. .... [ ]
13. .... [ ]	38. .... [ ]
14. .... [ ]	39. .... [ ]
15. .... [ ]	40. .... [ ]
16. .... [ ]	41. .... [ ]
17. .... [ ]	42. .... [ ]
18. .... [ ]	43. .... [ ]
19. .... [ ]	44. .... [ ]
20. .... [ ]	45. .... [ ]
21. .... [ ]	46. .... [ ]
22. .... [ ]	47. .... [ ]
23. .... [ ]	48. .... [ ]
24. .... [ ]	49. .... [ ]
25. .... [ ]	50. .... [ ]

Week 1

Big truth I learned: ____

One sin to confess or resist: _______________________________

One person to love or serve: ______________________________

One step I will take in 48 hours: ___________________________

Prayer request: ____

Week 2

Big truth I learned: ____

One sin to confess or resist: _______________________________

One person to love or serve: ______________________________

One step I will take in 48 hours: ___________________________

Prayer request: ____

Week 3

Big truth I learned: ____

One sin to confess or resist: _______________________________

One person to love or serve: ______________________________

One step I will take in 48 hours: ___________________________

Prayer request: ____

Week 4

Big truth I learned: ____

One sin to confess or resist: _______________________________

One person to love or serve: ______________________________

One step I will take in 48 hours: ___________________________

Prayer request: ____

Week 5

Big truth I learned: _______________________________________

One sin to confess or resist: _______________________________

One person to love or serve: _______________________________

One step I will take in 48 hours: ___________________________

Prayer request: ____

Week 6

Big truth I learned: _______________________________________

One sin to confess or resist: _______________________________

One person to love or serve: _______________________________

One step I will take in 48 hours: ___________________________

Prayer request: ____

Week 7

Big truth I learned: _______________________________________

One sin to confess or resist: _______________________________

One person to love or serve: _______________________________

One step I will take in 48 hours: ___________________________

Prayer request: ____

Week 8

Big truth I learned: _______________________________________

One sin to confess or resist: _______________________________

One person to love or serve: _______________________________

One step I will take in 48 hours: ___________________________

Prayer request: ____

Week 9

Big truth I learned: ____

One sin to confess or resist: ____________________________

One person to love or serve: ____________________________

One step I will take in 48 hours: ________________________

Prayer request: ____

Week 10

Big truth I learned: ____

One sin to confess or resist: ____________________________

One person to love or serve: ____________________________

One step I will take in 48 hours: ________________________

Prayer request: ____

HERE'S ANOTHER BOOK BY JAMES NORTHWELL THAT YOU MIGHT LIKE

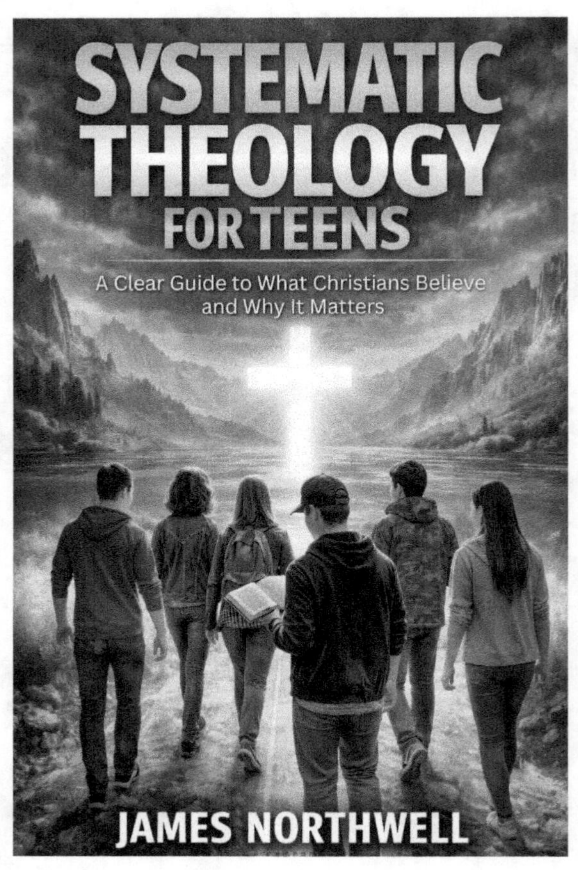